AMERICAN PRISONS

PATTERSON SMITH SERIES IN
CRIMINOLOGY, LAW ENFORCEMENT & SOCIAL PROBLEMS
A listing of publications in the SERIES *will be found at rear of volume*

PUBLICATION NO. 17: PATTERSON SMITH SERIES IN
CRIMINOLOGY, LAW ENFORCEMENT & SOCIAL PROBLEMS

AMERICAN PRISONS

A STUDY IN AMERICAN SOCIAL
HISTORY PRIOR TO 1915

"Reformation in our enlightened day is considered
one of the main objects of punishment."

—NEW YORK MANAGERS OF THE REFORMATION
OF JUVENILE DELINQUENTS, *Report* (1827)

By

BLAKE McKELVEY, PH.D.

Montclair, New Jersey

PATTERSON SMITH

TO

ARTHUR MEIER SCHLESINGER
SOCIAL HISTORIAN

PREFACE

The history of American prisons records the labors of several fairly clearly defined generations of builders and reformers and traces their notable strides toward penological realism. For more than a century the authorities have been chiefly absorbed in the struggle to accommodate growing convict populations and to reduce the burden of their maintenance, but each successive generation has made more or less significant changes in the correctional philosophy, the institutional technique, or the emotional appeal to the public. Only when able leaders succeeded in meeting insistent problems with workable programs and in rousing popular feelings to their support did concerted developments occur. Modern penologists have been somewhat inclined, because of their radically new conceptions of criminality, to depreciate the contributions of their predecessors; but, like every generation before them, they are coming to realize, after several years of practical administration, that they have inherited institutions and traditions whose evolution merits close study.

The task of tracing the fibers of culture that have woven in and out of American prison developments has provided an illuminating experience to the historian. Suggestive evidence concerning the nature of American society in its various historical and sectional stages has emerged from a consideration of the geographical, industrial, and cultural factors that have determined penal trends. The study has presented an opportunity to balance Europe's contribution of standards and techniques over against the ingenious native adaptations to practical problems. The rapid growth and partial industrialization of the nation have emerged as the primary influences, readily accounting for the greater development of American as contrasted with European penal systems. America's failure, in spite of many earnest attempts, to provide an adequate correctional system according to the standards of the day challenges the historian to discover the conditioning fissures in the social development of the nation, but such an undertaking would require a comprehensive study of the history of crime in America and must be left for another student.

In planning the present project certain boundaries were demar-

ix

cated which it has been difficult to maintain. Considerations of changing trends in crime and criminal law have intruded in spite of the necessity to avoid a thorough analysis of those distinct fields. The establishment of juvenile institutions has come into the story as an important reform of jail and prison conditions, but an adequate consideration of the later development of juvenile treatment would require a volume of its own. On the other hand, even within the limits set for study, it has been impossible to make the exhaustive researches some might desire. One friendly warden has advised that the true history of prisons can never be written, because no student can disinter the factional rivalries and personal ambitions that have so largely dominated the affairs of most prisons. Necessarily, these undocumented struggles among the authorities as well as the case histories of all but the few articulate convicts remain obscure. Nevertheless I venture to set forth the story as the records reveal it, puppet show though it may be, and any curious reader can verify portions of the account by a visit to one of the penal fortresses in his neighborhood or by a brief glance at his daily paper.

Bibliographical notes have been attached to most of the chapters in lieu of more detailed references, and the student may consult A. F. Kuhlman's extensive *Guide to Materials on Crime and Criminal Justice* (New York, 1929) for further leads. I am obliged to the authorities of the Massachusetts State Library for the opportunity to spend several months working through their remarkably complete collection of official reports gathered throughout the past century from practically every state in the Union. The authorities of the Harvard Law Library graciously opened their excellent collection of criminological and penological materials to protracted use. Access was likewise enjoyed to additional materials in Widener Library, the New York Public Library, Harper Library of the University of Chicago, and the Russell Sage Foundation Library in New York. The courtesy of the Massachusetts, New York, New Jersey, Pennsylvania, and federal prison authorities made possible frequent and instructive visits to institutions representing every stage of our prison history.

This study was undertaken at Harvard University under the stimulating direction of Professor Arthur Meier Schlesinger whose catholic interest in America's development has encouraged more than one excursion off the beaten track of political and economic developments. Dr. Sheldon Glueck of the Harvard Law School, Dr. A. Warren Stearns, former Commissioner of Corrections in Massachusetts, Dean George W. Kirchwey of the Russell Sage Foundation, Austin H. MacCormick, Commissioner of Prisons in New York City, and most recently Miss Edith Abbott, Dean of the School of Social Work, the University of Chicago, have each read major portions of the manuscript in various stages of its preparation and have given helpful suggestions or encouragement. Among many friends who have rendered generous assistance, acknowledgment is due especially to Mrs. Elizabeth Stearns and Mr. James Havighurst. Finally, more than to anyone else I am indebted to my wife, Jean Trepp, for the unflagging interest and co-operation that have helped to bring this study finally to conclusion.

TABLE OF CONTENTS

TABLE OF CONTENTS

CHAPTER I

THE ORIGIN OF PRISONS

The grim walls of century-old prisons still darken the streets of several of our eastern cities. Drab symbols of punishment, they have long defied the advance of civilization. Fires, riots, and renovations have transformed their interiors, and new institutions have been erected partially to relieve their congestion, but these massive stone embattlements continue to entomb and debase the lives of thousands of prisoners annually.

To the historian there is a majesty about some of these old structures, weighted down as they are with the traditions of a century-long struggle against crime. If the babble of contemporary penological disputes can be stilled long enough to permit us to hear the faintly echoing steps of the hundreds of able men who have administered and inspected these monuments of correction, and if their words of praise and criticism can be detected amid the clamor of brutalities, corruptions, stupidities, and insanities that reverberate through the halls, we may gain a new appreciation of these massive works of man.

BACKGROUNDS AND EARLY MAKESHIFTS

The penitentiary was one of the products of the social and humanitarian revolution that contributed so generously to the founding of the American nation. The philosophical concepts of natural and equal rights as advanced by Montesquieu, Voltaire, Rousseau, and their rationalistic followers were applied to the crime problem by the thoughtful Italian, Cesare Beccaria. His famous *Essay on Crimes and Punishments*, first published in 1764, clearly reasoned that punishment can be just and effective only when penalties are equally administered to all and when confinement in a humane environment encourages the prisoner to reform. Meanwhile, in England, John Howard, and Jeremy Bentham after him, extended the range of an indigenous humanitarian movement to include the welfare of jail inmates. Still an earlier stream of influence sprang from the Quakers, many of whom, from William Penn on, urged a more modest and charitable treatment of offenders.

As is usually the case, this philosophical fermentation did not immediately produce results, and it was not until the mellower days of Franklin and Jefferson that the righteous desire to cut off the wicked from the face of the earth began finally to give way. Romilly in England and Jefferson in Virginia advocated the abolition of capital punishment for the great majority of offenses, but it was the Quaker stronghold of Philadelphia that led the world in the adoption of humane criminal laws. Between 1783 and 1796 Pennsylvania gradually substituted imprisonment for the inexporable penalty of death in all offenses except first-degree murder. As the other states and the countries of Europe slowly followed this example, the modern world assumed the new responsibility of providing a means for housing criminals during the years of their confinement.[1]

The original inspiration of the penitentiary was rationalistic, but the successful establishment of prisons and the determination of their early character were more directly influenced by the reviving religious idealism of the early nineteenth century. Beccaria justified punishment in terms that suggest the modern concepts of social defense,[2] and Kant and Hegel merely clothed the theory scantily in theological terms when they held that punishment was the necessary expiation of sin, the retribution that completes or complements the criminal act. The humble parson and the early legislator, following doctrine only vaguely, regarded imprisonment as a charitable kindness, enabling the convict to work out his penance on earth where his suffering would serve as a warning to others. The benevolent Quakers considered imprisonment a sufficient punishment and held themselves responsible for brightening its dull monotony by friendly visitation in the spirit of Jesus. The evangelical sects, as well as Bentham, who stemmed more directly from the rationalists,[3] held society duty-

[1] Boston Prison Discipline Society, *Report* (1835), pp. 40–46. English law still recognized 240 capital offenses in 1780, but 94 per cent of the 1,192 average annual death sentences between 1823 and 1829 were commuted to transportation. Between 1814 and 1823 six American states, whose combined population was just under one-third of that of England, sent an average annual total of 760 to prison.

[2] *An Essay on Crimes and Punishments* (English trans. from Voltaire's French trans.; Dublin, 1777), p. 34: "The end of punishment, therefore, is no other than to prevent the criminal from doing further injury to society, and to prevent others from committing the like offence."

[3] *An Introduction to the Principles of Morals and Legislation* (Oxford ed.; 1907), p. 179. Bentham's assertion that "the value of the punishment must not be less in any case than what is sufficient to outweigh that of the profit of the offence" is a nice example of his moral calculus.

bound to make aggressive efforts toward the reformation of the convict without, however, lessening the deterrent purpose of the punishment. The whole age took for granted the free and individual will of the criminal and earnestly believed that imprisonment afforded the best opportunity for teaching rational men the folly of sinful acts.

The jail, the chief prison at hand when imprisonment was first heralded as the proper cure for crime, was unsuited for any additional functions. This oldest of prisons, known since the beginning of recorded history, had existed for several centuries in England in the form of local detention houses, and as such had been carried to America by the earliest colonists. But the jail was just at this time being exposed by the extensive investigations of John Howard, and no states, as proud of their capacity for self-government as were the young American commonwealths, could place a new responsibility upon such discredited establishments.

Another local institution, the workhouse or house of correction, had a long if somewhat indistinct tradition and offered at least a few suggestive ideas to the reformers. The English houses of correction, starting with the Bridewell of London in 1555, had been closely allied with the administration of poor relief during the first century of their existence and then had slowly lost their distinctive character as they became in practice secondary gaols. Thus a tradition of confinement at productive labor as a means of checking vagrancy and other minor evils was attached to the name of these institutions, independent of Continental developments of a more specific character; and it was probably the English tradition which William Penn and the Quakers of Philadelphia carried a step forward in 1682 when they planned houses of correction as a major instrument of justice. The two or more houses of correction provided in colonial Pennsylvania were duplicated at least in Boston and Hartford as Massachusetts in 1699 and Connecticut in 1727 directed the courts to sentence "sturdy beggars" and other minor offenders to hard labor. The principle of confinement was thus established as an alternative to corporal punishment, but the difficulty of making these institutions self-supporting caused the authorities to turn to branding, whipping, gagging, the pillory, the stocks, and fines in their endeavor to enforce an increasing number of minor puritanical regulations. Even the Pennsylvanians were beginning to apply these severer penalties before 1718 when English criminal law and practice largely superseded Penn's enlightened measures. Parliament's revision of the benefit-of-clergy law in 1706, empowering the courts to commit all first offenders of a minor character for short periods to local jails or houses of correction, further strengthened the tradition that imprisonment might serve as a corrective punishment; but at the same time this law helped to destroy the distinction between the two types of institutions.

Fortunately John Howard's Continental tours brought to light several developments which offered a much more suggestive pattern for penology. The oldest of these models was the combination prison and house of correction established by Pope Clement XI at Rome in 1704, but the most remarkable was the *maison de force* established at Ghent in 1773. Each provided for the separation of various classes of inmates and for the housing of the criminals in individual cells, and each had shops for the employment of the inmates at productive labor.[4] Howard discovered similar provisions for the inmates in a few of the jails of Switzerland, Holland, and Germany and at a new house of correction being erected at Milan. The meticulous detail with which Howard described each of the wretched gaols of England as well as these foreign models created a sharp contrast that challenged Parliament to action. Able men, such as Popham, Blackstone, Bentham, and Romilly, rallied to Howard's campaign for national penitentiaries to replace the transportation system which the revolt of the American colonies was just then interrupting. But disagreements over the choice of a site for the first penitentiary delayed the program, and the opening of new transportation outlets in Australia, with the economies it promised, again postponed for sev-

---

[4] John Howard, *State of Prisons* (2d. ed.; Warrington, 1780), pp. 94–95, 131–35. When Howard first visited Ghent, 260 individual cells, ranged in four tiers and opening on an open-air courtyard, were already completed in the section of the prison assigned to male criminals who at the time numbered 159. Professor Thorsten Sellin has made the most fruitful study of the European antecedents of our penal system and finds that the line leads back to the monastic prisons of the Middle Ages where an ecclesiastical spirit of penance and labor in solitary cells provided the root ideas for later houses of correction, penitentiaries, and reformatories; see his scholarly articles: "Filippo Franci —a Precursor of Modern Penology," *Journal of Criminal Law and Criminology*, XVII, 104–12; "Dom Jean Mabillon—a Prison Reformer of the Seventeenth Century," *ibid.*, pp. 581–602; "The House of Correction for Boys in the Hospice of Saint Michael in Rome," *ibid.*, XX, 533–53.

eral decades the development of a penitentiary system in England. Meanwhile the model provisions laid down for the proposed penitentiaries in the law of 1779 were extended to local gaols and houses of correction by a series of laws culminating in the first general prison act of 1791. Although no central authority was created to see that these provisions were applied, several counties did undertake to build new institutions on the patterns approved by Howard and his followers. The most significant of the new structures was the model Norfolk prison erected and managed by Sir Thomas Beevor in 1784.

Philadelphia, the most important city of the New World, was the proper stage for statesmen eager to build a new society. Inspiration enough could have been derived from the programs of William Penn, but the city was the focal point for liberal European influences; Benjamin Rush, William Bradford, Caleb Lownes, and others interested in penal problems were in close touch with foreign friends, and, like Thomas Jefferson in his *Declaration*, they were not concerned for originality. While the promising jurist, William Bradford, prepared the code that was to inaugurate a new era in the criminal law of the Western World, a group of Quakers and friends associated themselves as the Philadelphia Society for Alleviating the Miseries of Public Prisons. An earlier society, organized in the same city in 1776 but disbanded during the war, had been content with a charitable collection of food and clothing for the prisoners; the new society, starting in 1787, was the first in the modern world to assume the responsibility of planning a satisfactory penal system.

When we consider [said the preamble of the Society's constitution] that the obligations of benevolence which are founded·on the precepts and example of the Author of Christianity, are not cancelled by the follies and crimes of our fellow creatures . . . . it becomes us to extend our compassion to that part of mankind who are subjects of these miseries. By the aids of humanity their undue and illegal suffering may be prevented . . . . and such degrees and modes of punishments may be discovered and suggested as may, instead of continuing habits of vice, become the means of restoring our fellow creatures to virtue and happiness.[5]

The Society soon put this admirable resolution into effect by urging before the legislature that "solitary confinement to hard labor and a

[5] H. E. Barnes, *The Evolution of Penology in Pennsylvania* (Indianapolis, 1927), p. 82.

total abstinence from spirituous liquors will prove the means of re-forming these unhappy creatures"[6] whose labor in chains in the city streets was causing so many riots and whose undisciplined confine-ment in crowded jail rooms was a public scandal.

The Society was able to carry forward its program by urging the example of Parliament's activity and citing the Norfolk prison as a suitable model. The legislature in 1790 ordered the erection of a cell house in the yard of the Walnut Street jail for the solitary confine-ment of men convicted of felonies, designating the old building for the separate detention of suspects, witnesses, and misdemeanants. The act directed the Walnut Street jail authorities to receive con-victs from other counties until similar provisions could be made in their jails, thus providing a state prison without committing the legislature to that policy. The act further stipulated that labor should be provided in the several departments and that a rigid discipline should be maintained; more surprising was the authority given the sentencing court to release a convict before the end of his term in case an investigation revealed that he had been reformed. When to all of these details are added the activities of the Society in supplying Bibles, religious counsel, and instruction to the inmates, it becomes apparent that the main lines of American penal develop-ment for the next half century were envisaged at this early date.

During the first years Caleb Lownes was in charge, and the prison fully realized its promise. A wide variety of handicrafts was intro-duced, including "shoe-making, weaving, and tayloring; chipping logwood, grinding plaister of Paris, beating hemp, sawing and polish-ing marble; occasionally swingling flax, picking oakum, wool, cotton and hair; carding wool for hatters, sawing wood, etc."[7] But it soon became evident that the building plans had been miscalculated, for the twenty-four cells, each 6 by 8 and 9 feet high, and the thirty-six rooms, each 20 by 18 feet, although adequate for the seventy-two convicts plus additional detention cases in 1795, were crowded to capacity by 1800. Caleb Lownes retired in disgust the following year when the unrelieved congestion made industrial activity im-possible. Fifteen years later a population of 225 convicts together

---

[6] *Ibid.*, p. 90.

[7] Caleb Lownes, *An Account of the Alteration and Present State of the Penal Laws of Pennsylvania* (Boston, 1799), pp. 14-15.

with numerous detention cases had crowded all semblance of discipline from the prison, and a series of riots compelled the authorities to consider measures of reform.

Meanwhile other states were revising their criminal codes, substituting imprisonment in place of the death penalty for many offenses, and new prisons had to be provided. The optimistic reports of the early years of Walnut Street jail made it the model for prisons erected at Newgate, New York, in 1796, Charlestown, Massachusetts, and Baltimore, Maryland, in 1804, and Windsor, Vermont, in 1809; unfortunately these prisons copied the congregate rooms rather than the individual cells of their model. In Virginia, Thomas Jefferson, consulting a plan borrowed from a French architect, unwittingly followed the cell pattern of Ghent when designing Richmond penitentiary, built in 1800.[8] Other early prisons established at Frankfort, Kentucky, in 1798, at Columbus, Ohio, and at Concord, New Hampshire, in 1812, can hardly be credited with any considered pattern; Connecticut for its part continued to use an old copper mine as a makeshift prison. The remaining states and territories, in so far as they dispensed with corporal punishment—which was very cautiously south of Virginia—relied entirely on their old county jails. Thomas Eddy, a prominent New York Quaker, provided excellent management and high standards of discipline for a few years at Newgate prison but resigned in protest when the state turned the industries over to a contractor in 1803. Serious overcrowding and the consequent disruption of industry and discipline rapidly converted all these prisons into riotous dens of iniquity and roused a wave of popular indignation that in turn prepared the way for a new era of prison reform. The stone fortresses that were erected on the ruins of the first scanty prisons of the young states are the grim bastilles that still defy time and progress in several of our eastern cities.

THE ESTABLISHMENT OF PRISON SYSTEMS

Whatever the intentions of the first generation, the dawn of the "Era of Good Feeling" found the American states struggling along with totally unsatisfactory prisons. Fortunately the increasing stability of the states enabled several of them to tackle the problem with

[8] *Writings of Thomas Jefferson* (H. A. Washington, ed.), I, 46–47.

new vigor, and four fairly distinct penal systems shortly emerged. The persistent theories of the Philadelphia Society finally crystallized into the solitary system of Cherry Hill penitentiary; but before that model was securely established, a practical compromise between separate confinement and congregate labor was worked out at Auburn and embodied in an architectural plan which, with the aid of an aggressive society of New England reformers, won the country to its silent system. While these developments were in process, determined philanthropists in New York, Philadelphia, and Boston planned houses of correction for misdemeanants and established reform schools to take the children out of jails and prisons. The creation of these four institutional patterns provided the models for the next half-century of prison development.

The incessant growth of New York state promised anything but relief to Newgate prison where seven hundred inmates were already desperately overcrowding the prison twenty years after its establishment. Accordingly, two new prisons were provided for, and the first was started at Auburn in 1816 following the old congregate pattern. But a small band of reformers, profiting from contacts with the Philadelphia Society and after 1820 re-enforced by John Griscom, fresh from his European tour, was able to secure legislation in 1819 and 1821 directing the construction of solitary cells at Auburn. The building contractor, seeking economy, erected small inside cells, each $3\frac{1}{2}$ by 7 and 7 feet high, and these soon had appalling effects on their idle inmates. John Cray, Elam Lynds, and Gershom Powers, the men in control at the prison, undertook to correct this unfortunate state of affairs in 1823 by a compromise which confined the men in the cells only at night and employed them during the day under rules of silence in congregate shops. In an effort to repress all forms of communication John Cray devised a severe discipline which included such regulations as downcast eyes, lock-step marching, no prisoners ever face to face, no talking, and constant activity when out of the cells. Confident of the success of these methods, New York built a cell block at Auburn with four hundred inside cells and in 1825 started a second prison at Sing Sing on much the same pattern but designed to include one thousand cells.

Only the earnest efforts of the Philadelphia Society had won even the temporary achievement Pennsylvania had enjoyed after her courageous revision of the criminal law; now again an organized body of reformers came forward as the self-appointed champion of the new system and made Auburn the model for practically the entire country. The Philadelphians had been animated by a philosophical and urbane benevolence, but the new Society in Boston was dominated by the zealous religious passion of its vigorous leader, Louis Dwight. For thirty years after its creation in 1825, the Boston Prison Discipline Society issued annual reports that served as the penal textbooks for governors, legislators, and prison officers throughout the country.[9]

Louis Dwight, born of devout New England parents and inculcated with stern Puritan morals, was preparing himself for the ministry at Yale College when in 1813 an accident in a chemical experiment injured his speaking voice. Although the handicap terminated his ministerial career, it appears to have increased his ardor for service. After graduation Dwight became the first agent for the American Bible Society, and in 1824 while on a horseback journey seeking to revive his health the indefatigable agent visited jails and prisons in order to carry Bibles to their unfortunate inmates. The vicious conditions, the degradation and misery of the prisoners whom he now visited for the first time, shocked his sensitive spirit and aroused strong feelings of righteous indignation. Instead of worrying with Immanuel Kant about the theoretical justification of punishment as a divinely ordained expiation for sin, Dwight passionately asserted:

There is but one sufficient excuse for Christians in suffering such evils to exist in prisons in this country, and that is, that they are not acquainted with the real state of things. . . . . When I bring before the Church of Christ a statement of what my eyes have seen, there will be a united and powerful effort to alleviate the miseries of prisons.[10]

There was, in this declaration, a fresh breath of the religious ardor that was stirring America in those years, and Dwight found little difficulty in organizing the strong Boston Prison Discipline Society,

[9] Dwight noted in his 1830 *Report* that orders from state legislatures and other subscribers had already exhausted six editions of the first report, three of the second and third, and two of the fourth.

[10] O. F. Lewis, *The Development of American Prisons and Prison Customs* (Albany, 1922), p. 290. Lewis is quoting from Dwight's papers.

of which he became the secretary and the dominant spirit until both passed away together in 1854.

The failures of the earlier generation had left a fallow field for Dwight's cultivation, and the elaboration of the silent system at Auburn provided a program suitable to his tastes. The salvation of the convict, as conceived by Dwight and the Baptist and Congregational ministers who rallied to his Society, was not the penitence of solitary souls but the redemption of unfortunate sinners, to be achieved with the aid of revivals and Sabbath schools and through the development of industrious habits under strict discipline in congregate shops. Unfortunately Dwight's strong belief in the righteous nature of his cause made it difficult for him to tolerate disparate programs, and it was not long before he was engaging in an acrimonious controversy with the Philadelphians that seriously marred his reputation. Nevertheless, the Bostonian's influence spread rapidly, making him the first national figure in American prison reform.

Several of the American states had attained stability and were enjoying a measure of prosperity when Dwight took up his labors. As yet, however, only one prison, that of New York at Auburn, had been provided with separate cells sufficient in number to accommodate its inmates; and the authorities at this prison, and Moses Pilsbury under difficulties at Concord in New Hampshire, were the only ones maintaining a semblance of discipline. It is true that the prisons of New York and New England had some provisions for the religious care of their inmates, but the $200 provided for this purpose at Charlestown was the most generous. One prison, that at Baltimore, had a fairly satisfactory department for the segregation of the women with a matron in charge, and New York City was undertaking to establish a special institution for the care of juvenile offenders, but these were lonely forerunners of the elementary principle of classification. Dissatisfaction was rife, and forces were active that were to enable Dwight to carry his program rapidly forward.

The first achievement was in the establishment of a model prison at Wethersfield, Connecticut. The staunch Puritanism of this commonwealth was easily aroused by Dwight's indictment of the vicious conditions in the old copper mine which had been used as a makeshift prison since before the Revolution. The governor and the legis-

lature undertook to replace the Old Newgate horror by erecting a
new prison on the Auburn pattern, and the first cell house was
rapidly completed at Wethersfield, fitted to accommodate 135 prisoners in separate night cells, each 7 by 3½ and 7 feet high. Thereafter, as Dwight toured the states, interceding before the legislatures
in behalf of their convicts, it was the Wethersfield structure built
at a total cost of only $30,000, rather than the already politically
corrupted Auburn, that served as his model. Connecticut had the
good judgment to call the able warden, Moses Pilsbury, from New
Hampshire to manage its prison; and for twenty years this self-made
administrator, and his son Amos who succeeded him, maintained the
best penal institution in the country. With the example of a practical achievement at hand, Dwight was able to persuade Massachusetts to erect a cell block at Charlestown, and a half-dozen other
states—New Hampshire, Vermont, Maryland, Kentucky, Ohio, and
Tennessee—as well as the District of Columbia fell in line before his
Society had rounded out its first decade.

Meanwhile Pennsylvania was perfecting the solitary system and
winning the plaudits of European visitors. After a decade of wrang-
ling the first stones were laid at Cherry Hill in 1829, and the Philadelphia Society proudly watched the completion during the next six
years of what they confidently believed to be the greatest prison in
the world. Branching out from a central rotunda, like the spokes of
a hugh wheel, the seven massive stone corridors of the prison provided easy access to the rows of cells that flanked them. Each of the
four hundred large solitary cells, 8 by 15 and 12 feet high in the
center of their vaulted roofs, could be entered only from these corridors, but each was provided with an individual exercise yard, likewise securely walled about to prevent any communication between
the convicts. The network of massive stone walls practically filling
the twelve-acre plot at Cherry Hill, surrounded by an imposing
outer wall, had been designed by the architect, John Haviland, to
perpetuate the best traditions of medieval castle architecture. The
ease with which the simple disciplinary regulations produced sub-
servience if not penitence among the inmates roused the envy of
distraught officers in other prisons, and if it had not been for the
$750,000 construction cost—a sum that staggered responsible au-
thorities in those days—Louis Dwight would have encountered a

more effective rivalry. As it was, New Jersey started a prison on this pattern at Trenton in 1833 and built 192 outside cells, each 7½ by 12 and 12 feet high, but neglected to provide individual exercise yards. Maryland constructed small outside cells in a new building at the Baltimore prison, but they were far from the Pennsylvania pattern and the authorities adopted the rival Auburn discipline and eagerly introduced congregate shops. Meanwhile Pennsylvania's Western Penitentiary at Pittsburgh, originally built in 1818 on the model of Bentham's Panopticon, was reconstructed in 1829 with 170 large outside cells. Thus only three state prisons in America maintained a genuine solitary system.

The agitation of Dwight and his Society was producing results in other fields as well. The Bible, the Sabbath school, and the preached gospel were indispensable features of their reform program. The Society in 1825 sent Rev. Jared Curtis and Gerrish Barrett as missionaries to the various prisons, maintaining them there until the states could be persuaded to provide for resident or part-time chaplains. Revivals were joyfully reported from time to time by the Boston Society's agents, and Sabbath schools became customary features during the winter months in many of the northern prisons. Thousands of Bibles were distributed, forming the nucleus out of which prison libraries were later to develop, and convicts were encouraged in a new rivalry at committing to memory selected passages of Scripture.[11] This program was more aptly fitted to prepare the prisoner for a satisfactory adjustment to society after his discharge than the twentieth-century man might suspect, although of course that was not the primary concern of Dwight and his associates.

No reformer could have selected a more fortunate plank than the third feature of Dwight's program, the encouragement of prison industry. A half century had not lessened the American distaste for taxes, and the increasing burden of supporting idle convicts had become a major cause for popular dissatisfaction with the first prisons. The thriving handicraft labor of the early days of Walnut Street and Newgate prisons had soon been snuffed out by overcrowding

---

[11] Boston Prison Discipline Society, *Report* (1829), p. 25; *ibid.* (1828), pp. 60–63. Barrett reports from Sing Sing that in eighteen weeks forty-two entire books of the Bible had been memorized by one or another convict and that one had committed 1,605 verses and another 1,296 in that time.

and the resulting disciplinary breakdown; nevertheless, the prison
at Auburn had scarcely been started when an enterprising citizen
applied for a contract to operate a factory within the walls—a circumstance which played an important part in determining the nature of the compromise that gave rise to the silent system. The factory system itself was just then gaining a place in industry, and the
merchant-capitalists who ventured into large-scale production in
those early days turned eagerly to the permanent supply of cheap
labor available in prison. By 1825 Auburn prison was a smooth-
running industrial plant, and it was not long before this prison and
those at Wethersfield, Charlestown, and Baltimore were realizing
small surpluses over and above their expenses, an irrefutable argument in support of the silent system. Mechanics' associations raised
protests in New York State, and a convention of ninety-nine of their
delegates gathered at Utica in 1834 and another in Albany in 1841
to fight the system; but, although a legislative committee investi-
gated the grievances and a feeble regulatory measure was adopted in
1835, no changes were made in the system as the authorities rejoiced
over their successful reduction of the tax burden. Indeed, whatever
their profits, the contractors considerably assisted the states in developing a stable penal system in America.

The two other systems evolved during these years were fortunately recognized from the start as correctional rather than penal. Yet
the agitation for juvenile reform schools and houses of correction
for misdemeanants resulted in each case from local attempts to
correct deplorable jail conditions. These institutions were early
attempts at penal specialization, and, while the basis of classification
was very superficial, the fundamental philosophy behind the reform
was revolutionary in significance. Here was recognized for the first
time the existence of crimes for which society rather than the individual was responsible, and the corollary easily followed that society
was obliged to train the neglected child and the unfortunate vagrant
or drunkard for a more wholesome life.

Several religious and charitable organizations in various cities of
Europe had early provided reform schools for juvenile delinquents,
usually in connection with older orphans' homes, but it was left for
a few humane-spirited men in New York City to plan and establish

the first public institution of this character in 1824. Europeans had a long experience with the problem of homeless and wayward boys and girls before the development of cities in America raised the issue here, but by 1816 New York City was thronging with so many waifs that leading citizens organized the Society for the Prevention of Pauperism. An investigation of juvenile delinquency by this Society revealed that, while many juries refused to convict children, an average of seventy-five lads had been sent to prison in each of the years from 1819 to 1821. Popular concern was aroused by the publication of this report, and a new Society for the Reformation of Juvenile Delinquents was organized. Professor John Griscom was active in both of these societies, urging the example of a privately supported home for juvenile criminals which he had recently visited in England. Private benevolence built the New York House of Refuge in 1825— a method of public action commonly followed in the creation of educational institutions in those days—but the legislature voted a grant of $200 a year for five years and the city supplied additional funds for operating expenses. After 1830 the institution was entirely supported by these appropriations, thus becoming the first public reform school of modern times.

That the building of reform schools was a part of the general prison-reform movement of the day is further evident from the leadership and inspiration of the two movements. John Griscom, Thomas Eddy, Joseph Curtis, Edward Livingston and many other men were active in both fields. The inclosure within walls, the regimentation in the dining rooms, and the Auburn cell block which was adopted for the new building erected at New York in 1827 and for all succeeding reform schools down to 1856,[12] reveal the influences of current penal methods. The reformers were convinced in the early twenties that the wretched jails and prisons of the day were, especially for the young, nothing but nurseries of crime, and New York, Boston, and Philadelphia each erected its reform school before achieving a satisfactory penal system. The subsequent advance of the larger movement distracted attention, and twenty years were to pass before other communities became actively conscious of a larger responsibility for their young wards.

[12] The Philadelphia school, opened in 1826, later provided separate night rooms; only Boston retained dormitories.

But the reform school, even in America, was not exclusively of penal origin. John Griscom, Nathaniel C. Hart, the second superintendent of the New York House of Refuge, and the Reverend E. M. P. Wells, in charge at Boston, were not only professional educators but alert students of European educational reforms. The discipline which these men evolved contrasts sharply with prevailing penal customs. In New York the children were graded according to their conduct, and Wells in Boston added a marking system to encourage the children to strive for advancement to a higher grade. School studies for four hours a day alternated with industrial work in programs designed to keep body and mind busy. Merit badges and other rewards helped to eliminate corporal punishments. Unfortunately these inspired beginnings were discarded after a few years, thus failing to supply a suggestive model for prison reform.

The local house of correction, the fourth distinct penal institution to be developed during the era, had long roots in the past. But most of the earlier attempts to maintain such institutions had failed after brief periods, and, although the use of the term "jail and house of correction" had kept the principle alive, no genuine house of correction existed in America at the opening of the century. New York City was gathering hordes of petty offenders into its jails together with the hardened criminals awaiting trial when in 1803 Edward Livingston as mayor proposed the construction of a city workhouse for their proper segregation. Several years passed before a city penitentiary was erected for this purpose at Bellevue. When the institution was relocated on Blackwell's Island in 1826, Dwight's influence was strong enough to secure the adoption of individual cells; nevertheless, throughout its long career the workhouse proved to be a very imperfect answer to Livingston's proposal. The Arch Street prison opened by Philadelphia in 1816 was considered insecure for major offenders, and only debtors, witnesses, and later vagrants were admitted; but its congregate rooms defeated any efforts at correctional discipline.

It remained for Boston to develop an institution fit for this class of prisoners. In 1822 Josiah Quincy as judge of Essex County recommended the establishment of a house of correction where reformatory influences could be brought to bear on petty offenders. Becoming mayor of Boston the following year, Quincy appropriated one wing of the local jail for this purpose and introduced handicraft industries for its inmates. Finally, in 1833, the Boston House of Correction was provided with a separate home in another part of the city, and a system of labor and discipline was so well developed that it became the model for other institutions of this character in later years. Significant contributions were to be made to prison discipline by these institutions in later years, but for some time they were slighted by the reformers too exclusively concerned with the major prisons.

THE STATE OF PRISONS IN 1835

After several bad starts the American states by 1835 had finally enjoyed a decade of active prison development. The criminal codes had quite generally been revised, and most of the states had substituted imprisonment for the traditional corporal punishments. Groups of public-spirited citizens had banded together into several societies and were endeavoring to secure satisfactory penal institutions. A score of prisons and a half-dozen special institutions had been established, and the time was ripe for the appraisement of these developments. Unhappily local rivalries had grown to such a point that in the absence of standard measures of achievement the authorities were stooping to a fruitless squabble.

Fortunately by this time the theories of Beccaria had gained an ear at European courts. Comprehensive surveys were being made of European prisons, and responsible commissions were sent to study in the democratic laboratory across the sea. France sent Gustave Auguste de Beaumont and Alexis de Tocqueville in 1831; five years later Frederic Auguste Demetz and two companions came to check the earlier report. England sent William Crawford in 1832; and Dr. Nicholas Heinrich Julius came in behalf of Prussia two years later. Other official and unofficial visitors arrived, and, after making more or less careful investigations, returned with lengthy reports, most of them loud in their praise of the idyllic Pennsylvania system just then appearing for the first time in its pure form at Cherry Hill. This unanimity of judgment was partially responsible for turning England in 1835, Belgium in 1838, Sweden in 1840, and Norway and Holland in 1851 toward at least a partial adoption of the separate or solitary system for their new penitentiaries.

But this very unanimity of judgment, running so directly counter to the general trend in America, deprived the European critics of the full measure of influence that their surveys might have been expected to bear on American developments. Louis Dwight, whose reports circulated throughout the nation, was antagonized by the preference for Cherry Hill. However, Francis Lieber, a liberal German refugee serving on the faculty of the University of South Carolina, partially frustrated Dwight's conspiracy to silence the critics when he translated the report of Beaumont and Tocqueville for a Philadelphia publisher. The sober judgment of these brilliant Frenchmen informed Americans that their prisons had certain advantages over those of Europe: they checked the mutual corruption of the prisoners; they encouraged habits of obedience and industry; and they provided an opportunity for the reformation of the criminal. These critics considered the rival prisons in America as variants of the same system, confinement in solitude, some using walls, others depending on rigorous discipline; they concluded that "the Philadelphia system produces a deeper effect on the soul of the convict . . . . while Auburn . . . . is more conformable to the habits of men in society."[13] The pious Bostonians found little consolation in this contrast.

There were, of course, conditioning circumstances that helped to determine foreign opinion. Sing Sing, the most frequently visited institution of the Auburn class, was under the shadow of the harshest disciplinarian of its history, Warden Lynds. Moreover both Auburn and Sing Sing with their combined equipment of 1,770 cells seemed greatly overexpanded in contrast with Cherry Hill and the standards of the day. Wethersfield was a happier example of the Auburn system, and William Crawford, the English commissioner who in 1833 visited all but two of the prisons of America, generously recognized its merits but warned his countrymen against being "too sanguine as to its results" which he attributed largely to the genius of the two Pilsburys who had managed it from the start.[14]

But the Europeans were concerned with more serious matters than the dispute between the two rival penal systems. They lauded the states for their success in abolishing corporal punishments and

[13] *On the Penitentiary System in the United States* (F. Lieber: trans.; Philadelphia, 1833), p. 59.

[14] *Report on the Penitentiaries of the United States* (London, 1935), pp. 22 and 32.

limiting capital offenses[15] as well as for their general provision of institutions for the attempted correction of malefactors. They were, on the other hand, practically unanimous in condemning the neglect of local jails, a phase of penal reform to which England in particular was already devoting careful attention.[16] Crawford had some pertinent remarks to make concerning wholesale pardoning, but it must be noted that the flagrancy of the practice at the time—one-fourth of those discharged in New York were pardoned—actually represented a fair improvement over the enormity of the abuse as it had existed a few decades earlier when in many prisons half of the inmates were discharged through pardons. The sum of the foreign comments was that America had undertaken a large task with energy and had set a fine example to Europe, but that the time had not yet arrived for the states to rest content with their accomplishments.

Indeed many of the states were entitled to a little boasting over their penal developments during one short decade. Louis Dwight could now list ten prisons operating on the Auburn plan.[17] Each of these was adequately equipped with individual night cells, usually 7 by 3½ and 7 feet high. Two additional prisons already under construction would soon add one thousand to the existing total of over thirty-three hundred individual night cells.[18] Practically all these prisons were operating prosperous industrial departments, mostly under the direction of contractors or lessees, and several of them were regularly defraying their expenses. Fairly satisfactory women's

[15] *Ibid.*, *passim*. Crawford abstracts the codes of nineteen states and finds only one capital offense in Pennsylvania, Ohio, and Tennessee; two in New Hampshire and Kentucky; three in New York, New Jersey, Maine, and Indiana; four in Illinois and Missouri; five in Vermont; six in Massachusetts and Connecticut; and seven or eight in five other states.

[16] *Ibid.*, pp. 23–24: "There is far more injury resulting from confinement in the county gaols of any of the States than benefit arising from its penitentiary."

[17] Auburn had 770 inside cells; Sing Sing, 1,000; Wethersfield, 232; Charlestown, 304; Windsor, 136; Concord, 120; and Washington, D.C., 214—all on the Auburn cellblock pattern; but Baltimore with 320 small outside cells, Richmond with 168, and Frankfort with 100 were following the Auburn system in all other respects.

[18] The first 200 cells at Columbus, Ohio, each 7 by 3½ by 7 ft., were opened in 1834, and the remainder of the 700-cell structure was already in process of construction; at the same time the 200-cell prison at Nashville, Tennessee, was well under way, following closely the Wethersfield model.

quarters were being maintained at Auburn, Baltimore, Washington, and Wethersfield; and these four, plus Charlestown and Sing Sing, employed chaplains and conducted Sunday classes for the instruction of their illiterates. The rules of silence, downcast eyes, and the like were rigidly enforced in most of these prisons, but half of the states had abolished the use of the lash for prison discipline, and Richmond was at this early date experimenting with a system of honor badges and other rewards as incentives to good behavior. Unfortunately the large numbers confined at Auburn and Sing Sing seemed to have made it necessary for the officers to use brutal physical punishments, the iniquitous "cat" among them, in their efforts to maintain silence. As yet only Auburn, Baltimore, and Frankfort had provided dining-room accommodations to ease the monotony of cell life. Such was the Auburn system at the end of the first decade of Dwight's ministry.

The solitary system had been successfully established at Cherry Hill, Pittsburgh, and Trenton, but only the two Pennsylvania institutions were supplying sufficient handicraft industries to employ all their inmates. Each of the cells of these prisons was provided with a primitive sort of privy and a faucet that delivered a limited quantity of water every day—unique features in prison architecture for several decades. Chaplains made periodic rounds, encouraging each prisoner to read his Bible and to cleanse his soul through prayerful repentance, and the officers found themselves only rarely confronted with disciplinary problems. Louis Dwight failed to substantiate his indictment of these prisons as insanity breeders, and indeed his attack seemed to have enhanced their deterrent value. At all events, Pennsylvania must be credited with two of the best prisons in the world in 1835.

Five other states had prisons that were anything but a boon to their self-esteem. Maine and Rhode Island were experimenting with their own adaptation of the solitary system. But the seventy-six underground pits at Thomaston, each $9\frac{1}{2}$ by $4\frac{1}{2}$ and $9\frac{3}{4}$ feet deep, were insufficient for the solitary confinement of Maine's ninety-one convicts in 1832, and fortunate it was, for the wretched fellows would have frozen to death without the warmth of a companion or two during the long winter months. Meanwhile the tiny inside cells that were being constructed in one wing of the Providence jail, with the object of housing the state's convicts in complete solitude, certainly belied the fair name of that city. Indiana and Illinois were still maintaining wretched structures after the style of the worst make-shift jails, and Georgia was vacillating between the trials of operating its equally unsatisfactory prison and the alternative of turning the prisoners over to the counties. The remaining states and the territories left the administration of justice entirely in the hands of local authorities—an arrangement which was proving, especially in the South, most unsatisfactory.[19]

The jails of the entire country were little better than those of the South. The criticisms of the Europeans prompted Dwight to seek for a model jail, but his search was without success until in 1836 one was erected at Hartford on the approved Auburn pattern. Philadelphia at the same time started the construction of a new city jail with large outside cells,[20] but these disparate patterns failed to arouse the rivalry among local authorities that was providing so much incentive to state prison officials. Instead, the wretched congregate jails remained to deteriorate with age and to contribute more to the making of criminals than toward their correction. Meanwhile the plan to create houses of correction, where misdemeanants could be confined and employed free from contact with the more serious detention cases, made little headway. Only Boston had succeeded in establishing a worthy institution of this type.

Likewise, the movement for juvenile houses of reform had come to a stand with the creation of the institutions in New York, Philadelphia, and Boston. It was just at this time that several interesting developments in the treatment of juveniles were going forward in Europe, but another decade was to pass before these examples were to stir Americans to new efforts. Indeed, the New World, with its many opportunities for the young people who in Europe comprised

[19] Crawford, *op. cit.*, pp. 23–24: "In the slave states, particularly, the county gaols are truly deplorable. It is the practice to commit a slave to the common gaol whenever it suits the convenience of the owner. . . . . From the number and various description of the prisoners, and the extremely limited space allowed them, these places of confinement exhibit scenes of great wretchedness and oppression."

[20] *Ibid.*, p. 17; American Prison Association, *Proceedings* (1928), pp. 217–19. No contemporary evidence has been found to support this print and description of the Burlington County jail and workhouse, allegedly built in 1808 on the plan later followed by Haviland at Cherry Hill.

the major portion of the delinquent classes, did not face very critical problems in this field until the development of industries and urban communities transformed the social landscape.

Thus a century ago our ancestors were tackling their criminal problems with the energy of a young people, unhampered by rigid traditions. Old theories and methods of punishment had been swept aside. The penitentiary and its associated institutions were as legitimate offsprings of the age as the young democracies themselves. These developments were alike manifestations of the current belief in the free will of the rational man, they shared the same optimism for the future of the race, and they were animated by similar romantic ideals. Europe justly paid honor to the Americans for having established the first genuine penal system in the modern world—an achievement which was in large part due to the zeal of Louis Dwight and to his practical skill in fusing righteous impulses, a program of industry, and a rigid discipline into a cheap but secure structural pattern.

BIBLIOGRAPHICAL NOTE

Cesare Beccaria, *An Essay on Crimes and Punishments*, may be consulted in the original or in numerous editions of several translations; the English translation of Voltaire's French translation, published in Dublin in 1777, was used. John Howard, *State of Prisons* (2d ed.; Warrington, 1780). Jeremy Bentham, *An Introduction to the Principles of Morals and Legislation* (London, 1823). Caleb Lownes, *An Account of the Alteration and Present State of Penal Laws of Pennsylvania* (Boston, 1799). John Griscom, *A Year in Europe* (2d. ed.; New York, 1824). Gershom Powers, *Brief Account of the Construction, Management and Discipline of the New York State Prison at Auburn* (Auburn, 1826). Valuable reports of the prison officers are printed in the early legislative documents of most of these states, but full detail on all the prisons is available in the Boston Prison Discipline Society, *Reports* (1826–54), an invaluable source.

The best descriptive studies by foreign visitors are G. de Beaumont and A. de Tocqueville, *On the Penitentiary System in the United States* (F. Lieber trans.; Philadelphia, 1833); and William Crawford, *Report on the Penitentiaries of the United States* (London, 1835). The views of a dozen other visitors are canvassed in the *Report of a Minority of the Special Committee of the Boston Prison Discipline Society* (Boston, 1846), and in the B.P.D.S., *Report* (1843), pp. 44–95.

Harry E. Barnes, *The Evolution of Penology in Pennsylvania* (Indianapolis, 1927), is a scholarly treatment of the history of this important state and includes many rare documents. Orlando F. Lewis, *The Development of American Prisons and Prison Customs* (Albany, 1922), is an exhaustive treatment of the institutional side of the developments down to 1845. Other volumes of special value are: *Reformatory Education* (Henry Barnard ed.; Hartford, 1857); Raymond T. Bye, *Capital Punishment in the United States* (Philadelphia, 1919); Alice M. Earle, *Curious Punishments of Bygone Days* (New York, 1929); F. W. Hoffer, D. M. Mann, and F. N. House, *The Jails of Virginia* (New York, 1933); Marcus W. Jernegan, *Laboring and Dependent Classes in Colonial America* (Chicago, 1931); Cyrus H. Karraker, *The Seventeenth-Century Sheriff* (Chapel Hill, 1930); B. K. Pierce, *A Half Century with Juvenile Delinquents* (New York, 1869); Sidney and Beatrice Webb, *English Prisons under Local Government* (London, 1922). Thursten Sellin has several excellent articles in the *Journal of Criminal Law and Criminology*, XVII, 104-12, 581-602; XX, 533-53. L. H. Gipson, "Crime and Punishment in Provincial Pennsylvania," *Pennsylvania History* (January, 1935); A. E. Smith, "The Transportation of Convicts to the American Colonies in the Seventeenth Century," *The American Historical Review*, XXXIX, 232-50.

CHAPTER II

FRESH THEORIES AND FAILURES

America had succeeded in establishing a penal system by 1835 but could boast of no great mitigation of crime. In the seventy years that had passed since Beccaria had first formulated the rationalistic theories of punishment the New World had been the chief scene of penitentiary developments. The original inspiration had given place to religious and romantic sentiments before stable prisons had been secured. In the practical struggles of the succeeding years the zeal of the leaders had been absorbed in large part by the material and technical problems of establishing institutions. More than a score of prisons already stood as tangible accomplishments, but society's interest in the convict had simmered down to the bloodless passion for his salvation that still animated a few reformers.

Fortunately in the late thirties the Western world was enlivened by a fresh current of humanitarianism. The interests of the common man were creating a host of generous reform movements that found expression in temperance campaigns, peace congresses, crusades against both wage and chattel slavery, and demands for education and opportunity for all men and women. In the midst of this ferment a more rounded program for the reformation of criminals was conceived. Like most of the idealistic programs of the day, the reformation of convicts was to enjoy a preliminary hearing, but its formal trial was deferred for several decades. Nevertheless, this era did witness the theoretical formulation of most of the principles that were to guide prison developments during the rest of the century.

The international exchange of inspiration and ideas played a large part in the new trends, but these revealed at the same time strong native characteristics. The dominance of Louis Dwight continued in all practical matters, but he had identified himself so closely with the propagation of the Auburn system that he began to appear as an obstacle to progress. The leaders who best represented the inspiration of the new generation were the erudite Francis Lieber, the energetic Dorothea Lynde Dix, and the compassionate Samuel Gridley

23

Howe. Theirs was, however, primarily a contribution of generous theories and programs, and even the auspicious outset of the New York Prison Association in 1844 failed to accomplish any considerable amelioration of the convicts. These intellectual stirrings awaited the development of a situation that would call their programs into being, and that occasion was not to arrive until after the close of the Civil War.

NEW CURRENTS OF THOUGHT

American reformers have not always been as erudite as they were resourceful, and they have seldom buttressed their programs with the available European citations, but the pioneers of this period, Lieber, Dix, and Howe, were frankly proud of the international horizons of their humanitarianism. On the other hand, it had not been homage for the young republic but determined agitation at home that had prompted Europe to send commissions to study prisons in America. The chief portion of the European agitation and of the programs there advocated was little different in spirit and character from those of the Pennsylvanians or of Louis Dwight and his school. A charitable concern for the oppressed and a religious interest in their salvation through solitude, prayer, and Sabbath instruction animated both movements.

There was, however, a new inspiration in England that envisaged a more aggressive attack on the problem, one that was closely allied with the newer trends in education and social ethics. Scholars have traced back as far as William Paley's lectures in the late eighteenth century on moral and political philosophy to find the origin of the theory that a labor rather than a time sentence is the correct way of stimulating criminals to reform.[1] Archbishop Richard Whately reasserted the idea a half century later in his oft-quoted letter to Lord Grey, and direct lines can be traced from here through the ticket-of-leave to parole, the indeterminate sentence, and the whole reformatory system.

[1] Thorsten Sellin, "Paley on Time Sentence," *Journal of Criminal Law and Criminology* (1931), pp. 264–66. Dr. Sellin quotes from Paley, *Principles of Moral and Political Philosophy* (Collins ed.; New York, 1837) II, 132: "I would measure the confinement not by the duration of time, but by quantity of work, in order both to excite industry and to render it more voluntary." It is interesting to note that several editions of this work were printed in America before 1830.

Two able administrators, acting independently and probably without knowledge of the earlier theorists, put these principles into practice with creditable results. First, Colonel Montesinos, who took charge of the old Spanish prison at Valencia in 1835, initiated a reformatory discipline coupled with a policy of releasing the men as soon as he became convinced of their reform. Unfortunately after a few years of remarkable success, political interference took away the power to grant releases, and Montesinos resigned. A more influential experiment was that of Captain Alexander Maconochie at Norfolk Island, Australia. On accepting his appointment as commander of the penal colony, one of the last outposts of the English transportation system, Maconochie declared that a labor sentence was the only enlightened basis for the correction of offenders, and that it must be combined with a system that provides first "specific punishment for the past" and, in a second stage, "specific training for the future."[2] Although denied the authority to put the theory of labor sentences fully into operation, Maconochie's administration, by "providing a field for the cultivation of active social virtues" and thus "preparing for society in society," transformed some fruitful ideas into practical penological experience.[3]

England in the thirties, as in Howard's day, had been saved from commitment to a rigid solitary system by the economy of transportation. The national penitentiaries finally erected in England on the solitary pattern had become punishment prisons where convicts were confined for a year or two in solitude before transportation. But this simple method of distinguishing the punishment and correctional stages broke down when the indignant opposition of the colonies put an end to the transportation system, forcing England to solve its penal problem at home. Maconochie received a hearty welcome when he returned to England in 1845, and his advocacy of progressive-grade treatment was indorsed by a large group of reformers, among them Frederick and Matthew Davenport Hill and Mary Carpenter. These leaders had gained faith in more aggressive reformatory methods from their experiences with juvenile offenders. The end of transportation brought them the opportunity to lead

[2] Mary Carpenter, *Our Convicts* (London, 1864), p. 96. Miss Carpenter is quoting from a pamphlet published by Maconochie at Hobart Town in 1839.

[3] Alexander Maconochie, *Norfolk Island* (London, 1847).

England, and especially Ireland, toward the development of a system of graded prisons, and their program was most successfully embodied a decade later in Sir Walter Crofton's famous Irish system. The new program called for three distinct stages of treatment—punishment in solitude for two years, follow: ' by congregate labor under a marking system that regulated priv ,eges and determined the date of discharge, and finally conditional release under a ticket-of-leave. Unfortunately for England this promising experiment was emasculated after a few years by political interference, but not until after it had fructified developments in America.

Several aspec ; of an educational penology were already developing in the New World. The Sabbath schools advocated by Louis Dwight had in many cases undertaken to educate the illiterates, and more elaborate programs of instruction were already in operation in the reform schoo s. Richmond penitentiary had experimented for a time with a grading system; Charlestown and a few other prisons were occasionally celebrating a holiday with entertainments. Scattered contractors were giving the convicts small bonuses for good work. Indeed, an increasing emphasis was being placed all down the line on positive aids to reform.

The most forward-looking programs of the era came from the theoretical reformers. Edward Livingston, dean of the group, had outlined, in his model criminal code for Louisiana, a diversified system including reform schools for juveniles, houses of correction for minor offenders, and two grades of prisons. The proposed penitentiary system, which incidentally antedated the experiments of both Montesinos and Maconochie, envisaged a prison for punishment and labor in solitude, from which a convict by accumulating certificates of good conduct would earn his promotion to better quarters where he would enjoy the privilege of association in classes and at congregate labor. Although rejected by Louisiana, the code gained a deserved repute in the Northeast and in Europe.

Livingston had likewise advanced, at least tentatively, another theory which, if seriously considered, might have significantly altered the course of American prison development. This theory followed as a corollary of the then popular "science" of phrenology and maintained that certain criminals could be detected by an examination of the lobes of their skulls. George Combe, an English visitor of the late thirties, was more actively interested in the theory, and if his lectures had stimulated scientific research rather than righteous indignation, he might h‿ve antedated the Italian Lombroso as the founder of modern penology. But the scientific method was gaining hesitant recognition only in a few universities, and the dominant belief in the equality of men, together with the religious faith in the salvation of all, was sufficient to reject the suggestion that some criminals were incorrigibles to be cared for indefinitely as d‿ngerous patients. The reaction to this idea is hardly surprising when it is recalled that the asylums which Miss Dix was persuading the states to build were provided only for the purpose of *curing* the insane.

Stirrings within the old reform societies and the establishment of a new one in New York brought several fruitful ideas to the fore but without much practical effect on the administration of prisons. A minority faction within the Boston Society attempted to secure a hearing for the foreign criticisms of the Auburn system and a more tolerant attitude toward the Pennsylvania prisons. In the course of their struggle Samuel Gridley Howe and Horace Mann, the minority leaders, explored the penological literature of Europe, and Horace Mann went so far as to exchange letters with Maconochie; but their revolt involved an issue of personalities, and Dwight's stronger position enabled him to maintain absolute control over the Society.[4]

The revolt against the sterile argument over the merits of the separate and silent systems received a more hearty response in New York. Judge John W. Edmonds, recently appointed inspector of Sing Sing, found the problems there too great for singlehanded action and issued a call for a convention to meet in New York in 1844 to plan a concerted program of reform. A variety of humanitarian and intellectual forces responded, and the assembled judges, professors, Unitarian divines, and Quakers organized the New York Prison Association. Professor Johann L. Tellkampf, a visiting lecturer at Columbia College, struck the keynote of the convention when he declared that reformation, "the avowed object of penitentiaries," could not be realized by a complacent reliance on either

[4] Maconochie's letter to Mann is quoted by Sanborn in the *Proceedings of the American Social Science Association* (1874), pp. 12–16, probably its first public notice.

silence or separation.[5] He proceeded to outline the system he and Dr. Julius had proposed to the king of Prussia the year before—a house of detention with strictly separate cells, a lunatic asylum for insane criminals, and three grades of penitentiaries through which the convict would advance from complete separation, after the Cherry Hill pattern, to strict silence but congregate labor on the plan of Auburn and finally into a responsible association with a select group of reformed convicts where he would serve the remainder of his term under liberal regulations. With such a comprehensive formulation of many of the best theories of the day teasing the imaginations of the reformers at the convention it is no wonder that William H. Channing, the young and erratic Unitarian minister who became the first secretary of the Association, could assert with conviction that "the passion of overcoming evil with good is becoming everywhere superior to the vindictive spirit." Channing voiced the opinion of the convention when he concluded that "the community is itself, by its neglect and bad usages, in part responsible for the sins of its children; and owes the criminal, therefore, aid to reform."[6]

The Association was soon called upon by scattered reformers to father divers theories and programs. Letters arrived from various sources urging the society to indorse the reformatory sentence—the first expressions of this doctrine that have been found in American literature. Samuel Gridley Howe, recently returned to Boston after an extended study of European educational, penal, and asylum institutions, expressed the new theory most precisely.[7]

The doctrine of retributive justice is rapidly passing away, and with it will pass away, I hope, every kind of punishment that has not the reformation of the criminal in view. One of the first effects of this will be, I am sure, the decrease in the length of sentence and the adoption of some means by which the duration and severity of imprisonment may in all cases be modified by the conduct and character of the prisoners. What we want now—what no system that I know of offers—is the means of training the prisoner's moral sentiments and his power of self government by actual exercise. I believe that there are many who might be so trained as to be left upon their parole during the last period of their imprisonment.

[5] New York Prison Association, *Report* (1844), p. 45.

[6] *Ibid.*, p. 31.

[7] *Ibid.* (1846), pp. 21–22; *ibid.* (1847), pp. 90–92, 128–30. These last citations refer to letters from Rev. Samuel J. May and Mrs. E. W. Farnham, matron of Sing Sing, each advancing views similar to those of Howe.

While this fresh whiff of Froebelian doctrine was not strong enough immediately to redirect penal trends in America, a group of Quakers, joining the Association, pledged it to some practical efforts in behalf of discharged prisoners. Friend Isaac Hopper was appointed special agent to help the prisoners find jobs and homes at the time of their release, and for many years this faithful Quaker continued to serve in that capacity, breaking the way for parole agents in the years to come.

The new society certainly did not suffer from a lack of ideas, but it was handicapped by an overabundance of visionaries. A charter was secured from the legislature in 1846, granting authority to investigate the prisons of the state, but Judge Edmonds was not reappointed at the end of his term as inspector, and the new authorities refused to co-operate. John D. Russ, succeeding Channing as corresponding secretary, occasionally noted European developments,[8] but his reports contributed very little to practical prison developments. The fact was that the Association found itself out of harmony with penal trends in America when the dominant Auburn system was still young and self-righteous. Losing its hold on the charitable resources of the community, the Association had to curtail its activities, and only the energies of Isaac Hopper kept it alive during the following decade as a local aid society. Thus, although the Philadelphia Society had meanwhile abandoned its traditional seclusion and was issuing and distributing public reports, Louis Dwight was able to continue his former domination of penological practice in America.

INSTITUTIONAL EXPANSION

The failure of the theoretical inspiration to take hold did not check the rapid development of prisons throughout the land. New prisons erected in the South and the West copied the Auburn pattern, or its Baltimore compromise, largely because of the relative economy of construction and the promise of profits from congregate labor. New disciplinary measures were occasionally devised, but usually as a result of practical problems of control, and the limited attention given to religious and educational matters was but an out-

---

[8] *Ibid.* (1851), p. 312. Russ notes briefly Maconochie's proposal that labor sentences be substituted for time sentences.

growth of Dwight's program. The development of prosperous prison industries was the most earnest concern of the wardens, and indeed the rivalry between the officers of different prisons over their financial records gradually pushed aside the argument between the two systems, leaving it to the cranks and the historians to settle if they could. Nevertheless, this era did witness the further development of several of the best ideas of the former generation, notably the construction of additional houses of correction and reform schools and the segregation of the women. In short the states were able at least to maintain former standards in spite of the tremendous growth in the area and population of their settlements.

In a very significant way the incessant growth of population and the rapid expansion westward have been vital aids to prison reform. Together they have necessitated the construction of new prisons, thus providing the reformers with opportunities for the application of their theories. But at this time the more advanced theorists did not have a program that was easily adaptable to frontier conditions, and in New York, where a growing penal population certainly afforded a splendid opportunity for an experiment with the system of progressive penal stages, politics was in the saddle. The program of Louis Dwight, with its relatively economical prison structures and its promise of prosperous industries, continued to dominate the responsible officers charged with housing criminals. It was, nevertheless, a real undertaking for a frontier community to attempt to meet even this standard, and the erection of a dozen prisons was a creditable accomplishment.

The development of a penal system in the South and the Old Northwest was no simple task. In the late thirties these regions were still a part of the frontier in many senses of that illuminating term, and two additional decades were required before even the most advanced of these states was able to develop relatively stable prisons. The liberal criminal codes adopted at the start were quickly modified as the legislatures displayed a reckless willingness to add old-time punishments to a cumulative list of offenses.[9] The rapidly growing populations soon created serious housing problems in the new prisons, and several of the states were never able to provide the institutional equipment necessary to carry out the fine phrases of

[9] Laws of Indiana Territory (1801–9), *Illinois Historical Collection*, XXI, 35–50.

their laws. These frontier communities were preoccupied with the major problems of new settlements, and the authorities all too frequently shifted the burden of maintaining prisons to the first person who offered to assume it.

Frankfort, the oldest prison in the West, had struggled along for nearly three decades, neglected by the politicians, when in 1825 an energetic merchant, Joel Scott, offered to pay the state $1,000 a year for the labor of the convicts for five years. The authorities gladly shifted the whole burden to his care and in so doing originated the lease system that was to play an important part in the development of American penology. Joel Scott's chief concern was to establish prosperous industries, but he was a canny man and realized that discipline and security were first essentials. Studying the reports of Louis Dwight, this first of lessees started the construction, with the aid of public funds, of 250 cells on the Baltimore pattern and paid more than nominal respect to the Auburn discipline. Kentucky gladly extended his lease, and, when he retired in 1832, gave it to T. S. Theobold on similar terms. In the midst of construction activities that provided a cell house, a dining-room, a chapel, and several factories, Scott and Theobold carried on a profitable enterprise, creating an attractive pattern for many of the new prisons of the West and South.

Ohio and Tennessee, already challenging the Western political leadership of Kentucky, each built new prisons on Eastern patterns during the early thirties. These institutions at Columbus and Nashville provided adequate accommodations for their growing populations until the mid-fifties, and eager contractors vied for the opportunity to employ the inmates at prosperous industries that largely defrayed the prison expenses. The officers in both cases applied the Auburn discipline, and Columbus, growing the more rapidly, came to rival Charlestown for the blue ribbon among the larger institutions of this type during the fifties.

Indiana and Illinois shifted along with jail-like structures at Jeffersonville and Alton until the late thirties when both states commissioned their contractors to build new cell blocks on the Auburn pattern. Wardens held a nominal authority for a time, but the contractors would brook no interference and secured the full rights of lessees at both prisons by 1850. Unfortunately their building programs proved to be entirely inadequate. The 180 cells available at Jeffersonville in 1855 were crowded with 280 convicts, and the 160 cells completed a few years later failed to satisfy the needs of the expanded population. The first 88 cells at Alton in 1845 were already insufficient, and a decade later 300 prisoners were crowding 188 small cells. Not until both states undertook the construction of new prisons in the late fifties was there a reasonable hope that the wretched conditions would be corrected; unfortunately the outbreak of the Civil War defeated this expectation.

The convicts of Missouri were crowded into a still more unsatisfactory prison. Early state laws had directed that criminals should be punished with solitary confinement at hard labor, and when the prison was first opened at Jefferson City in 1836, 40 outside cells seemed a reasonable equipment for 46 convicts. But the number of prisoners increased rapidly, and 40 additional cells failed to satisfy the needs. In 1847 the governor answered a petition for better accommodations with the argument that two and three prisoners had long occupied each cell with little difficulty. Another decade passed before the state resumed control of its prison, which had been surrendered to a lessee in 1842, and started the construction of a cell block on the Auburn pattern with 236 small brick cells. But this program was likewise delayed by the war, and Missouri has never been able to boast of possessing a satisfactory prison system.

Meanwhile the Gulf states were cautiously experimenting with penitentiaries. The Carolinas still relied on the counties to administer justice, chiefly through corporal and capital punishments, but the law codes of the younger states of the Lower South frequently substituted terms of imprisonment for the older penalties. The regulation of the slaves who comprised the major portion of the population was usually handled in an extra-legal fashion, but these growing states found it necessary to build small prisons in order to house the free Negro and white convicts.

Administrative incompetence marred the good beginnings at the first three prisons. Georgia had established a prison in 1817 on the old congregate pattern, but Dwight's far-reaching agitation had helped to expose its evils, and in the late thirties the authorities erected a new building with 150 cells on the Baltimore pattern. It was poorly located from the point of view of industrial activity, but successive governors, complaining against large annual expenditures, forestalled improvements, and the structure remained in a neglected state until burned by the Northern army during the war. Louisiana opened its new prison at Baton Rouge in 1835 and embarked upon a carefully planned industrial program. A cotton mill and a shoe factory were introduced not only to manufacture essential articles for slave wear but to train machine operatives and to fight the high prices of Northern capitalists. The 100-cell prison was constructed on the Wethersfield model, and during the first years under a board of three directors the institution prospered. But a rapidly growing population increased expenses, and the authorities leased the prison to an enterprising company. An addition of cells increased the number to 240, but the population grew more rapidly, and the outbreak of the war found the prison seriously overcrowded. Alabama turned its prison erected at Wetumpka in 1841 over to a lessee from the start; fortunately the 208 cells on the Baltimore pattern remained adequate for all demands.

Mississippi and Texas satisfactorily met the moderate demands of their early years, while Florida did nothing, and Arkansas delayed until the end of the period to start its prison. The 148 cells erected at the "Walls" near the Mississippi state capital in the early forties proved adequate for all needs throughout this period, and a model cotton mill supplied labor for the well-disciplined prisoners and largely paid maintenance costs. When Texas prepared to erect a prison, one of its commissioners visited the Walls of Mississippi and returned with such a favorable report that the Lone Star State adopted this interpretation of the Auburn system. The 225 cells erected at Huntsville remained adequate until the eve of the war. The 85 similar cells erected at the Walls of Arkansas in 1858 were scarcely completed before the war brought an unexpected function to this as well as to most of the other prisons of the South—that of housing deserters and prisoners of war.[10]

It was little wonder that the South and the West did not follow Livingston's elaborate program or that of the theorists of the New York Prison Association. The settlers here were still engaged in the elemental struggle over land, slaves, and export prices, and their

---

[10] N.Y.P.A., *Report* (1868), p. 65. A letter to the Association from a member of the Arkansas legislature supplies the only description found of this small prison.

rapidly increasing numbers repeatedly denuded all state institutions except in those parts of the South where the counties continued indifferently to manage these functions. With enterprising merchants eager to lease the cheap and sure labor supply in order to man a blacksmith shop, a cooperage, or a cotton mill it is surprising that so many of the states adopted the warden system before the end of the period. Most of these states were planning expansion along Auburn lines when the Civil War intervened, postponing construction in the Northwest and turning the convicts of the South back into the hands of irresponsible lessees.

The Auburn system was making a more successful advance into a northern fringe of new states at the same time that it was establishing its sway throughout most of the older communities of the East. The advance of New York-New Englanders into Michigan, Wisconsin, and Iowa carried with it a rich institutional heritage. Accordingly when Michigan territory established its prison at Jackson in 1839, Wethersfield served as the model, and a fair-sized cell house was erected. An agent was placed in control, empowered to install new cells as they were required, and when the 164 cells ready in 1850 were filled, others were added. Wisconsin, feeling unequal to the task of building a permanent prison at the start, erected a log structure at Waupun in 1851. But, unlike most of the makeshift prisons, Waupun was equipped with individual cells, each provided with an iron-grated door that was to be used in the stone prison when completed, and before the end of the decade the convicts had the latter well under way. Iowa apparently did not take such pains with its prison at Fort Madison after the first small cell house was completed on the Wethersfield model, for a new warden in 1857 reported the necessity of cleaning out the prison yard used by his predecessor to house a herd of cows. Nevertheless, these states had prisons with a sufficient number of cells and were ready to take an active part in the reform movement of the next decade.

As a final triumph for Dwight's campaign in New England, Maine and Rhode Island were persuaded to adopt the Auburn system. The authorities at Thomaston had repeatedly condemned their underground prison before the legislature was persuaded in 1836 to order the construction of a new cell block on the Wethersfield pattern; but, delayed by hard times, the 108 cells of the new prison were not ready for occupation until the late forties. Rhode Island gave up its pretense of maintaining the solitary system when a congregate shop was introduced in order to mitigate the evil effects of confinement in small dark cells without labor. Dr. Francis Wayland, a former member of Dwight's Society and soon to be chosen president of Brown University, was made chairman of the board of directors at the prison in 1851. The following year a new wing with 88 cells on the Auburn pattern was started, and the Providence prison soon became a creditable institution. Meanwhile Dwight himself had been named as one of two commissioners empowered to plan the enlargement of Charlestown prison, and when the 150 new cells were opened in 1852, this old bastille had an equipment of 454 cells besides an old dormitory section that was soon to be refitted on the Auburn pattern.

The Auburn system made some further advances in the Middle Atlantic states. Although the separate structure erected for women at Sing Sing in 1835 was provided with 90 outside cells, the Auburn discipline was applied to the inmates who were daily gathered into laundry, sewing- or schoolrooms. The establishment of still another prison at Clinton in the Adirondacks and the construction there of typical Auburn cells further attested the Empire State's unswerving adherence to the system already discredited by its Prison Association. Even the New Jersey authorities were swinging over to Dwight's side as plans for a cell block on the Auburn pattern were finally acted upon at Trenton in 1860. Pennsylvania alone remained steadfast in its faith in the solitary system.

By far the most important penal problems still centered in the local jails. Unfortunately the efforts of Louis Dwight, Dorothea Dix, and the many other reformers scarcely affected the character of these institutions. Petty politicians were still in control, reaping fat profits from the corrupt fee system. Food, heat, and clothing were frequently deficient; and the bucket system, feeding in cells, poor ventilation, and overabundance of bugs and mice—all contributed to the wretched squalor of these institutions; but the indiscriminate association of all classes in the corridors in complete idleness every day was the crowning damnation of most jails.[11] The only feasible attack on this evil appeared to be the old one of removing special classes into separate institutions. The most promising reform of this sort was the widespread attack on imprisonment for debt. However, the complete abolition of such imprisonment made slow headway, and the relief enjoyed by local prisons from this source was more than offset by the rapid growth of towns and cities with their aggravated police problems. More was achieved as a score of workhouses for vagrants and several new reform schools were established, but even with the many new jails erected during the period the desperate conditions of the local lockups were scarcely alleviated. The one bright spot in this field was the success of several of the special institutions in evolving new disciplinary devices that were to play a significant part in later penological developments.

The petty offender was proving to be a decided nuisance in growing cities, especially during the winter months when he frankly sought refuge in the crowded jails. Albany determined in 1843 to correct this evil by building a local penitentiary for the confinement at hard labor of short-term drunkards and vagrants. The legislature was persuaded to grant the necessary authority, and Amos Pilsbury was called from Wethersfield to take charge. The achievements of this institution, notably its success in defraying expenses from the labor of the inmates, provided an attractive model for other cities. The New York Prison Association indorsed the program, and Rochester, Syracuse, Buffalo, and Erie and Kings counties in New York as well as Cincinnati and Detroit established such institutions during the next few years. Eleven counties in Massachusetts had meanwhile followed Boston's earlier example, but only two of these houses of correction were entirely separate from the county jails Several other scattered cities built new workhouses, most of which did little more than provide labor for the inmates.

All these institutions except the Moyamensing workhouse in Philadelphia had adopted the Auburn-type cell block, but no pre-

---

[11] Dorothea L. Dix, *Remarks on Prisons and Prison Discipline* (Boston, 1845), pp. 94–102. Miss Dix found only six jails worthy of honorable mention in 1845; three on the solitary pattern in Dauphin, Chester, and Philadelphia counties in Pennsylvania, and three on the Auburn pattern at Hartford, New Haven, and Boston.

tense was made of enforcing the silence system, and the absence of hardened criminals relieved them of the customary atmosphere of armed fortresses. Sabbath schools, libraries, and industry were standing these institutions off in sharp contrast with the great majority of the jails of the country, and a liberal discipline was differentiating them from the state prisons. Massachusetts, Michigan, and New York adopted the policy of sending most of their female convicts to these prisons, thus greatly relieving their state institutions. In 1856 New York passed a law permitting the commitment of young first offenders guilty of major crimes to the local penitentiaries and by this measure instituted a significant classification. But these institutions were only beginning to reveal their possibilities, and it was not until the sixties that the young and resourceful Zebulon Brockway made the new Detroit house of correction the most significant experiment station in the whole world of penology.

An equally creditable advance was being made in the field of juvenile institutions. The three reform schools established in the twenties had continued to develop in spite of the general diversion of interest to the state prisons. Now in the late forties an increasing recognition of public responsibility for the welfare of children brought a new impetus to the movement. State schools were established in Massachusetts and New York, but it was in the growing cities that this responsibility was most keenly felt, and Baltimore, Cincinnati, Pittsburgh, Providence, and Rochester were among the score of cities that established reform schools before the Civil War.

The authorities had recognized from the first the desirability of distinguishing these schools from the general penal system, and the breach was widened during this era. In spite of an excessive amount of disciplinary repression in many places the silent system was never attempted, and supervised games became a regular feature in several schools. The obligation of the school to provide general elementary instruction was conceded if not always fulfilled, but the boast that the active trade departments provided a valuable industrial training was seldom justified; a school ship launched by Massachusetts in 1859 probably came nearer than any other reform school to achieving this latter objective. The children were usually committed to the care of the school authorities during their minority, but the managers were generally empowered to indenture them to tradesmen or householders as soon as their reform was evident; this arrangement, together with the experiments with internal classification, progressive grading, and honor systems, supplied precedents for similar innovations in adult prisons a few decades later, but the direct line of succession was to be very indistinct. Meanwhile Horace Mann, Calvin E. Stowe, and other American educators who explored the European field returned with glowing accounts of the cottage system of the Rauhe House in Germany and Mettray in France, and that pattern was adopted at Lancaster, Massachusetts, in 1855 and at Lancaster, Ohio, in 1857. But again the gap between the trends of the reform school and the penitentiary system restrained the latter from profiting by this innovation until in the next century the application of the cottage system to women's reformatories broke down the bars of the Auburn cell-block tradition.

PENOLOGY IN PRACTICE DURING THE FIFTIES

The new currents of idealism that had enlivened penological theorists in the early forties failed to exert any considerable influence on prison practice. In Europe, where most of the countries were attempting to establish a penitentiary system somewhat after the Cherry Hill model, one or two significant experimenters were applying the new principles, most notably Sir Walter Crofton in Ireland; but Americans were at the time almost totally unaware of these developments. The American penitentiary had been projected and organized around the principle that each individual prisoner should be entirely cut off from his fellows. This simple negative program had early been modified in numerous respects, chiefly through the development of religious and industrial activities; now a moderate relaxation of the rigid disciplinary regulations and the introduction of new methods of control contributed to the same end Nevertheless, the American prison system of the late fifties was still very much as Louis Dwight had shaped it.

The dominant reform influences and reformatory agencies were, characteristically, religious. The campaign to supply Bibles, to provide chaplains, and to organize Sabbath schools had been largely successful. The growing power in the community at large of such denominations as the Methodists and the Baptists, with their emphasis on evangelism, was reflected in prison by an increasing num-

ber of revivals among the inmates; and, true to their higher responsibilities, many of the chaplains were more concerned over the soul
of one condemned man than over the preparation of his fellows to
return to society. No other incident sheds so much light on the reforms of this period as the heroic curtain call of Louis Dwight's
career. Rising from his death bed in 1854, this forthright servant of
God, long a leader in the morning prayer services in Old South
Chapel, drove to the Boston Lunatic Asylum to deliver a comforting
sermon to the inmates on "The Temptation of Christ."[12] The general American temper of the day placed great reliance on religion,
and it was not entirely as a figure of speech that wardens sometimes
addressed their reports to "Our Father" as well as to the "Gentle-
men of the Legislature."[13]

This widespread recognition of the function of religion in penology
helps to account for the fact that Enoch Wines and Theodore
Dwight, in their epoch-making investigation in the last year of the
Civil War, found all the wardens agreed that a major object of imprisonment was the reformation of convicts. This was not lip service, for, in the tradition they had inherited from Louis Dwight, God
was the great reformer of sinful men. The two investigators, reviving
the long-dormant ideals of the New York society, were the heralds
of a new era. While they praised the achievements of the past, not-
ing especially the progress in Boston, Philadelphia, Detroit, and
Albany, they nevertheless concluded "there is not a state prison in
America, in which the reformation of the convict is the supreme
object of the *discipline*."[14]

The all-absorbing concern of the wardens was to make the prisons
pay their expenses. Louis Dwight had made prison industry one of
his foster children. After the termination of his reports in 1854, the
occasional interstate communications were little more than acrimonious arguments over the financial merits of the various prisons.
Only the directors of Cherry Hill maintained a philosophical indifference toward large unearned expenditures, and the explanation
of this exception may be found in the unique custom of charg-

[12] Boston P.D.S., *Report* (1854), obituary notice.

[13] Connecticut State Prison, *Report* (1870).

[14] Wines and Dwight, *Prisons in the United States and Canada*, pp. 287–88 (author's
italics).

ing the board of each prisoner to the county in which he was convicted.

Only such administrators as succeeded in making their institutions largely self-sufficient gained the opportunity to consider the other functions of imprisonment. In the incessant political turmoil none but financially successful wardens could live through a change in parties. It was not a chance circumstance that, with the sole exception of Cherry Hill, all the prisons gaining honorable mention from Wines and Dwight at the end of the period had outstanding economic records. The Pilsburys, Haynes, Cordier, Rice, and Brockway, the ablest wardens of the day, had all won distinction in this respect before they did any experimenting in the reformation of their charges.

In the hard world of the prisoner this was not an indictment, and, when contrasted with the wretched idleness in local jails, it appears in its proper light as a genuine achievement. The abler wardens managed their prison industries with the aid of the institution's credit, but contractors dominated the scene in all but three or four of the prisons, frequently returning to the states more than enough to cover prison expenses, as was the case in 1852 when nine prisons reported a combined surplus of over $23,000.[15] The use of convict labor to help construct prisons, capitol buildings, and other public works was fairly general throughout the country but most frequent in the younger states of the West. The diversified methods of exploiting prison labor at the time enabled the authorities to avoid effective opposition, but the struggle to maintain prosperous industries frequently caused the authorities to lose sight of the interests of the prisoners; Wines and Dwight were disappointed to find that "one string is harped upon, ad nauseam—money, money, money."[16]

One of the inevitable results of this preoccupation with profits was a relaxation of the original methods of discipline. The construction program had provided a fairly adequate cell capacity so that most of the convicts, at least those of the Northeast, were supplied with individual cells throughout the era—a condition that was never

[15] Boston P.D.S., *Report* (1852), p. 103. Wethersfield had annually reported small profits from 1833.

[16] Wines and Dwight, *op. cit.*, pp. 289, also 265–68.

to be realized on such a wide scale after the Civil War. Meanwhile the additional features of the silent system were receiving a more diversified application, and the intrusion of educational and other activities was breaking down the rigid character of the old Auburn pattern.

Silence at all times, lock-step marching, downcast eyes except when addressed by an officer, no gazing at visitors, no clothing or other articles except as supplied by the prison, striped uniforms—these were the traditional features of the Auburn system, but Connecticut and New Hampshire were the only states to enforce all of them rigidly. The prison in Maine and that at Clinton, New York, went so far as to permit talking at labor "when necessary" and, together with Vermont, discarded the lock step. Several of the wardens favored a radical modification of the whole system, and already complete "freedom of the yard" had been granted on national holidays in Massachusetts, Michigan, and Missouri. In most prisons discipline had become customarily lax on these special days; talking in the dining-halls and the uproarious powwows in the cells at Sing Sing gained the authority of ancient custom. There was just a suggestion here of what the American prison system might have become, might yet become, if the prisoners were idle at all times. Wines and Dwight concluded as to the actual force of the silent system: "Communication, then, we must believe, takes place among convicts continually and in most prisons to a very great extent."[17]

The growing faith in public education and the popularity of circulating libraries had their influence on prisons. School classes had been a feature of juvenile institutions from their beginning; the Boston house of correction started classes in 1841, but the New York law of 1847 providing two instructors for each state prison was the first effective application of this policy to the major prisons. However, these teachers simply passed from cell to cell as occasional chaplains had done before, instructing in the three R's, and the periods between their visits were so long that the value of their services was questionable. By 1865 instructors in New York and Pennsylvania, as well as chaplains in Connecticut and New Hampshire, made their rounds in this fashion; only Ohio maintained regu-

[17] *Ibid.*, p. 177.

lar classes conducted by the chaplain three evenings a week. Education in the other prisons rested with the Sabbath schools.

The provision for prison libraries was the next step in many prisons. Early chaplains had occasionally loaned books to trusted prisoners as a supplement to Bible reading. Probably the first prison library supplying more than Bibles and religious tracts was that established at Sing Sing in 1840 by Warden Seymour and Governor Seward. New Jersey and other states made similar provisions, but in 1847 New York was the first to start the custom of making annual appropriations. When Wines and Dwight made their survey, they found libraries of a sort in all state prisons. Unfortunately, pious religious books, discarded by thrifty parsons, stuffed the shelves; their service was little more than that of providing an escape to readers bored with the drab realities of their prison home. Neither the libraries nor the elementary instruction can be credited with solving the indignant question of one convict: "Better thoughts! Where shall I get them?"[18]

The disciplinary problem was naturally more complicated in the prisons where the silent system held sway. The punishment records revealed that Maine, with its liberal policy toward talking, had the smallest percentage. A closer study showed that in the average prison the majority of punishments were for offenses against the rule of silence, and that short-term men and new arrivals received the largest share of these. The means of punishment were quite varied, but the severe methods of earlier days had been considerably modified. At least six prisons still permitted the lash and occasionally the "cat," but the trend was in the direction of leniency. New York had made the questionable reform of substituting the "crucifix," "bucking," and the "shower bath" for the unpopular lash. All the states permitted the dark cell with a bread-and-water diet, and this was the only punishment aside from the withdrawal of good time permitted in New England and Ohio.

There were several developments during this period that represented positive achievements. Thus the introduction of the practice of commuting sentences for good behavior was a considerable advance over corporal punishment as a means of maintaining disci-

[18] *Ibid.*, p. 221.

pline. The provision of paltry sums for the aid of discharged criminals and the appointment of agents to assist these outcasts to make a
new start in life were enlightened additions to the penal system. At
the same time the success of the agitation of Dorothea Lynde Dix
for public hospitals for the insane made it possible to relieve the
jails and prisons of many of these unfortunates.

The principle of commutation was not original with this era.
New York had had a good-time law as early as 1817, though it had
not been applied. The early reformers had not distinguished clearly
between commutation, the labor sentence, and the ticket-of-leave
procedures that were being proposed in England during the period,
all which modifications of the simple time sentence had indeed been
foreshadowed by Pennsylvania's action in 1790 in giving judges the
power to release men they had sentenced in case they found them
to be reformed before their terms were completed. But the distinguishing feature of commutation was the bid it made for obedience
to prison rules, and Tennessee, beginning in 1836, was the first state
to apply such good-time reductions of sentences over a period of
years. The procedure did not gain wide popularity until, in 1856,
Cyrus Mendenhall secured such a law in Ohio. Eight Northeastern
states followed within a decade, as the authorities quickly saw the
disciplinary value of the scheme of granting the prisoners a few
days' reduction of sentence for each month of good conduct. The
reformatory value of these laws depended very largely on the character of the officers, but, at least during the first years of their application, commutation laws seemed to stimulate many convicts to
try to become good citizens as well as good prisoners.

Meanwhile the humanitarian temper of the age was directing
attention to the problems of discharged prisoners. Quakers in and
out of Philadelphia had early given aid and comfort to prisoners on
their release from jail, but the New York Association was the first
to organize the work under the kindly services of Isaac Hopper.
Charles and John Murray Spear organized the Prisoners' Friend
Association in Boston in 1845, and for several years, rallying friends
to their assistance through the pages of their journal, *Prisoners'
Friend*, these compassionate brothers aided the men discharged from
the prisons of Massachusetts. The Philadelphia Society followed
these leads in 1853 when it appointed William J. Mullen agent to

care for the discharged and eventually secured government funds for his support.[19] Charitable citizens of Maryland, New Jersey, and Rhode Island likewise organized societies for this particular purpose. Massachusetts stepped forward into the next era when in 1845 the philanthropic John Augustus was appointed state agent and given government support in the care of the discharged. Another decided step in advance was taken in the same year by the New York Association when its women's branch founded the Isaac T. Hopper Home for discharged women prisoners, thus following the example of Elizabeth Fry in England. Amos Pilsbury, whose views on prison affairs carried weight, declared that this type of public charity had larger reformatory value than any amount of education within the prison.

Another forward-looking movement, the campaign of Dorothea Lynde Dix to persuade the states to undertake the cure of the insane, was beginning to exert an important influence on prison developments. As a result of the campaign the states, by the end of this period, had built asylums to a capacity that practically equaled that of the state prisons, and many serious cases were thus eliminated from the jails and prisons.[20] A few states provided that insane prisoners might be transferred to the asylums, but New York, troubled with the largest number of these cases, determined to erect a special asylum for insane criminals outside the walls at Auburn prison, and the new institution was opened in 1859. Ohio and Illinois took steps in this direction a few years later, but unfortunately the buildings they erected were within their prison yards and followed the solitary-cell pattern rather than that of the asylum ward already developed at Auburn and the better asylums. Another half-century was to pass before more enlightened views concerning insanity were to help revolutionize penology.

Meanwhile hardly anything had as yet been attempted in the most vital phase of prison reform—the organization of agencies for controlling policy. Except in Pennsylvania politics was everywhere actively in charge. The selection of prison inspectors by the state Supreme Court had secured a stable, if conservative, administration in the Keystone State. Massachusetts, Vermont, and Maine claimed

[19] *Philanthropist* (March extra, 1856).

[20] Boston P.D.S., *Report* (1852), pp. 103 and 137. Dwight reports the population of seventeen prisons as 4,515, and that of twenty-four asylums as 4,943.

that their prisons were free from politics, but this was due either to the continued dominance of one party or to the economic efficiency of a given warden. No state had as yet vested control over its entire prison system in any central body as England and France had done. The Massachusetts Board of State Charities, organized in 1863, was only a timid step in this direction, while the New York Board of Prison Inspectors had long been a most disappointing experiment in centralized management. Most of the prisons were controlled by an authority carefully suspended in good American style between a board of inspectors and a warden, each appointed separately and for varied short terms by the governor, legislature, or the two acting together. Massachusetts paid her warden $2,500, while all the others scaled from $2,000 down to $700.[21] Naturally these several features had discouraged able and honest men from seeking such insecure positions.

In the complex hierarchy of prison authorities there was yet another and most disturbing element—the governor's power to pardon. While it may have corrected many evils in the dispensation of justice, the frequent use of the pardoning power in an attempt to relieve overcrowded and unhealthy jails and prisons had undermined the discipline of many institutions.[22] The prisoners could see no certain standards of conduct where luck, religious "mush," or outside "pull" seemed to determine one's fate, and it was true that the more desperate criminals got most of the "breaks." Discipline was difficult and reformation almost an impossibility where one out of six prisoners received a pardon. The wardens were all opposed to the practice, but, when Wisconsin moved to require the recommendation of the warden, few of these practical officers considered the advantage worth the risk of the charge of favoritism. But at least the authorities were alive to the serious nature of the problem, which

[21] Wines and Dwight, *op. cit.*, pp. 77–82 and 119.   [22] *Ibid.*, p. 302.

ABSTRACT OF PARDON STATISTICS

CATEGORIES	MASS.	EASTERN PA.	OHIO	WIS.
	40-Year Aver.	10-Year-Period Aver.		
Convicts pardoned........................	12¾ per cent	13½ per cent	18¾ per cent	20 per cent
Lifers pardoned...........................	50 per cent	....	40 per cent	33 per cent
Average years of lifers in prison.............	7¾ yrs.	....	6½ yrs.	6 yrs.

made them receptive to the parole system when it was brought forward in the next era.

Thus, by and large, America had a fairly adequate penal system at the time of the outbreak of the Civil War. Except in Pennsylvania, the Auburn system was decidedly predominant and, although modified in minor details, retained its strongly religious ideology and its active industrial program intact. However, its Baltimore architectural compromise had been copied extensively in the South and West, and the leasing arrangement of Kentucky was substituted in several of these outlying states for the more general contract system. Only in the Northeast was the equipment sufficient to provide each prisoner with a separate cell, but even the states west and south of Ohio, where this standard was seldom realized in practice, had laws and projected programs of construction that indorsed these precepts. It is true that the young states of the Far West and the wide-open territories shared few of these traditions, but in that rough and ready frontier practically the only criminals of consequence were the fast-shooting highwaymen and the half-breed cattle thieves whose careers frequently ended with their capture. "Strong jails" occasionally served there, as throughout the South, and still to a deplorable extent in the Northeast, housing an indiscriminate assortment of cases; only a score of local institutions in the more populous centers of the Northeast were struggling to correct some of the evils of this weakest link in the American penal system. Some forward-looking principles had found expression without much effect during the forties, and, although it was not suspected by the penal authorities of the late fifties, the time was near at hand when these theories were to play a part in an extensive reorientation of the entire penal system.

BIBLIOGRAPHICAL NOTE

Edward Livingston, *Code of Reform and Prison Discipline* (Quebec ed.; 1831); Alexander Maconochie, *Norfolk Island* (London, 1848); Mary Carpenter, *Our Convicts* (London, 1864); William Paley, *Principles of Moral and Political Philosophy* (Collins ed.; New York, 1837); and especially the early *Reports* of the New York Prison Association (1844———), are of primary importance for a study of the new theoretical trends. More of the annual reports of the prisons are preserved for this period, and they are supplemented by the Boston Discipline Society, *Reports* (1826–54); Dorothea Lynde Dix, *Remarks on Prisons and Prison*

Discipline (Boston, 1845); George Combe, *Lectures on Phrenology* (New York, 1839), and his *Notes on the United States of North America* (Philadelphia, 1841); and by Enoch C. Wines and T. Dwight, *Prisons in the United States and Canada* (New York, 1867).

Again O. F. Lewis, *The Development of American Prisons and Prison Customs*, is authoritative down to 1845. For the individual states, in addition to the volume on Pennsylvania prisons by H. E. Barnes, should be added his *A History of the Penal, Reformatory and Correctional Institutions in the State of New Jersey* (Trenton, 1918); Philip Klein, *Prison Methods in New York State* (New York, 1920); Clara B. Hicks, *The History of Penal Institutions in Ohio to 1850* (Columbus, 1924); William C. Sneed, *A Report on the History and Mode of Management of the Kentucky Penitentiary* (Frankfort, 1860); and Elizabeth Wisner, *Public Welfare Administration in Louisiana* (Chicago, 1930). Other important volumes are David Dyer, *History of the Albany Penitentiary* (Albany, 1867); R. D. and F. D. Hill, *Memoir of Matthew Davenport Hill* (London, 1878); and David S. Snedden, *Administrative and Educational Work in American Juvenile Reform Schools* (New York, 1907). Articles of value are: H. C. Mohler, "Convict Labor," *Journal of Criminal Law and Criminology*, XV, 530–63; and E. L. Ryan, "Imprisonment for Debt—Its Origin and Repeal," *Virginia Magazine of History and Biography*, January, 1934.

CHAPTER III

THE DEVELOPMENT OF A REFORM MOVEMENT

The Civil War, ringing in a new era in many phases of social history, helped to co-ordinate in time and character the scattered strands of normal penological development. The compelling urgency of growing populations, the inspiration of native and foreign achievements, the zeal of new agencies for social control, and popular confidence in high ideals were opportunely brought together at the close of the war in time to assist a band of energetic reformers in an effective movement for prison reform. The first stage of the movement saw the best theories of the forties incorporated together with some new ideals into ambitious programs, and if the leaders were somewhat too optimistic, they nevertheless charted most of the developments of the next half-century.

The war helped to bring the movement to a head in the late sixties by checking a premature attempt at collaboration among prison officers. When Louis Dwight and his Boston Society finished their labors in 1854, a real opportunity for new leadership had appeared. The New York Prison Association was handicapped at the time by poverty, and the mace passed to the hand of Frederick A. Packard of Philadelphia, editor of the *Quarterly Journal of Prison Discipline*. Unfortunately Packard was so firmly committed to the Pennsylvania system that, while greatly assisting the movement for reform schools[1] he was unable to give hearty approval to the new ideas that his European correspondents called to his attention. His *Journal*, although widely circulated, could not buck the Auburn tradition in America.

Whether stimulated by these journals or propelled solely by a personal desire for guidance in building his new state prison, Edward M. McGaw, commissioner of Wisconsin prisons, corresponded with several wardens and reformers suggesting a conference in Philadelphia. When the Convention of Friends of Penal Reform gathered in September, 1859, seven states and three prison societies were

[1] *Journal of Prison Discipline* (Philadelphia, 1858), p. 104; *ibid.* (1859), p. 92.

represented. Gideon Haynes and five other wardens were among the twenty delegates. Most of the time was spent debating the relative merits of the Pennsylvania and Auburn systems, and, although the delegates lacked enthusiasm, they organized the American Society for the Improvement of Penal and Reformatory Institutions and called a second convention to meet in New York the following year.[2]

Several of the outstanding men in the field were present at the second gathering. Judge John W. Edmonds, Dr. John Griscom, and Professor Francis Lieber from New York, together with William Parker Foulks and Frederick Packard from Philadelphia, were all old in the service; Zebulon Brockway, down for the occasion from his county penitentiary in Rochester, was just making his reputation as a thrifty warden. Again the old debate raged between the rival systems, and a long philosophical discourse by the aged patron of the past, William Parker Foulks, failed to stir the creative genius of the young Brockway.[3] There is no evidence that the third convention under the presidency of Dr. Griscom ever convened as scheduled in Baltimore in 1861. Meanwhile Packard's quarterly, with its resources diverted by the war, was taken over by the Philadelphia Society, and, as an annual journal, became the official report of that organization. All articles now had to be approved by a vote of the Society, and Philadelphia was saved the embarrassment of nurturing a movement that might outgrow the faith of the fathers.

The war helped in another way to unify and to time the movement. Whether the army had absorbed the potential criminals, afforded a refuge for fugitives, or supplied a convenient commutation of sentence, the result was the same—a decided reduction of male commitments in all the states of the North. The survey in the summer of 1865 found most of the prisons equipped with reasonably adequate housing accommodations and fairly prosperous industries. The sudden increase in commitments following the close of the war crowded the prisons, placed penal problems on the front page in both popular and legislative journals, and presented all the prison administrators of the country with a common housing problem.

---

[2] *Ibid.* (1859), pp. 184–87. The prisons of Wisconsin, Michigan, New York. Massachusetts, Pennsylvania, New Jersey, and Maryland and the societies of New York, Philadelphia, and Baltimore were represented at the conference.

[3] *Ibid.*, (1861), pp. 34–36.

THE EMERGENCE OF NEW LEADERSHIP

The war had failed to absorb all the energy of the Northerners, and in New York, in particular, philanthropists as well as capitalists and laborers had their minds on other matters. After several lean years, during which the New York Association had been almost forgotten by the rapidly changing city, new friends began to rally to its cause. Judge John David Wolfe joined and became president in 1861. Although at first inclined to wait until the war had been won before pressing his cause, within a year the new president was pounding at the doors of the legislature, hat in hand. The real leadership, however, was to come from E. C. Wines, the new corresponding secretary appointed in 1862.

Dr. Enoch Cobb Wines was ripe with experience when the Civil War snuffed out the City University of St. Louis, of which he had just been chosen first president. After leaving his father's New England farm and graduating from Middlebury College, Wines had instructed in boys' schools, on a naval training ship, and, after several years of ministry in a Congregational church in Vermont and later in a Presbyterian parish on Long Island, had become a lecturer at Washington College, Pennsylvania. For a short time in the forties he had edited the *Monthly Advocate of Education*, urging the need for state normal schools and free public education. Added to all these rich experiences was the strength which comes to a man who, in the memory of his son, "never had a religious doubt." When he was called to the New York Prison Association as its new secretary in 1862, Wines responded in the spirit of a laborer assigned to a new vineyard, and he soon proved himself to be worthy of his hire.

Most of his fellow-workers had had long experience in the work. Professor Francis Lieber and Judge Edmonds were still active members. Dr. John H. Griscom, son of the noted founder of the first house of refuge, was carrying on in his father's spirit, while Abraham Beal was faithfully bearing the mantle of Isaac Hopper. Theodore W. Dwight, scion of the noted Dwights of Yale and soon to become first head of the Columbia Law School, joined the group shortly after the arrival of Wines. But these kindly spirited citizens and their growing Association needed the zeal and organizing ability of Dr. Wines to translate their high ideals into action.

Like his predecessor in Boston, Wines was essentially a pulpit reformer and for eighteen years used his post to proclaim many and vàried ideals, all looking toward the reformation of criminals. Again and again he called for more earnest support, declaring, "Our work is mainly a work of humanity and benevolence. . . . . It is a philanthropy akin to that divine benevolence that calls backsliders to repent."[4] Animated by a persistent zeal himself, Wines instilled a new enthusiasm into the New York Association and won for it the leadership it had failed to gain in earlier days.

But zeal and organizing ability never of themselves create great movements, and energetic leaders are fortunate when they find scattered forces in the field, ready for guidance toward co-ordinated expression. Wines found an abundance of such forces active in the early sixties, and rejoiced with Theodore Dwight over the many signs of growth noted on their tour. Wardens such as Cordier in Wisconsin, Rice in Maine, Hubbell in Sing Sing, as well as Haynes and Brockway were struggling to solve their growing problems; if there was to be any genuine reformation of criminals, it would be their job, and each was busy with his experiments.

Gideon Haynes, at Charlestown, Massachusetts, was enthusiastically commended by Wines and Dwight for making real progress toward a reformatory discipline. His efficient industrial program, although in the hands of contractors, was supplying healthy activity to the prisoners. A liberal interpretation of the rules of silence, a careful application of the commutation system, and the practice of granting occasional holidays in the yard to those in good standing had eliminated the necessity for the use of the lash and greatly reduced the problem of discipline. In 1867 Haynes added a good library, an active Sabbath-school program, and a third educational feature in the form of lectures once or twice a month. When in the following year the legislature appropriated $1,000 for these purposes, schoolbooks were purchased and classes for illiterates conducted two evenings a week. There was ample justification for ranking Charlestown as the model state prison in the land in the late sixties.

The best expression of the point of view of wardens awake to their opportunities came from Zebulon Brockway. Few men are able to project their future careers so concisely as did the superintendent of

[4] N.Y.P.A., *Report* (1863), p. 51.

the Detroit house of correction in 1865, revealing as well a clear understanding of the factors that were to bring success.[5]

I feel [Brockway wrote to Wines] that there are very gross defects in the prison system of the land, and that, as a whole, it does not accomplish its design; and that the time has come for reconstruction. There are doubtless in operation in the prisons of this country, religious and moral agencies, physical and hygienic regulations, and a system of employment for prisoners which if combined in the management of one institution, would produce a model prison indeed. To find them, combine them, and apply them, is, in my mind, the great desideratum. . . . . In my own quiet corner here, I am at work at this and trust that by next year the practical operation of our system of labor and partial gradation of prisoners will add at least a mite to the progress of prison reform. . . . . This is an age of demonstration, and the practicality of the improvement proposed must be demonstrated at every step to secure its adoption.

Thus the movement enlisted sturdy officers for its field activities. All the congresses, investigations, and reports, all the "I was in prison and ye came unto Me" sermons, were significant only in so far as they helped awaken and enrich the experimenting imagination of the wardens and secured for them a free hand, a stable tenure, and public support. But this was service enough for any reformer, since without it enduring progress was impossible. Already Franklin B. Sanborn and Samuel Gridley Howe in Massachusetts, the Quakers in Pennsylvania, Dr. Francis Wayland, the elder, in Rhode Island, and less prominent groups in other states were busy at the task.

The tour of Wines and Dwight in the summer of 1865 and the organization that winter of the American Association for Promoting the Social Sciences[6] officially launched the movement. By 1868 Wines was able to report that "more has been published in the quarterly, monthly, weekly and daily journals of the country within the last two years than during the ten years preceding."[7] To this literature should be added the comprehensive report of Wines and Dwight, the publications, now fat volumes, of the New York and Pennsylvania prison societies, of the Massachusetts Board of State Charities, and of several special investigating commissions in New Jersey, Pennsylvania, and other states. A growing appreciation of the public's responsibility for its criminals was an encouraging fea-

[5] Wines and Dwight, *Prisons in the United States and Canada*, pp. 343–44.

[6] N.Y.P.A., *Report* (1866), p. 35. This organization was later renamed the American Social Science Association.

[7] *Ibid.* (1868), p. 63.

ture of this literature, and the need to place control in capable and non-partisan hands was clearly expressed.

ORGANIZATION FOR CONTROL

The decentralized American democracy was being knit together in post–Civil War days as problems of control received attention in industry and politics, and the fields of charity and correction profited from this trend. A growing concern over poverty, insanity, and crime and a popular reaction to cruelty, debauchery, and corruption acted in varying proportions in different states to prompt the creation of central authorities for inspection and control. Politics, a desire for economy, and the hang-over of local traditions frequently retarded developments, but the commanding necessities of housing and other problems pushed reforms ahead in those states where the march of affairs was in "seven league boots." Massachusetts, New York, Pennsylvania, Ohio, and Illinois each organized its board of charities before 1879. Rhode Island, Michigan, Wisconsin, and North Carolina quickly followed their example. These boards were to have a quite varied influence on prisons, but the trend toward central control had nevertheless set in.

Civic pride, social righteousness, and public charity have always been considered strong points of the Bay State, but the creation of the Board of State Charities was frankly conceived as a move toward economy. An earlier board of commissioners of charities created in 1856 with restricted authority over almshouses had proved inadequate, and the new board with seven members was organized in 1863 and empowered to investigate all public charitable and correctional institutions in the state and "to recommend such changes and additional provision as they may deem necessary for their economical and efficient administration." Franklin Benjamin Sanborn, neighbor and disciple of Emerson, was chosen secretary, and the venerable Samuel Gridley Howe was shortly made chairman of the board. In the midst of many other responsibilities Sanborn found time to canvass the world's literature for ideas on correction and brought together in a special report on prisons in 1865 the first complete surveys in America of the English ticket-of-leave and the Irish-Crofton systems. Howe and Sanborn quickly made their board the model governmental agency of the decade.

New York had long been struggling with the problem of prison control, but both the board of inspectors and the New York Prison Association had failed to perform this function. The three inspectors, one elected each year, had large powers of control, but in practice each assumed full authority over one of the three prisons and proceeded to give his henchmen their share of the jobs, the orders for supplies, and the contracts for labor and construction. In 1859 Governor Morgan had recommended that complete authority be given to one inspector who should be appointed for a long term by the governor. When the legislature failed to act, Morgan undertook to demonstrate the value of the procedure by appointing Amos Pilsbury as his special investigator in 1862; but the regular inspectors blocked the work of even this seasoned veteran, claiming that they, rather than the governor, were responsible for this function. Central responsibility was impossible in such an arrangement.

It was largely due to this impasse that Enoch Wines and Judge Wolfe found the legislature responsive in 1863 to their appeals for funds to aid their inspection of prisons.[8] Good fortune had placed Tallock on the board of inspectors and Hubbell as warden of Sing Sing, thus opening prison doors to frequent inspection. When these friends were removed within a year or two, Wines became convinced that progress was impossible while politics was in the saddle. At his suggestion the Association began to prepare for New York's periodical constitutional convention, the reformer's heyday, just around the corner. A committee was created to draft an amendment providing centralized control over the prisons, and Wines and Dwight made their famous tour in order to collect facts and experiences for its use.

This committee, comprised of Dwight, Lieber, Griscom, Gould, and Wines, was supported by Judge William F. Allen and Mayor John T. Hoffman, soon to become governor. They drafted an able amendment, designed to eliminate politics from prison control. A prison commission of five members, one to be appointed every two years for a ten-year term, was to have full charge of all state prisons, to appoint and remove the chief officers, to make regulations and grant orders and contracts. The consitutional convention appointed

---

[8] *Ibid.* (1870), pp. 157–64. Wines raised $12,768 in 1863, $5,000 each from the city and from the state; the average expenditures of the Association during its first seventeen years had been $2,349.

its own prison committee, and, following Governor Morgan's proposal, a majority of this group recommended a single, all-powerful, prison superintendent; but vigorous lobbying on the part of Wines persuaded the convention to substitute the Association's amendment for that of the committee. With victory so near, it was a considerable disappointment when the entire constitution was rejected at the polls in 1869. Nevertheless, a high standard had been raised and an ideal program had received favor and indorsement by responsible authority; the New York reformers were still optimistic of final success.[9]

Ohio, like New York, was experiencing tremendous development. Her state prison at Columbus, with its 1,050 cells, had the questionable distinction of ranking with Sing Sing as the largest in the land. Already it was becoming crowded. Several attempts to perfect its management culminated in the law of 1867 which applied the New York idea to the board of directors, providing six-year appointments for its three members, one every two years. This body was given the power to select the major officers, to create the rules, and let the contracts. Meanwhile the seventy-seven counties with their dilapidated jails urgently needed central supervision, and, following the lead of Massachusetts, a state board of charities was created in 1867. Five non-salaried members were appointed for three-year terms, and powers of inspection and recommendation for all penal and charitable institutions in the state were conferred on them. As no funds were supplied to employ a secretary, the prison loaned the services of its chaplain, Albert G. Byers. For several years thereafter this Methodist minister and one-time army chaplain secured free passes on the numerous railroads and traveled his extended circuit throughout the state, visiting jails and almshouses, insane institutions and reform schools, and occasionally returning to his home base in the prison. In company with the president of his board, Byers visited major institutions in New York, Pennsylvania, and Massachusetts, and worked out a well-considered program for the expansion of the state penal system; their most noteworthy success was in the counties where they stimulated the erection of new structures on a model borrowed in part from Boston.

[9] The New York Board of Charities, created in 1867, does not come into this discussion because it had nothing to do with either jails or prisons.

The reputation of the central board of supervision was spreading, and three more states created such boards in 1869. In Pennsylvania the Philadelphia Society called attention to the valuable work of the Massachusetts Board, and the legislature was finally persuaded to create a similar one. Unfortunately its influence was dissipated by responsibility for the inspection of all eleemosynary institutions, and with few powers it could do little more than undertake the education of county and state officers. In Illinois the number of state charitable institutions had increased from three to eight during the decade, emphasizing the need for central management, and a board of public charities was created in 1869 with authority to inspect all public institutions except the state prison. Frederick Howard Wines, son of the New York reformer, was chosen as secretary for the board, and in succeeding years the county jails and especially the several correctional institutions of Chicago profited greatly from his persistent prodding. In Rhode Island a legislative committee, appointed to consider the state's need for an insane asylum, proposed in 1868 that such an institution be built together with a state house of correction on a state farm and further recommended that a single board be created to supervise them. These proposals met the approval of the legislature and a board of charities and correction was organized and given not only supervisory authority but full power to create the new state farm and to manage it thereafter. Thus was created the first board of control in America; its scope was gradually extended as additional institutions were erected on the 400-acre farm, and a decade later, when a new prison was built at the farm, that institution as well was brought under its control.

Other states were shortly to follow these leads, and in the meantime public-spirited citizens were organizing prison societies. Maryland, New Hampshire, and far-western California witnessed the formation of societies on the New York pattern, and at least one of these, that of G. S. Griffiths in Baltimore, was destined to exert considerable influence over local penal developments. Agitation for reform in New Jersey and Indiana found vent in special investigating commissions, but their comprehensive reports suffered from the lack of the follow-up work of the boards of charities in other states. Much more remained to be done in 1870 than was realized at the time, but progress in the direction of central inspection and control had at least been encouraging.

ORIGIN OF THE REFORMATORY PROGRAM

One of the first results of reorganization was the creation of a class of men who quickly came to regard themselves as professional penologists. The members of the several boards of supervision, and especially the secretaries, usually saw longer service than the earlier managers had enjoyed, and several of them became active leaders of the reform movement. Enoch Wines and his son, as well as Richard Vaux, Albert Byers, and G. S. Griffiths made their reputations in this work; Franklin Sanborn, the two Francis Waylands, Samuel G. Howe, and Theodore Dwight served the cause faithfully in spite of their larger interests in other fields. Brockway, Cordier, Rice, Haynes, Felton, Vail, and the Pilsburys among the wardens enjoyed longer tenures and advancement from one position to another, partly as a result of the influence of the new controls. These were some of the men that gave the movement form and personality, making its history much more than a statistical abstract.

Among the men who were presuming to show the American public how to reform its criminals, very few considered it necessary to make a protracted study of the problem. They had the feeling that their natural equipment of Christianity and common sense required only the baptism of experience to secure them good standing in the calling. They quoted the Bible to prove the reformability of criminals, but their faith more frequently came out of a warm experience; Brockway was one of many who gained strength at the altar.[10] This element was so prominent in the early days that its importance can scarcely be overestimated; its practical disappearance in the course of the next fifty years was to be a significant factor in the story.

Many of the leaders were already so old in prison service that the new organizations at first brought simply a greater zeal and force to ideas inherited from a century of reformers. Wines and Dwight in their report had applauded several new developments, but most of their attention was directed toward the stimulation of the old programs for education, religion, industrial activity, and human kindness.

Efforts to improve the educational facilities opened week-day classes in Wisconsin, Ohio, and New Hampshire prisons and in the Detroit house of correction. Following the example of Haynes in

[10] Z. Brockway, *Fifty Years* (New York, 1912), pp. 63–65. Brockway tells about his conversion in Rochester, the "city of revivals," in the late fifties.

Massachusetts, lectures on advanced subjects were provided in these prisons and in that of Rhode Island. Connecticut, as well as New York and Pennsylvania, now had instructors going from cell to cell each evening, while all the others continued to provide Sunday-school classes. Prayer meetings, first introduced in 1862, numbered five within a half-dozen years. A general improvement of the libraries brought the total number of books in all the prisons up to 15,250 by 1868.

A similar agitation for improved living conditions was showing results. Elaborate plans for model prisons and jails were published by the several boards and societies, especially those of New York, Massachusetts, and Ohio; and these not only influenced the builders of new prisons or cell houses but also encouraged the remodeling of old structures. The full-length windows introduced at Charlestown replaced the dingy windows of the old Sing Sing pattern, and most of the prisons introduced gas lights. The drive for larger cells and for more adequate ventilation was already active before the New York Prison Association published Dr. Griscom's "Essay on Prison Hygiene," but Griscom's argument for a ventilating system that would supply four cubic feet of fresh air per minute to each prisoner appeared to enlist the authority of science behind the reform. No prison realized the recommended ideal, but the larger cells of the Joliet pattern became the order of the day.[11]

Wines and Dwight hailed with enthusiasm the good-time laws and other innovations discovered on their tour. Commutation of sentences for good behavior quickly spread into twenty-three states by 1869, and only Indiana among northern states had failed to adopt such a law. The New York Association won its first national victory when a federal commutation act it had sponsored was signed by President Johnson. Meanwhile agitation for the better care of women in prison was prompting the appointment of matrons in an increasing number of prisons. Massachusetts and Michigan removed their women entirely from the state prisons and confined them in local houses of correction. New York continued to maintain its women's prison at Sing Sing as the only separate prison for women

[11] N.Y.P.A., *Report* (1867), pp. 44–65. Incidentally, the cells of Joliet were 7 by 4 by 7 ft. and contained 196 cu.ft. in contrast with the 169 cu.ft. in Sing Sing cells and the 315 cu.ft. in the new cells being erected at Elmira.

in the country; but Wisconsin and Illinois had fine women's buildings and yards within the walls of their state prisons, although the latter never used the structure for this purpose. Massachusetts and Indiana were already considering radically new innovations.

This was an era of remarkable prosperity for prison industries. Machines with steam power were replacing the old handicrafts and became for a few years the basis for a healthy prison atmosphere. Many wardens developed a zest for the reformation of their prisoners when successful industries brought freedom from concern over tenure. Growing populations at first favored the industries by supplying more laborers and reducing overhead costs, but the prisons soon became congested, thus seriously handicapping efficient production. At the same time protests were arising again from the struggling labor organizations, and both the professional reformers and their sympathizers began to criticize the profiteering contractors. Meanwhile the problems of overcrowded cells and congested factories joined to supply the urge that prompted several states to build new institutions, thus providing the reformers with a fighting chance to win the adoption of some of their best ideals during the succeeding decade.

In other words, there was a native substance to the reform movement, a program and a technique that was growing up within the four gray walls of American prisons. But this was only part of the story. While most of the new leaders were men of affairs, depending on their common sense and the heritage of tradition, a few of them, notably Wines and Sanborn, sought far and wide for new methods and theories. The movement was in this way considerably enriched and stimulated by foreign influences.

The expanding horizon of Dr. Wines was characteristic of the movement. His first reports reveal a close study of the earlier reports of his Association and the Boston Society and disclose a knowledge of the writings of the European critics of the thirties. By 1864 Wines was corresponding with the venerable Frenchmen, Lucas, Tocqueville, and Beaumont, and with the English inspector of prisons, Colonel Jebb. The following year he prepared a paper on the "Progress of Prison Reform in England," using the excellent memoir of

John Clay,[12] and thus learned of the work of Maconochie and Clay but little of Ireland. Wines did not begin to correspond with the Hill brothers, Sir William Crofton, or Miss Carpenter until after his extended tour of American prisons, and his first reaction to their system was colored by the prejudices of his first English correspondent, Colonel Jebb. Beginning in 1866, however, the reports of the New York Society were full of Crofton's system. Gaylord Hubbell, former warden of Sing Sing, while on a trip to Europe in that year made a special visit to the Irish prisons, and his account beggared the most enthusiastic reports of its European friends. During the next decade all the descriptions and criticisms of American prisons by Wines and his Society were strongly under the influence of the Irish ideal.[13]

This was not the first knowledge of the Irish system to reach America. As early as 1856 the *Pennsylvania Journal of Prison Discipline*, still the liberal quarterly edited by Frederick A. Packard, had a note on the ticket-of-leave idea; two years later it presented a fair discussion of the Irish system. The merits of the new methods were recognized, but even the liberal Pennsylvanians could see no possibility of improving their system, and nothing more was heard of Ireland.[14] The real apostle of the Irish system was the young Emersonian, Franklin Benjamin Sanborn. As secretary of the Massachusetts Board of State Charities he learned of Crofton's work sometime during 1864 or 1865, thus antedating Wines by a few months. But the matter of priority of discovery was not so important; it was in the zeal of his apostleship that Sanborn excelled. His impatience for a demonstration of the ideal in Massachusetts produced no little hard feeling in Charlestown, proud of having the best prison in the land.

The Maconochie-Hill-Crofton group had more influence on the development of penology in the New World than in the Old. While

[12] W. S. Clay, *The Prison Chaplain: A Memoir of Rev. John Clay* (Cambridge, England, 1861).

[13] The influence on Americans of English writings during this era must not be overlooked. Pre-eminent among these were: Mary Carpenter, *Our Convicts* (London, 1864); Clay, *A Memoir of Rev. John Clay* (Cambridge, England, 1861); Frederic Hill, *Crime* (London, 1853). It is interesting to note that several Americans, wishing to praise the report of Wines and Dwight, compared it with Miss Carpenter's book.

[14] *Pa. Journal of Pris. Disc.*, January, 1856, p. 53; *ibid.*, January, 1858, pp. 16–25.

the forms of this system were adopted in several places in Europe, they were shortly discarded or corrupted. America, on the other hand, never exactly copied the Irish system, but its methods and theory of punishment came at just the right time to enrich and inspire a strong native movement. The Americans were the aggressors; their movement appropriated these foreign theories and made them the basis of its new gospel. The grading of criminals according to the degree of reformation; the use of a mark system as a check on this process and as a restraint against disorders; the recognition of religion, education, and congregate labor as reformatory agents; and finally the release on ticket-of-leave as soon as reformed—no single one of these measures was wholly new to America. Crofton's significant service was to combine them into a unified experiment on adult prisoners. His achievement fired the imaginations of American reformers and provided a new pattern free from the old rivalry between the Auburn and Pennsylvania systems. The new pattern was fortunately in harmony with American trends and helped to knit them together into an elaborate reformatory program.

The humanitarian idealism of the forties came to dominate the movement, supplying it with a charitable attitude toward the criminal. The frequent use by Wines of the term "backsliders" rather than "sinners" when referring to convicts was indicative of the changed attitude which regarded prisoners as potential citizens deserving to be educated for society into which they were to be released as soon as their satisfactory readjustment was assured. This last conception, although arising as a common-sense interpretation of the function of imprisonment, made a clean break from the traditional ideal of justice which sought to make the punishment fit the crime. The elaborate legal and judicial technique that had grown up in the administration of the older ideal stubbornly resisted the advance of the newer conception; fortunately several practical modifications of the older procedure helped prepare the way for the adoption of the reformatory sentence in the next era.

The free use of the pardoning power, long a vicious feature of state government, was steadily undermining the tradition that courts should mete out carefully measured sentences for specific crimes. Reformers, seeking to modify the effects of the system on prison discipline, proposed that at least politics might be eliminated by the creation of pardon boards, but many feared that such a recognition of the power would encourage jail deliveries. Massachusetts happily re-enacted in 1867 an old common-law provision for conditional pardon, and this attempt to curb one of the dangers of too frequent pardons provided an instructive precedent for the parole laws of the next generation.

The increasing concern for discharged prisoners was likewise important in this connection. In 1866 Massachusetts provided a special agent to visit the boys and girls released on permits from its juvenile institutions. Regular police officers had previously performed this function in Ireland and a few other places, but Gardiner Tufts, the new agent, was the first special parole officer, and in 1869, when he was further directed to inspect the cases of children before trial, he acquired probationary functions as well. The humanitarian labors of John Augustus, dating back to 1841 when he had first "bailed out" the Boston jail, had antedated the probationary functions of Gardiner Tufts, but when Augustus was made state agent to aid the discharged, his energies had been diverted. Thus the recognition of the state's responsibility to watch over the readjustment of conditionally released offenders first developed in connection with the evolution of juvenile treatment, but it was not to be many decades before all criminals would gain the status of state wards.

This new attitude received its first application to cases of drunkenness, vagrancy, and prostitution. It was becoming clear that the states, in branding liquor and certain practices as social evils, forfeited the right to hold the victims entirely responsible. Again a Massachusetts law of 1866 led the way by authorizing magistrates to release persons committed to houses of correction for vagrancy as soon as such an individual "had reformed and is willing and desirous to return to an orderly course of life."[15] In 1869 Rhode Island established its state house of correction and conferred the power to release reformed inmates on the board of state charities and correction.[16]

Meanwhile, working with a smiliar class of prisoners in Detroit,

[15] Massachusetts Board of State Charities, *Report* (1870), p. 13. An earlier law of 1860 had suggested this provision, but its vague instructions had not been applied.

[16] Rhode Island Board of State Charities and Correction, *Report* (1870), p. 24. The board asserted that "The object of the sentence to the Workhouse is not punishment but reformation. . . . . The persons committed are the wards of the State and the sole

Brockway complained of the futility of short sentences. Two years of agitation finally secured the adoption in 1869 of his famous "three year law" giving him the power to detain Detroit women sent up for sex offenses until they were reformed—not exceeding three years. Brockway had urged in behalf of the law:[17]

Experience has demonstrated that to sentence such persons (prostitutes, vagrants, confirmed pilferers, and those whose persons and appetites are beyond their control), to imprisonment for definite periods of time frequently subverts the purpose in view. . . . . To commit these persons to the House of Correction until they are reformed will be a strong inducement for them to enter immediately upon the work of self-improvement.

These developments, as well as the commutation laws, were all pointing in the direction of reformatory sentences. They were deviations from the simple method by which a blindfolded goddess was supposed to measure out punishment in proportion to the gravity of the offense. They had come about as practical adjustments to actual problems, but they were disjointed practices, foreign to the system of which they pretended to be a part. It remained for the leaders of the reform movement, inspired by liberal theories, to co-ordinate them into a new reformatory system.

Possibly some of these beginnings had been stimulated by foreign theories. Sanborn had advocated the Irish system a year before the Massachusetts vagrancy law was adopted. But it was a far jump from the one system to the other; the Irish program dealt only with long-term prisoners, and after 1864 it had lost its indeterminate-sentence clause and was stressing the reformatory discipline of its intermediate prison; Massachusetts, on the other hand, was facing a totally different problem with a very special class of prisoners. In Detroit Brockway cited English precedents in recommending his house of shelter in 1868 but did not refer to the Irish developments in connection with his three-year law.[18] These vagrancy laws mean-

object of their commitment should be reformation. It is not expected that those committed will remain for the whole term of their sentence, and in practice this is rarely the fact."

[17] Detroit House of Correction, *Report* (1868), pp. 11–12.

[18] It is interesting to note that among the Brockway papers deposited in the Russell Sage Library in New York is a copy of Joseph Adshead's *Prisons and Prisoners* (London, 1845) with occasional marginal notes by Brockway; these notes were possibly made at the time of his first reading of the pamphlet, evidently in 1860. But while the pam-

while had a long ancestry, and plenty of precedents could be found in English and colonial law for the principles here adopted. The significant point was that these ideas were now applied to offenders against newly enacted laws by officers who were soon to be in a position to extend the application of these principles to a broader class of criminals.

The far-reaching significance of these practical developments did not appear, however, until foreign theories helped to enliven American thinking. This was notably true in the case of Enoch Wines and Franklin Sanborn. The latter had not been advocating tickets-of-leave very long before he discovered the little-used conditional-pardon law and hailed it as a possible means to his end. In 1867 he secured an amendment of the law, giving the warden the responsibility to recommend candidates for such pardon and the duty to order the arrest of any released man who failed to conform to the conditions imposed. Gideon Haynes, fearful of showing favoritism, hesitated to assume the responsibility, and the governor's council proved unable to resist demands for full pardon, so that it was several years before a workable parole system was developed. But the reform was gaining support elsewhere, and in 1869 Enoch Wines rejoiced to note that recommendations had been introduced in the Michigan, New York, and Ohio legislatures favoring the indeterminate sentence. His report quoted with pleasure from the official message of the kindly governor of Ohio, Rutherford B. Hayes:[19]

It may seem to be in advance of the present day, but it is, as we believe, but anticipating an event not far distant, to suggest that sentences for crime, instead of being for a definite period, especially in cases of repeated convictions, will, under proper restrictions, be made to depend on the reformation and established good character of the convict.

ANTECEDENTS OF THE REFORMATORY

A movement begins to reveal real strength when costly institutions are erected and dedicated to its ends. The excellent disciplines of Haynes at Charlestown and Hubbell at Sing Sing passed away

---

phlet urges the adoption of grades, tickets-of-leave, rewards for good discipline, and industrial training, Brockway's notes are all related to the attack on solitary confinement as a sufficient aid to redemption. Of course this would not prevent the natural infiltration of the other and more constructive ideas.

[19] N.Y.P.A., *Report* (1869), p. 162.

with these wardens, but the building of Elmira Reformatory was a lasting achievement. The American reformatory institution was a mutation resulting from the junction of developments in two distinct classes of prisons. A growing demand that the states undertake the reformation of misdemeanants encouraged the creation of institutions on the pattern of the better local houses of correction. In some instances the agitation resulted in distinct institutions of this character; more frequently it combined with a growing campaign to remove the youthful offenders from the state prisons, thus producing the typical adult reformatory. The enthusiasm for the indeterminate sentence and the other correctional devices predisposed the leaders to favor the development of special institutions where these methods could be applied under the most favorable conditions. Finally it was the insistent demand for more adequate prison accommodations that provided the opportunity for the creation of a radically new type of institution.

The remarkable developments at the Detroit house of correction made significant contributions to the development of adult reformatories. This institution had resulted from agitation begun by prominent citizens in 1856 against the abuses and expenses of the local jail. Brockway's reputation as the head of the self-supporting Monroe County penitentiary had spread, and he was called to Detroit in 1861 as the first superintendent to organize the new enterprise. The first concern was the industrial program, and for this Brockway was well fitted; but the young superintendent had recently gained a strong religious conception of the higher nature of his calling. With the co-operation of sympathetic friends in the city, he promised jobs to all who maintained good disciplinary records and in 1865 granted wages for overstint production. Brockway organized a Sunday school for the men and helped the matron establish an evening school for the women; in 1866 he called a chaplain to his assistance and provided morning chapel services in both departments. Most significant of all, he developed an experimental grading system in the women's branch in 1865, the first application of the theory to adults in America.

But all these efforts were greatly handicapped by the short terms of confinement, and accordingly Brockway began the campaign for longer sentences which resulted in the three-year law of 1869. A house of shelter was opened adjacent to the prison in this year as a home where discharged women could labor until they found respectable positions. This was soon converted into a secondary prison to which the better women could be removed and detained under a more liberal and homelike discipline until the expiration of their sentences. It became in a sense the first women's reformatory in America. With the able assistance of Miss Emma Hall, the head of the house of refuge, and of Professor H. S. Tarbell, superintendent of the union schools of Detroit, Brockway, by providing lectures of the lyceum character and experimenting with reading assignments, made his educational department more than a dull reading-and-writing school. When his proposed comprehensive indeterminate-sentence law was defeated in 1871, Brockway resigned, but the institution was so well established that, in spite of the abandonment of the house of shelter, it continued for many decades as one of the outstanding penal institutions in the country.

These houses of correction were essentially city rather than county institutions. Even in Massachusetts only the two or three counties containing large cities developed institutions worthy of the name, notably the Boston house of correction on Deer Island. They were largely concerned with drunkenness, vagrancy, and prostitution—offenses against local order and decency, social evils for which society considered itself in part responsible. Just as in the case of public education, so now in jail reform the cities were the first to assume responsibility; nevertheless, Francis Wayland agitated for a state house of correction in Rhode Island, and a few other states considered such proposals. Massachusetts was the first to establish a state workhouse when it appropriated the almshouse at Bridgewater for this purpose in 1866. Other New England states followed this lead, partly because the laws in that section gave more attention to this kind of offender, and partly because most of them were small enough to permit the gathering of short-term prisoners to one site without bankrupting the state with transportation charges. The proposals brought forward in other states did not get very far at this time.

The other root idea of the reformatory had gained recognition in America as early as 1822 when the Society for the Prevention of Pauperism had proposed that criminal youths should be taken out of the penitentiaries. The reform schools that resulted were primarily for misdemeanants although the judges had usually been given discretionary authority to commit very young criminals there as well. Several states had made sixteen the minimum age at which a person could be convicted of crime, but the first legislative recognition of a class of young men criminals occurred in 1856 when New York directed that all under twenty-one years who were convicted of the first offense should be sent to the local penitentiary where such existed. By 1872 there were three hundred young men segregated in this way. When the Detroit house of correction was being erected, Michigan adopted a law committing all its male first offenders under twenty-one to this institution; unfortunately a judge of the state Supreme Court declared the law unconstitutional, and Brockway's experiments with this class were delayed until 1877.

The Empire State with its teeming criminal classes was the cradle for the adult reformatory. In 1863, anticipating the end of the war and a flooding of the prisons, A. B. Tappen, one of the state inspectors, proposed the building of a new institution. After collaborating with the leaders of the Prison Association he suggested that it be called a state penitentiary and be used as an intermediate link between the county penitentiaries and the state prisons, and further that without elaborate walls or bars it might house the younger and less vicious criminals in a location where convenient industries would supply a valuable training. The Association indorsed the proposal, suggesting the addition of a grading system and rewards. The reformers gradually elaborated their ideal until in 1868 they saw it as an opportunity to introduce the Irish system and to create a truly model institution.

Forced to action by the expanding prison populations, the legislature created a commission to select a site and recommend plans for a reformatory. Theodore Dwight and Gaylord Hubbell were both named to the commission, thus assuring the influence of the Association. A 250-acre farm outside of Elmira was chosen for the site, and a most progressive program was outlined in the report of the commissioners to the legislature in 1869:[20]

It is apparent that the law under which we act [said the Commissioners] does not contemplate simply another State Prison. In referring to a reformatory we assume that the design of the Legislature was that there should be a selection from the mass of convicted criminals, of such persons as are most likely to yield

[20] Commissioners of New York State Reformatory, *Report* (1870), pp. 2–3.

to reformatory influences. . . . . We recommend that no person be sentenced to the proposed reformatory whose age is less than sixteen or more than thirty years, or who shall be known to have been previously convicted of any felonious offense. . . . . He [the inmate] will learn that a record will be kept from day to day of his conduct, and that it will be made to tell in his favor. . . . . Privileges will be conceded to him. . . . A portion of his earnings may be set aside for his use on the expiration of his sentence. . . . . It has been a favorite theory . . . . of Mr. Recorder Hill of England that criminals should be sentenced not for a definite term of years, as at present, but until they are reformed, which may, of course, turn out to be for life. While we do not propose to recommend this rule in full, yet we think that it has much to commend it in principle and that it may safely be tried in a modified form.

The commissioners further recommended that a special agent be appointed to supervise the young men after their release until their final discharge. One of the most valuable proposals was that the institution be placed under the control of a non-partisan commission to be organized along the line of the Association's proposed prison commission. Thus all the best ideas of the day were woven into the plans for Elmira reformatory. Unfortunately financial difficulties in the state delayed construction, and the institution was not ready for occupation until 1877.

Nevertheless, the prison-reform movement appeared at full flood in 1870. The gradually accumulating heritage of a half-century of builders and reformers had been enlivened by a new spirit since the war. A rapid increase in the number of convicts had forced prison problems before the public eye. New and impartial agencies of inspection had brought a clearer understanding to the problem. Foreign experiments had been hailed as showing the way for a more satisfactory solution of the difficult task of reforming criminals. Scattered achievements in a few state prisons and in several progressive city institutions were adding to the enthusiasm of optimistic idealists. One very considerable undertaking had already been indorsed by New York State, and great things were expected from the new reformatory being erected at Elmira. Great things were hoped for all along the line, and all that these forces seemed to lack was a central co-ordinating agency to direct their proper fulfilment. Enoch Wines was already planning a vast gathering at Cincinnati which should formally inaugurate the new era. Nobody suspected the disappointments just around the corner.[21]

[21] See the Bibliographical Note to chap. iv.

CHAPTER IV

COURSE AND DISAPPEARANCE OF
THE MOVEMENT

The imagination of Enoch Wines had been stirred by the wide-spread clamor for reform. Inspiring theories quickened his spirit. He would not have been true to himself had he been content, after his tour of 1865, to settle down quietly in Bible House, New York. His thoughts soared above annual reports into a glamorous dream of a world-organization in which the outstanding men of all nations would join to plan an ideal prison system. And indeed the records reveal how he carried his American and European friends off their feet with him and how, in the space of a few years, they convened several congresses and sent resounding calls for prison reform around the world. But these men overestimated the power of the idea. The organizations they established were poorly designed to force their theories upon governments, and the first suggestion of their futility practically disbanded them. The death of the bolder leaders left to the generation that followed little but a heritage of idealistic programs set forth in a voluminous literature. Nevertheless, a few younger men had gathered inspiration from the heights and were patiently building for the future.

ORGANIZATION OF THE MOVEMENT

Wines determined that the first step toward an international gathering of prison reformers was the organization of an American association sufficiently representative to call such a convention.[1] In response to an inquiry sent out in 1868 forty replies from various states favored the gathering of a national congress. The New York and Philadelphia societies hesitated to assume responsibility, but Wines

---

[1] National Prison Congress at Cincinnati, *Transactions* (New York, 1870), pp. 253, 267–75. The earlier international congresses on prison reform—the first at Frankfort-on-Main in 1845, the second at Brussels in 1847, and the third and last again at Frankfort in 1857—undoubtedly influenced the thought of Enoch Wines. Other unofficial gatherings had discussed international standards for statistics of crime and charity at Brussels in 1853, Paris in 1855, Vienna in 1857, and London in 1860. The United States had sent delegates only to the first Frankfort congress.

and a few friends took the initiative and sent invitations to all parts
of the country for a congress on prison reform to meet in Cincinnati
in 1870.[2] Governor Rutherford B. Hayes welcomed the 130-odd delegates who gathered from twenty-four states, Canada, and South
America. Wardens, chaplains, judges, governors, and humanitarians
—they made a distinguished assembly; and the conspicuous absence
of the eastern Pennsylvanians freed the convention from the usual
acrimonious debate over the rivalries of the fathers. Indeed, the
delegates concerned themselves largely with the future, and after
eagerly discussing many papers and addresses they unanimously
adopted a declaration of principles so forward-looking that for several decades their successors were able neither to better it in theory
nor to exhaust its possibilities in practice.

There were some very remarkable papers among the forty presented to the congress. Several had been written by English and
French reformers, but the majority were by budding American penologists. The Irish system was ably described by its founder, Sir
Walter Crofton, as well as by its enthusiastic American admirers,
Sanborn and Hubbell; Matthew Davenport Hill sent a fine paper on
the indeterminate sentence, elucidating its theoretical aspects. Such
age-old problems as executive pardon, jail systems, after-care of
juveniles and adults, and prison hygiene received considerable attention. Dr. Wines, true to his major purpose for convening the congress, read a paper advocating an international gathering.

The most able address of them all, however, was Brockway's
"Ideal for a True Prison System for a State." Here the best thinking
of the New York group and of the foreign experimenters was
gathered into one system along with the practical experience of a
skilled administrator. Brockway proposed that a non-political commission, such as that recommended in New York, be created and
given full power to build and control juvenile reform schools, district
reformatories or houses of correction, reception prisons for male
adults in which each convict would be examined and the incorrigibles

---

[2] "Minutes of the Acting Committee of the Philadelphia Society" (MS) (Philadelphia Society Library, 1867–73), pp. 125–28, 146–51. These records show the cool
reception Wines received from this old society at the same time that his own associates
in New York were hesitating to act. Nevertheless, such diverse leaders as Daniel C.
Gilman, F. B. Sanborn, Theodore Dwight, and Amos Pilsbury indorsed the call for
the convention.

retained for life while the others would be transferred to industrial or intermediate reformatories, and lastly reformatories for women. He recommended that discipline be regulated by grades and marks and that these be administered in connection with indeterminate sentences so as to release each prisoner as soon as he was reformed. Brockway's paper, with its inspiring ideals full of revolutionary significance, soon became the center of a stormy discussion; in the end the declaration of principles approved most of his recommendations.[3]

The convention was in the hands of reformers who had arrived with prepared speeches while the traditions had no spokesmen. Overwhelmed with inspired addresses, with prayer and song and much exhortation, even the hard-headed wardens were carried up for a mountain-top experience.[4] In their enthusiasm for the ideal they rose above the monotony of four gray walls, men in stripes shuffling in lock step, sullen faces staring through the bars, coarse mush and coffee made of bread crusts, armed sentries stalking the walls. They forgot it all and voted for their remarkable declaration of principles: Society is responsible for the reformation of criminals; education, religion, and industrial training are valuable aids in this undertaking; discipline should build rather than destroy the self-respect of each prisoner; his co-operation can best be secured with an indeterminate sentence under which his discharge is regulated by a merit system; the responsibility of the state extends into the field of preventive institutions and to the aid and supervision of prisoners after discharge; a central state control should be established so as to secure a stable, non-political administration, trained officers, and reliable statistics.

[3] Cincinnati Congress, *Transactions* (1870), p. 54. Brockway recommended that "all persons in a state, who are convicted of crimes before a competent court, shall be deemed wards of the state, and shall be committed to the custody of the board of guardians until, in their judgment, they may be returned to society with ordinary safety and in accord with their own highest welfare."

[4] N.P.A., *Proceedings* (1887), pp. 311–12. Brockway at this time looks back over the seventeen years intervening and recalls that at Cincinnati in 1870 he had had an experience similar to that of the disciples on the Mount of Transfiguration. He had felt himself strengthened by "a mysterious, almighty, Spiritual force . . . . I was going to have a grand success . . . . but it did not work. . . . . I found that there was a commonplace work of education to do with these persons whom I hoped to inspire . . . . That did not suffice. The industrial training of prisoners was taken up, and that is drudgery. Getting down to drudgery, and even lower than that. . . . ." Thus he warns the younger men that hard work must follow inspiration.

Wines was in fine feather when the leaders of the convention and prominent men throughout the nation signed up as charter members of the National Prison Association. Congress was persuaded to adopt a resolution inviting the nations of the world to send delegates to an international congress on prison reform to meet in London in 1872, and an appropriation of $5,000 was made to provide for a commissioner to carry forward the American part of the program. Wines resigned his New York post in order to accept the secretaryship of the new Association and the appointment as United States Commissioner tendered him by President Grant. In his new capacity Wines made a special visit to many of the European capitals and national penitentiaries in 1871, and it was largely as a result of his campaign that twenty-two nations sent official representatives and a total of four hundred delegates gathered from all parts of the world to London in July of 1872.

The Americans took a prominent part in the London sessions. Representatives from nineteen states joined Wines in London, and when the voluntary visitors were added the delegation totaled seventy. Several European countries and Japan as well were stimulated to new efforts in behalf of their convicts. But the Americans who contributed so much to the congress were able to take back from the meetings little more than the satisfaction to be derived from the delegates' half-hearted indorsement of their Irish gospel. The numerous reports made to the legislatures, including that of Wines to Congress, might have produced larger results had it not been for the changing economic and political scene of the mid-seventies. Nevertheless, the London congress had all the appearances of a glorious success when the National Prison Association gathered in its second convention a few months later.

Horatio Seymour, governor of New York, presided over representatives of twenty-one states gathered at Baltimore. Unfortunately the enthusiasm that might have enlivened this convention had been expended at London. Papers were read and discussed, but the novelty of the occasion had passed, and no attempt was made to write a new set of resolutions. It was not only that the declarations of Cincinnati and London were still satisfactory to the leaders, but, with the largest delegation hailing from Pennsylvania, dissension had developed, rendering a vote on principles dangerous both to the unity of the movement and to the authority of the faith.

Brockway, absent because of sickness, sent a report for the committee on prison discipline urging the indeterminate sentence with conditional release under police supervision, but this time, in the discussion that followed, the weight of opinion was on the side of older traditions. Richard Vaux, chairman of the directors of Cherry Hill, and delegates from Ohio, Missouri, and New Jersey assailed the proposals with vigor. Dr. Wines as secretary reported the proceedings, but most of his friends of Cincinnati and London were absent, and he found himself and his program somewhat pushed aside by the new men representing the changing authorities in the states. The activity of the Philadelphia Society at the Baltimore meetings prompted the election of Richard Vaux to preside over the third congress scheduled for St. Louis in 1874; but Vaux found little pleasure in his office and reported to the Philadelphia Society that nothing was accomplished at St. Louis.

Thus the reform movement, which had gathered, like a stormy religious revival, around the inspired leadership of Enoch Wines, was losing its force. In making the world his parish, Wines had severed connections with many of the vital forces in institutional penology. He should have considered more soberly the fact that prison problems in America had never gained much attention from the national government. Five thousand dollars had been appropriated only because James G. Blaine, recalling an investigation during his younger days of the prisons of New England, had by good fortune been Speaker of the House at a time when an astute man could get an appropriation through Congress. Such federal philanthropy could not continue, and to borrow on its favor, as Wines did in 1872, was to court disaster.[5] Two years later the Association was bankrupt and unable to print the proceedings of its St. Louis gathering. Meanwhile the New York Association, with its problems right at the doors of its patrons, was able to continue through the period of economic depression with only moderate retrenchments. The National Association, handicapped by a lack of funds and further crippled by the death of Francis Lieber and other leaders, was able to assemble only a few local friends to its fourth congress in New York in 1875, a sorry reminder of the ambitious expectations of the Cincinnati gathering five years before.

[5] N.P.A., *Baltimore Transactions* (1873), p. 488. Wines had collected $7,068 from friends, $5,000 from the United States treasurer, and had borrowed $4,925.

LEGISLATIVE ACHIEVEMENTS

After all, the real goal of the reformers was not the national organization, with its mutual edification, but the reformation of prisoners. The program envisaged the enactment of new and more liberal methods of punishment, the erection of prisons suitable for the new objects of confinement, and the practical development of a reformatory discipline under stable administrations. The central association, with all its high-flown speech-making, was much less important in the struggle of the various states toward these ends than the plodding local bodies.

Unfortunately the state boards of charities, although they increased in number during the seventies, failed to fulfil the expectations of their founders, at least in respect to state penal institutions. Michigan, Wisconsin, and Connecticut were the first to create such boards during this era, and, like most of their predecessors, their major concern was the inspection of county institutions. Kansas, on the other hand, created a board of trustees of state charitable institutions, but this board of control had no authority over the prison. This shift toward control was characteristic of the period, although it was not carried into effect in many states for some time.

Franklin Sanborn had early recognized the need for real control over all the prisons of Massachusetts, and his first report had recommended the creation of a responsible prison commission. Various conditions, especially the plight of the female prisoners, forced the general court to act, and a prison commission was created in 1871. Its original powers were, however, limited to local correctional institutions and responsibility for the care of the women, and not until the reorganization of 1879 was its authority extended to include the prison. Massachusetts thus achieved a centralized system of management for its prisons that was rivaled only by that of its tiny neighbor, Rhode Island, when the erection of a new prison on the state farm in 1879 brought all charitable and correctional institutions under the responsible control of the state board.

Meanwhile reformers in New York did not accept as final the defeat of 1869 when the entire constitution had been rejected. Governor Hoffman as well as Enoch Wines proposed that the prison amendment be submitted separately for a popular vote. While the legislature procrastinated, the county penitentiaries, under stable administrations and largely free from politics, continued to defray their expenses in sharp contrast to the growing deficits of the three state prisons, mounting as they did from $366,000 in 1867 to $588,000 in 1874. Accordingly, when the amendment was finally submitted and approved, the model commission of five, aiming primarily at non-political statesmanship, was discarded in favor of the more efficient single superintendent. Other factors, such as the scandals centering around the old Canal Commission, had made the public suspicious of such independent bodies. The withdrawal of Wines from the New York Association and the death of other prominent leaders weakened the influence of the disinterested reformers and permitted the politicians to centralize the system without freeing it from party control. Louis D. Pilsbury, son of the "Nestor," was to make a creditable financial record as the first superintendent, but that was about the extent of his control over state prisons, and he had no jurisdiction over the many and important local institutions.

Meanwhile the trend toward centralization was scarcely evident in the remaining states. The Ohio board of charities, failing to secure financial support, discontinued its activities during several critical years, and, when it was revived by Governor Hayes in 1876 and a salary of $1,200 provided for its hard-working secretary, the board had to remain content with its former powers of inspection. The North Carolina board likewise failed to gain financial support and remained dormant for many years; no other state in the South made even a beginning in this direction for another decade. New Jersey and Indiana were equally inattentive to their needs for central control, while Illinois failed to bring its state prisons within the scope of the board of charities, and its citizens remained ignorant of many evils in these supposedly model institutions. Only California in the Far West, by a reorganization in 1880 in which it adopted verbatim the New York Association's model for a non-political commission, acquired a system of control that ranked it with the more efficient states of the Northeast.

Fortunately the waning of the national movement and the failure of many states to achieve central control over their prisons did not entirely check the advance of the new ideology. Both the belief that criminals would become better prisoners with the aid of a little friendly assistance after their discharge, and the theory that they should be discharged as soon as they were reformed, gained increasing favor, and the country was prepared for their more hearty indorsement in later decades.

The discharged prisoners received increasing attention from both state officers and charitable societies during the seventies. While several prisons slightly enlarged the meager sums designed to provide an outfit and a ticket home for each of its discharged, Pennsylvania in 1870 supplied funds to employ an agent at each penitentiary to supervise this system, thus matching the earlier appointment of a state agent by Massachusetts. In 1877 New York State, when an amendment cut off all incorporated organizations from public funds, assumed full responsibility for the support of the extensive work of John Russ, the New York Association's agent for the discharged, and Russ was named state agent by Superintendent Pilsbury. The prison societies in these states did not discontinue their aid to the discharged, and at least one new society, that organized by the younger Francis Wayland in Connecticut, undertook the job in a new field.

Meanwhile the theory and significance of the indeterminate sentence was being noised about. New York had tentatively adopted the principle for its new institution under construction at Elmira; Brockway, rejoicing over the success of his three-year law at Detroit, made a gallant fight for a comprehensive indeterminate-sentence law in Michigan, and although defeated in 1871 was able to enlist many supporters who later carried the measure through in a compromised form. Proposals for comprehensive reforms in Connecticut, Illinois, Ohio, and Wisconsin incorporated the indeterminate sentence as a main feature, but none of these programs was adopted at the time. Many responsible authorities held back until the new theories should have an opportunity to demonstrate their merits in actual practice, and for this service everyone looked hopefully to Brockway as he took charge at Elmira in 1876.

PARTIAL REDIRECTION OF INSTITUTIONAL EXPANSION

The major concern of the era was the housing problem. At no other time during the second half of the century did the prisons suffer so persistently from serious overcrowding as during the ten years following 1868. A few of the states, notably New Jersey, Indiana, Illinois, and Missouri, never succeeded in freeing their prisons from the evil of two or more men to a cell, but most of the other northern states approximated the standard of a cell for each man except during this decade. Furthermore, overcrowding was more of a problem for management at this time than in the early years of the next century, for the silent system still had a strong hold on prison traditions during the seventies. The attempt to correct over-crowding gave the reformers an opportunity, and where they were strongly organized they were able to secure new institutions after their own mind. Everywhere expansion occurred, and by the close of the decade most of the states of the Northeast were equipped with prison structures that were to serve them for the rest of the century with only occasional additions.

The slow progress of construction at Elmira, delaying the opening of the reformatory until 1877, deprived the reformers of a model which might have tipped the balance in favor of their programs in Ohio, Illinois, New Jersey, and California, each engaged in the expansion of its regular prisons. A more favorable result rewarded the reformers in Michigan, Indiana, and Massachusetts. Brockway's long agitation in Michigan, supported by Governor John Bagley, prevented the enlargement of Jackson prison and secured instead the creation of the Ionia house of correction and reformatory to relieve congestion at Jackson. When the first cell block was opened in 1877, the three hundred cells, each 8 by 5 by 7 feet high, soon duplicated in a second cell block, provided a creditable equipment. But a shift in politics left the legislative and administrative organization of the institution in inexperienced hands, and neither indeterminate sentences nor grades and marks were provided for. Ionia soon became in practice a prison for young men where an active industrial program was the only reformatory device.

Meanwhile, as prison populations increased beyond capacity, the problem of segregating the women from the men became more difficult. Numerous scandals roused popular indignation in several states, adding incentive to the move for complete separation. Thus Indiana's success in building the first entirely separate institution for women was the fortuitous result of a series of scandals, rather than the work of reformers. Yet it takes leaders to direct public indignation, and the Annual Meeting of Friends in 1866 started the public protest. Two of their number were chosen to investigate, and the report of Charles and Rhoda Coffin was instrumental in rousing Governor Conrad Baker and the legislature to action. A long postponed plan for a girls' reform school reinforced the movement, and in 1869 a reformatory for women and girls was created. Sarah Smith, a prominent Friend, was placed in charge when the new institution was opened in Indianapolis four years later, and a kindly, maternal discipline was developed. But there was no board of charity or other instrument in the state to bring in new ideas, and the continuing interest of a committee of Friends succeeded only in preserving the human touch. For many years the major concern of the officers was to prevent the older women from corrupting the girls of the reform-school department.

The fortunes of convict women in other states varied considerably. While Connecticut and Missouri were erecting new cell houses with separate yards for the women, Illinois was crowding them into the fourth story of the warden's house and using the admirable women's building for the overflowing male population. Except for New York and Massachusetts, the other states continued their earlier arrangements, usually with a matron in charge of the dormitory or small cell house located within the state prison. Michigan's provision in 1872 for the removal of all women to the Detroit house of correction lost the character of a satisfactory solution when Brockway and Miss Emma Hall retired from control there, and the adjacent house of shelter was soon abandoned. Except for the Cincinnati women's jail and the provision for misdemeanant women in Detroit, Indiana, New York, and Massachusetts, no attempt was made at this time to remove the women from local jails.

Overcrowding was one of the factors that forced the removal of the women from Sing Sing. The one hundred outside cells in a separate building on the hill above the main prison had been overcrowded almost from the start, and the law of 1856 permitting the courts to sentence women felons to the county penitentiaries had failed to solve the problem. In 1872, when Mrs. Van Courtland assumed the duties of volunteer agent for the women's branch of the New York Association, she found 133 hopeless women crowded in the Sing Sing prison while many of the same class were as securely confined in several county penitentiaries without suffering the stigma of a Sing Sing record. On the basis of these facts agitation was begun for a women's reformatory, but the state was too busy building Elmira and enlarging Auburn and Clinton to consider another institution at the time. The superintendent compromised by removing all the women from the infamous association with Sing Sing to King's County penitentiary. Two more decades were to pass before New York provided for the care of some of its women felons in special reformatories.

The development of an enlightened program for the care of women prisoners in Massachusetts was closely bound up with the careers of two Christian women. Hannah B. Chickering, as a young woman, had felt a strong urge to use her talents in public service but did not find the channel until a visit to some Quaker friends in Philadelphia opened her eyes to the many needs of the women in prison. Back home in Dedham, Miss Chickering established a library in the local jail and in 1874 opened an asylum for discharged females. Her efforts to extend the services of this institution to women from all parts of the state attracted the co-operation of F. B. Sanborn, the secretary of charities, and Mrs. Ellen C. Johnson whose interest in the hardships of homeless and vagrant women had been aroused by her contact with them during war work. Together these reformers stirred up a state-wide agitation for a women's prison. The general court chose to side-step this demand by creating a prison commission, another of Sanborn's proposals, with power to transfer the women to a suitable house of correction. Greenfield jail was selected in 1871 for the use of the women of the western part of the state, and Miss Chickering was named as one of three women advisers in cases of transfer; but the local jail authorities refused to co-operate, and the makeshift failed. Continued growth of state and local prison populations forced a return to the earlier proposal, and a women's prison was provided for in 1874 and opened three years later at Sherborn. Its three hundred outside rooms and two fifty-bed dormitories were soon crowded with major and minor offenders from all parts of the state; fortunately a new law soon permitted the transfer of certain cases to the jails, thus relieving congestion. But it was not until 1884 when Mrs. Johnson finally assumed control that a fine discipline based on a graded system was developed, making Sherborn the model institution for women in America.

The main construction activities of the seventies were directed toward the enlargement of the older prisons. The state authorities were still striving to provide a cell for each prisoner, and while this standard was fully maintained only in New England, the majority of the northern states were fairly adequately equipped by the end of the decade. The construction of additional institutions on the Elmira pattern was put off until the next era.

Charlestown, model prison of the sixties, suffered from serious overcrowding during most of the following decade. The institution was cramped by its narrow confines, and, as the land values were high, the general court decided to sell the old site and build a new and larger prison at Concord with the proceeds. The arguments of the reformers for two small prisons with limits of 450 convicts each, in order to facilitate the segregation of the young, the accidentals, and the drunkards from the vicious and the repeaters, were defeated by the prospect of securing one large and economical prison at little or no cost. Meanwhile the removal of the women from the jails to Sherborn opened the way for a compromise; all men with sentences of three years or less were committed to the local institutions, and the plans for Concord were reduced from 1,000 to 750 cells. The prison commission, hoping that this law was but the first step in the transformation of all local prisons into state district institutions, proposed that the Fitchburg house of correction be altered for use as a young men's reformatory. But the value of the Charlestown site suddenly declined, and the state, faced with the necessity of paying hard cash for Concord, refused to consider additional outlays for prison reform. Massachusetts had sufficient cells by the end of the decade, but the rearrangement of the penal system that converted Concord into a young men's reformatory was not achieved until the next era.

Each of the other New England states made a fairly satisfactory solution of its population problem. Rising land values in Providence induced Rhode Island to sell the city jail and build its new prison at the state farm; the desire for a better industrial location prompted New Hampshire to erect a new 248-cell prison at Concord; and Vermont provided equivalent accommodations by completing its partially constructed prison at Windsor. Connecticut and Maine were content to enlarge their older prisons to satisfy the needs of slowly growing populations. Rhode Island and Vermont each built state workhouses to correct unsatisfactory jail conditions, following the earlier lead of Massachusetts. Vermont, inspired by the Elmira pattern, renamed its workhouse a state house of correction and admitted the less vicious young felons at the discretion of the directors and judges, thus preparing the way for the development of a real reformatory when circumstances became favorable.

Four additional states in the North made a fair advance toward a solution of serious housing problems. New York opened Elmira and expanded Auburn and Clinton, and only the isolation of the latter in the Adirondacks prevented the full utilization of its facilities to relieve Sing Sing, where the flood of commitments continued to crowd two men into many of its tiny cells. In a similar manner Michigan, adequately equipped after the completion of Ionia, tolerated a faulty distribution of state and local offenders. Ohio provided a sufficient number of cells at Columbus by the close of the decade, but this achievement equipped the state with the largest prison in the world, and the state board of charities found little cause for elation over this unwieldy institution. Meanwhile a revolution in the control of the Western Penitentiary in Pennsylvania placed Edward Wright in the warden's office, and a new cell building was erected on the Auburn pattern, thus satisfying the population demands by a break from the state's traditional pattern. At the same time Allegheny County built a new workhouse and brought Cordier from Wisconsin to organize its industry and discipline, with the result that it soon became a model local prison, the rival of Detroit, and shamed the reformers of Philadelphia into establishing a new house of correction for the eastern city.

Serious overcrowding in the prisons of Indiana, Illinois, and New Jersey continued in spite of repeated indictments by progressive investigators. Missouri likewise belonged to this group but as its most renegade member. Possibly these states would have done better had they provided permanent boards responsible for the supervision of prisons, but scandals and corruption absorbed the attention of their politicians. The Quaker agitators in Indiana were fortunate to get a women's prison. Illinois, after long delay, was forced by the danger of insurrection at the overcrowded 1,024-cell Joliet prison to start a new institution at Chester, but her politicians failed to heed the suggestion that it be made a reformatory. Chicago built a new house of correction and imported the able Charles E. Felton from the Buffalo penitentiary to take charge, but the cells were so tiny and convicts were so continuously crowded two, even three, to a cell that the institution deserved rather the title of house of corruption.

Of all the northern states, Missouri maintained the most diabolical prison conditions. The intense feelings and hostile factions inherited from the Civil War still dominated state politics. As power shifted from radical to liberal Republican and then to the Democrats the major concern in regard to the prison was that it should be as small a financial burden as possible. And yet, when the state was head over heels in debt, it did enlarge its old prison and erect a women's building outside the walls. The Democrats regained political control in 1873 and turned to the lease system that was rapidly becoming popular in the South. After two years of bad management the bankrupt lessee surrendered the disorganized institution to the state authorities, but renewed efforts to organize discipline and industry were handicapped by a steadily increasing population, which by 1878 numbered 1,333 men in 460 cells and rooms, besides 164 women in the separate 146-cell building.

Wisconsin, Minnesota, Iowa, Kansas, and West Virginia were still in many respects on the frontier of the advance of northern penological institutions; nevertheless, they were able during the decade to equip themselves with fairly adequate prisons. The Wisconsin authorities failed to carry through a comprehensive reorganization of their penal system along lines similar to those advocated by Sanborn in Massachusetts, and yet the end of the decade found the prison at Waupun only slightly overcrowded. Minnesota had no difficulty in expanding the recently established prison at Stillwater to meet the halting growth of its criminal population. Iowa, boom state of the era, started a second prison before the first was completed, only to face the difficulty of supporting two inadequately staffed and partially occupied institutions. Kansas stuck doggedly to what many had considered an overambitious program and was able to report in 1880 the completion of the entire prison structure. With 688 up-to-date cells patterned after those of Joliet it was, without a rival, the best prison west of the Mississippi. Nevertheless, so serious were the social problems of this frontier state that the convicts had constantly overcrowded the available cells as they were completed and now exceeded the capacity by at least one hundred—a condition which was to be aggravated as the next era advanced.

The leaders of West Virginia faced north from the first. When in 1866 the legislature appropriated $50,000 for a state prison, the pattern of the new cell house at Pittsburgh was adopted, and the state energetically pressed the construction of its prison at Moundsville. By 1880 it had finished the wall, one of the cell blocks, and a small women's building, as well as a dining-hall and several shops. The 223 cells here provided were sufficient at the time for the needs of the state and represented the only genuine Auburn prison south of the Mason and Dixon line. In the interests of economy the southern lease system was frequently proposed but it was always defeated, and this state became in respect to penology a true daughter of the North.

Thus the northern states in the decade of the seventies opened eleven new state prisons or reformatories, at least four of which were dedicated to a special class of criminals. When taken in connection with the considerable additions to older prisons and with the new houses of correction, this era of construction might well be regarded as successful in spite of the disappearance of the organized movement—successful, that is, in supplying fair accommodations in most of the states and in clearing the ground for other reforms in succeeding years.

When in 1873 Miss Mary Carpenter visited prisons in the United States, she quickly discovered, true to the genius of English visitors, the weakest part of the American system:

The existing jails are insufficient both in size and number, and the overcrowding of the prisoners necessarily causes great demoralization among them. . . . . The female prisoners are not properly separated from the males, nor are they under proper supervision. . . . . I saw in the cells two or three prisoners together, without anything to prevent them spending the whole day in idleness and injurious conversation.[6]

The few jails that she visited suffered by contrast with institutions of the same grade in England, for it was in this very important class of prisons that the mother country was making the greatest improvements. While there was some resentment among American reformers

[6] N.Y.P.A., *Report* (1872), p. 119.

who would have liked to have Miss Carpenter visit Detroit and a few other prisons they proudly named, they were nonetheless aware of the truth of her indictment, and many of them were earnestly facing the problem.

The attack on the jail evil came from two directions. The first problem was to find a competent leadership, for county responsibility was hopelessly transitory unless the community had become so populous that vital interests made for strong party factions. In such cases the critical nature of the jail problem played into the hands of the reformers, and some excellent houses of correction were the result. The other attack was through the state authority over all local political divisions. But local self-government was a strong tradition, and even the best of the boards of charities and prison commissions found it difficult to get any real power over local jails. Nevertheless, great improvements in inspection and standardization were made in Massachusetts, Michigan, Ohio, Wisconsin, Illinois, and to a degree in Pennsylvania and New York. But excellent comprehensive proposals brought forward in New York, Massachusetts, and Wisconsin were not seriously considered.

The best of these achievements was not very good. In spite of a law against sending children to jail, the Massachusetts commission found ninety-seven so confined in 1869, and only with the most persistent agitation was it able to reduce the number to twenty-five three years later. The New York Association found in 1878 that but five out of sixty jails had carried out the mandatory regulations for the segregation of women, children, and witnesses; a strenuous campaign the following year brought only ten more jails into line. When such was the performance in the most advanced state, the Americans had little response to make to their candid English visitor. The Michigan penal commission might well have spoken for the whole country when it reported that "the jails . . . . have escaped reform and are in Michigan today as wretched as they have been in England or America at any time in their existence."[7]

SLIGHT IMPROVEMENT OF DISCIPLINE

When all the legislatures have had their say, when their laws have been interpreted and their appropriations have been spent, the final

[7] *Report* (1876), p. 9.

problem still remains. The impact of these measures on the internal life of the prison is the alpha and omega of penology, and it is with this that the prisoner is chiefly concerned. If the old "cons" had not heard of it through speeches and sermons, it is certain that many of them, whose terms spanned the era, would scarcely have known of the world-wide reform movement. Many of them must have told their younger buddies of the good old days. Yet the story was not one-sided, and on the whole the prisoners got the better "break" at the end of the period.

The general standards of prison schools gradually rose during the era. Unfortunately several of the more brilliant experiments were either discontinued or considerably modified. Thus the excellent school system which Brockway had developed at Detroit deteriorated sadly after he and Miss Hall departed. In a similar fashion the lecture system of Haynes at Charlestown was modified by his successor, sacrificing much of its educational value. A lesson had nevertheless been learned by the administrators concerning the disciplinary value of school classes. Accordingly when the depression hit prison industry in Massachusetts and many of the contractors laid off their men, Warden Chamberlain relieved the strain of idleness by expanding the evening schools into day schools; but a revival of trade two years later converted even the regular schoolrooms into factories. Meanwhile the occasional evening schools of 1865 had spread until all the state prisons in New England and those in Michigan, Illinois, and Iowa, as well as New York and Pennsylvania, provided such opportunities to learn to read and write. New York appeared the model of generosity, spending $7,500 a year on teachers, chaplains, and books, but when this was divided among the teeming populations of New York prisons and administered cell to cell, as was the normal practice, it did not transform much gray-matter.

The prison library was another department potentially of large value to the convict. Wines and Dwight had found libraries in all the state prisons of the North, but the books had been contributed by charitable persons, and were for the most part antiquated religious treatises, of little interest or value. Some of the states were already assuming responsibility for supplying small annual sums to replenish the libraries. This custom spread, but there was little care to apportion these funds, ranging between $25 and $200, so as to secure desirable books and magazines. In 1877 the New York Association compiled a catalogue of one thousand suggested titles covering a wide variety of interests, listed so as to guide chaplains seeking to provide a library of fifty to one thousand books. This might have had a large influence had it come when the reform movement was in full flood, but no record has been found of any prison that used it. Many of the prisons did work out reasonably efficient distributing systems, enabling the convicts to make use of the books available, but no adequate accounts were kept of the expenditures, and, with petty graft on the one hand and thrift drives on the other, even the meager funds provided did not always reach the library shelves.

The county jails supplied plenty of education, but it was as "seminaries of vice and crime." Outside of Massachusetts almost no organized instruction was provided; the commissioners of that state worked diligently and succeeded in establishing a library in every jail and in developing good schoolroom instruction in Lowell, Lawrence, and South Boston houses of correction. Sabbath schools and libraries existed in scattered jails elsewhere, but the former were usually dependent on the whims of local parsons. The work of Miss Linda Gilbert in establishing libraries in the large jails of such cities as Chicago, New York, St. Louis, and Buffalo during these years was of great service to the thousands of prisoners who flocked through those portals. Nevertheless, in the great majority of the jails, if the idle unfortunates wished to occupy their minds they had to depend on books or papers supplied by their friends, and this was a privilege not always granted.

The rudiments of education were about all that any prison supplied. Their contribution was more in relieving the monotony of prison life than in fitting men for society. Possibly the better prisons through these agencies were helping to Americanize an increasing number of aliens, but the schools and libraries were in favor with the wardens largely because of their disciplinary value. They supplied a basis for a system of rewards, while in another important respect they aided in the relaxation of the silent regulations, so difficult a problem for indolent officers. Prison education for its own sake was not yet the reformatory panacea that it was to become a decade or so later.

The one reform which all the wardens praised during these years was the commutation system. This was one of the few practices that spread not only throughout all the northern states but into the Far West and South as well. Many of the laws were carefully administered and possessed a disciplinary value that they were to lose in time. However, only Michigan and Vermont tried to carry out the full intent of their laws, going so far as to add wage payments to the good-time earnings.

There were many other scattered changes in prison discipline, although they fail to reveal any general trends. On the one hand, Michigan removed John Morris, whose strict discipline in attempting to stamp out the use of tobacco had made Jackson prison notorious, and inaugurated an era of liberal discipline under Warden Humphrey and Chaplain Hickox; in the same year Indiana replaced Warden Shuler, who had eliminated the "cat" from Jeffersonville, and gave control to A. G. Howard, a strict disciplinarian who used the lash freely. In general, the punishments applied were much the same as in earlier years, for, while several of the states had regulations against the "cat" or the "shower bath," Sanborn was of the opinion that these regulations were not strictly followed.

The most important disciplinary trend, the gradual relaxing of the silent system, was not so much the work of reformers as the inevitable result of overcrowding. Silence was possible as long as each man could be locked in a separate cell and carefully supervised at labor; but with two in many cells or with scores sleeping in corridors or in the chapel, silence was no longer pretended. The system remained in its worst possible form—a law not generally obeyed but which could be enforced at the whim of an officer. In this form it became a major cause for the prison atmosphere of repression. The frank abandonment of these regulations in the higher grades at Detroit and Elmira was to be a significant contribution to reformatory discipline in later years.

Prison industry was a major concern of administrators and reformers alike. From the first penitentiary days, when fierce debates raged over the merits of labor in solitude versus labor in association, there have always been conflicting theories. Industry gained its place in prison discipline because where it was omitted revolts, mutual corruption, and waves of insanity always appeared. A few hard-headed reform wardens, as Amos Pilsbury and Zebulon Brockway, grasped the equally significant fact that the only sure basis for a permanent administration was relative economic self-sufficiency. The Wines school, on the other hand, took the theoretical stand that, as the purpose of prisons was the reformation of criminals, the first concern should not be the economic one.

A sharp argument had occurred during the first day at Cincinnati between Enoch Wines and Amos Pilsbury over this difference of opinion. It was never settled. Wines failed to persuade a single state government to support a prison administration that sought only the reformation of its inmates; even Elmira did not slight the economic factor during the first years. On the other hand, the prosperity of prison labor came to smash in 1873, and during the following years in the North only rare administrations were able to insure their tenure by paying all the prison expenses. The dispute was in reality only a tactical one and it was soon overshadowed by the agitation against contract labor.

The right of way of the contractor had long been a characteristic of the prison world, and so it remained for many years, in spite of the reformers. The New York Association started a campaign to stop this exploitation of penal servitude, and in the hard times following the panic their arguments were reinforced by the petitions of the competitors of prison contractors both employers and laborers. One result was a series of state investigations of the prison labor problem in the late seventies. Several of these shed considerable light on the subject, but while they condemned the contract system, they hesitated to recommend its abolition until some other system had been partially introduced.[8] As any other system seemed to demand large state appropriations to start with, no one of the responsible boards was very definite in its recommendations. A few suggestions, such as that aiming to prevent concentration in one industry by limiting the percentage to be employed in each trade, were happy inspirations to quiet the protests of the competitors; on the whole no permanent contribution to the solution of this problem was made during the

[8] U.S. Commissioner of Labor, *Report* (1886), pp. 307–68. Carroll D. Wright here reviews the many state investigations, notably those in New York in 1841, 1867 (Wines), 1871 (Wines), 1879 (L. D. Pilsbury); Ohio in 1877; Pennsylvania in 1877; Massachusetts in 1878, 1880; New Jersey in 1879; and Connecticut in 1880.

decade. The only law of any consequence was that in New York centralizing control in the hands of the state superintendent and directing him to diversify production. The war against contractors was a total failure. Even Wisconsin abandoned the state account system and called in contractors to manage her industries. Nevertheless, the very zeal with which the undaunted contractors pushed their cheap goods onto the public market helped to call down on their heads the storm of laws that dominated the next period.

In spite of a partial realization of its objectives, the organized movement gradually disintegrated. The constantly changing personnel was an influential factor in this decline. Prison officers have never enjoyed secure tenure, and although in the period following the Civil War a few able wardens had served year after year, most of them were turned out by political shifts in the mid-seventies. The death of several of the unofficial reformers crippled the movement even more seriously. Thus the passing of Francis Lieber, Abraham Beal, and Judges Edmonds and Wolfe was a serious blow to the New York Association. Wines, Sanborn, and Byers unfortunately withdrew from their key positions at a critical time in the mid-seventies. The removal of Gideon Haynes from Charlestown after he had sold his soul for five thousand greenbacks, the removal of Shuler and Sullivan in Indiana, the transfer of Cordier from Wisconsin to Pennsylvania, and the resignation of Brockway from Detroit —all seriously checked important developments. The death of Amos Pilsbury carried away an important link between the theoretical reformers and the hard-fisted wardens. Only Brockway remained, and his job, as he accepted his new post at Elmira, was to build for the future.

The views of many of the new officers were aptly expressed by the new Ohio board of directors in their 1873 report:[9]

The management of penitentiaries has, until lately, attracted very little attention, except so far as pecuniary results were concerned. Some excitement was created a few years since in regard to crime generally and the reformation of criminals, and several conventions have been held at which a number of subjects were discussed. We are not aware that our officers have derived any practical benefit from these conventions. The excitement and the discussions have passed away leaving a very slight impression in the world.

[9] Ohio State Penitentiary, *Report* (1873), pp. 31–32.

But the Ohio directors were badly misinformed. Dr. Wines was already a world-figure, and the movement he had organized in America was stimulating important developments in Europe, South America, and Japan. As president of the International Prison Association he was busy arranging for its second congress, to convene at Stockholm in 1877, and in last-moment preparation he called the Prison Reform Congress at Newport in the early part of that year. However, Wines admitted his American defeat by failing to invite all prison men to this gathering; only his select friends had an opportunity to vote on resolutions of still a broader nature than those of 1870. The gathering had little significance and its resolutions are interesting only because, even at this date, they idealized the Crofton system, long since abandoned in Ireland.

In his presidential address at Stockholm, Dr. Wines reviewed the progress of prison reform. In almost every nation the newer principles had had some effect, but the veteran reformer was a bit overpleased with these achievements. A large share of credit was due to the state of external and internal peace which the European countries were at last enjoying. Yet, as penal systems were developed, the movement, coming at an opportune time, exerted its influence. However, in place of the practical experimenters taking charge of American prisons, a legalistic profession was gaining control of the prisons on the Continent, and had Wines lived long enough he would have seen the Europeans become skeptical of the optimistic claims of the American reformatories. Already he noted the passing of Recorder Hill, Miss Carpenter, and other outstanding members of the group that had organized the world-wide reform movement. Enoch Wines was almost the last of the unshaken idealists; fortunately he remained long enough to finish *The State of Prisons* and leave it as a monument to the era that had ended.

An era had ended indeed—that is, provided the history of institutions ever lends itself to procrustean terminology. Perhaps it would be better to say that a generation had passed. What a generation it had been! All but Sanborn and Brockway had been men of advanced years, and yet such had been their idealistic enthusiasm that they had defied the old Hebrew prophecy. Marvelous were the visions they had seen: contrite convicts working earnestly for merits with which to gain their freedom; conscientious officers serving their states as long as they could create a new spirit in their prisoners; Christian friends administering public aid to released prisoners and helping them toward useful citizenship; and great national and international conventions pointing the true road to life. Their compassionate idealism had carried them not only far ahead of contemporary attitudes toward the criminal but somewhat out of the realm of practical penology; nevertheless, they succeeded in implanting their major principle—that the criminal was an erring brother deserving of society's special care until he should be refitted for a normal life in its midst—in the newly established Elmira reformatory, "free college" for the criminal youth of New York State.

The rise of Enoch Wines and his movement had been attended by many fortuitous circumstances. Not only did this generation profit from the experiences of a century of reformers, but the older rivalries and traditions were waning as the new leaders came upon the stage leaving them free to make fresh combinations of old principles. The opportune discovery of the Irish model supplied an ideal pattern at the same time that the newly created organizations for inspection provided agencies for the advancement of reform programs. The industrial boom of the late sixties gave many of the wardens the opportunity to enjoy the zest that comes from running a thriving concern, thus raising them above the drab worries of repressive discipline and supplying them with the two essentials for success: optimism and long tenure. By the same token the prisons were advanced in the public esteem, and an eager rivalry in the construction of adequate plants took place. The erection of new prisons was largely a response to the pressure of population growth, but here again circumstances played into the hands of the reformers, who in several cases succeeded in shaping the building programs.

By the late seventies, however, fortune was turning against the reformers. Political upheavals were playing havoc with their friends; economic reversals were blighting their optimism; legislative defeats were compromising their programs; and finally death was claiming its own. The generation passed, but it left a clearly formulated program, a few promising experiments, a rich literature, and a quickened public responsibility for the reformation of criminals.

BIBLIOGRAPHICAL NOTE

The sources are enriched, beginning with this period, by the regular reports of the newly created state boards of charities and corrections, notably those of Massachusetts, Ohio, and Michigan, in these years. The official reports of all the northeastern state prisons are also available, and those of the Detroit house of correction are important. E. C. Wines and T. Dwight, *Prisons in the United States and Canada* (New York, 1867); The New York Prison Association, *Reports*, especially after 1862; the *Journal of Prison Discipline* (Philadelphia, 1856——); the National Prison Congress, *Transactions* (1870); the National Prison Association, *Proceedings* (1873-75); and the International Penitentiary Congress, *Transactions* (1872, 1877), are all of primary importance. John Augustus, *Report of Labors of John Augustus, 1841-1852* (Boston, 1852); Linda Gilbert, *Life and Work* (New York, 1876); Gideon Haynes, *Pictures from Prison Life: An Historical Sketch of the Massachusetts State Prison* (Boston, 1869); Enoch Cobb Wines, *The Actual State of Prison Reform Throughout the Civilized World* (Stockholm, 1878), and *The State of Prisons* (Cambridge, 1880), are all useful.

Later works of special interest for this period are: Zebulon Brockway, *Fifty Years of Prison Service* (New York, 1912); Anderson W. Clark, *State Control and Supervision of Charities* (Lincoln, 1905); Sarah E. Dexter, *Recollections of Hannah Chickering* (Cambridge, 1881); Eugenia C. Lekkerkerker, *Reformatories for Women in the United States* (The Hague, 1931); Sir Evelyn Ruggles-Brise, *Prison Reform at Home and Abroad* (London, 1924); and Lucien V. Rule, *The City of Dead Souls* (Louisville, 1920). The volumes of H. E. Barnes on Pennsylvania and New Jersey prisons, and that of P. Klein on New York prisons, noted under chaps. i and ii above, are valuable for this period as well. The Russell Sage Foundation's *Penal and Reformatory Institutions* (New York, 1910), Vol. I, contains biographical sketches of the leaders and a survey of the reforms of this period.

CHAPTER V

CONVICT LABOR AND PEDAGOGICAL PENOLOGY

American prison developments became increasingly complex in the northern states as the nineteenth century entered its last quarter. The heritage of a century of reformers and a half-century of builders had supplied a considerable equipment of customs and cells. Recent building programs had measurably allayed the demands of expanding populations, and in several instances reformers had successfully directed construction toward the creation of promising institutions. These new reformatories together with a number of forward-looking organizations found themselves in the eighties in the midst of a complex play of forces, dominated by the struggle of organized labor and "free" industry for legislative protection from prison competition. In state after state anti-contract laws were adopted that exerted a far-reaching influence on prison developments.

In the mid-eighties the survivors of the older generation found the younger men eager to join in reviving the National Prison Association in order to discuss their mutual problem, the anti-contract threat. Zebulon Brockway had by this time sufficiently elaborated his reformatory discipline at Elmira to provide a model for new institutions, and the revival of the reform movement was greatly aided by this practical demonstration of its ideology. The annual congresses became increasingly popular and supplied a convenient agency for the education of the officers and inspectors regularly brought into power by political changes within the states. Thus pedagogical penology, elaborated in the reformatories, was made the standard for all prisons by the end of the century, and many of them were to meet the emergency resulting from labor laws by a partial application of the new technique.

THE DOMINATION OF THE LABOR PROBLEM[1]

The Industrial Revolution was already at full tilt in America. Two of its phases in particular exerted a large influence on prison

[1] The author is grateful to the publishers of the *Journal of Criminal Law and Criminology* for permission to use portions of his article printed in Vol. XXV of that *Journal*.

developments: the substitution of machine industry for handicraft production, and the organization of the labor forces. Both of these had been in process for some time, and already the former had transformed prison industry and given it into the hands of contractors. Many of the prisons had become prosperous factories and remained such, at least for the contractors, except when the depressions of the mid-seventies and the mid-eighties destroyed their markets. Many of the reformers, who, a few years before, had bitterly attacked the subversive influences of the contractors, now elaborately defended the system as better than idle prisons. The public, for its part, hesitated to trust the transient politicians in charge of the prisons with the management of large industries.

The question might have been tabled in this fashion had it not been for the constant growth of organized labor during a period of sharp political rivalry. It was one thing for the National Labor Party to insert an anti-contract clause in its platform, and for the Knights of Labor as well as the Federation of Organized Trades and Labor Unions to follow this lead; but it was quite another thing when the district assemblies of the Knights and the state federations took up the agitation. State politicians had their ears to the ground in the early eighties, and they revealed some ability at *Realpolitik* if not in penological statecraft.

The industrialization of America was taking place chiefly in that belt of nine states reaching from Massachusetts to Illinois. Led off by New York in 1864, all but two of these had state federations of labor by 1889, and Pennsylvania and Ohio, the two exceptions, were centers of the growing Knights of Labor with its energetic local and district assemblies. All except Indiana had, before 1887, set one or more special commissions to the investigation of prison labor, and as for the Hoosier State it remained until the nineties not only the most backward in prison reform but the least advanced industrially of the group. But the old subterfuge—commissions for investigation—did not suffice. The parties in power in Illinois and New Jersey hearkened to this demand of the labor forces, as did the Democrats, when in the early eighties, with the aid of many labor votes salvaged from the Greenback-Labor party, they turned out the Republicans in Massachusetts, Pennsylvania, New York, and Ohio. The same party, capturing the White House, was able by

1887 to pass a law forbidding the contracting of any federal criminals.[2] This legislative onslaught was shaking the foundations of the
old American prison system of Lewis Dwight. In desperation the
wardens and responsible reformers revived their national association
and convened annual congresses where they could share their fears
and debate possible solutions. They were all agreed that the prisons
could not be administered properly without labor to fill the long
hours of the convict's day.

In the midst of this hubbub Zebulon Brockway proposed his piece-
price scheme to the revived National Association in 1883, proclaim-
ing it as the long-sought-for solution. Indeed from the point of view
of the warden it had great advantages. It proposed to eliminate the
disturbing influence of the contractor within prison walls by giving
the officers full control over discipline of the convicts and management of the industries. On the other hand, it proposed that the
warden contract with outside companies to supply machinery and
thus free himself from the necessity of waiting on state appropriations. The scheme would make possible as large a diversification of
industry as the warden saw fit or his managing ability allowed;
further than this, it avoided the ill-repute of the contract system and
insured a rich market.

The new proposal received a varied reception. Many of the leaders hailed from states where the current of opinion disregarded labor
protests, and they were naturally little inclined to encourage even a
modification of the existing system; thus Professor Wayland from
Connecticut and various leaders from Michigan were constant critics
of the proposed plan. Michael Cassidy joined in this attack but
from entirely opposite premises; his Philadelphia prison was still
operating on the old solitary system, supplying handicraft labor, un-
affected in the least by the necessity for self-support, the machine
age, or the labor unions. On the other hand, leaders from Ohio, New
Jersey, and Illinois were immediately attracted by Brockway's
scheme, and politicians were plentiful who, after satisfying labor
with laws against contractors, agreed to save the public taxes by
permitting the prisons to earn a part of their expenses at piece-price
agreements. In fact, of the states that abolished contracts, all but

---

[2] U.S. Commission of Labor *Report* (1886), p. 368. In Part II of this report all the
laws of the states on convict labor are quoted in full; see pp. 507–604.

Pennsylvania very quickly reorganized their prison industries on this new plan.

The prisons weathered the severest phase of the storm of labor agitation before the end of the eighties. The growing disharmony within labor ranks, the return of the Republicans to power, and the discovery of the magnitude of the bills of idle prisons brought a lull in anti-contract agitation. At the same time the weight of the reports of numerous special investigations and of the several state labor commissioners and finally in 1886 of the United States Labor Commissioner was all on the side of cautious, moderate regulation rather than complete abolition of contracts. Most of these minimized the importance of prison labor as a competitor of the free workers. Carroll D. Wright, the United States Commissioner, made a special study of the quantity and value of products displaced and concluded that $28,753,999, the total product of 45,277 convicts in 1885, was a very small figure when compared with $5,369,579,191 produced by 2,732,595 free laborers five years before.[3] This rapidly became a major argument and was not seriously challenged until the end of the century.

But the labor forces were not the only interests that had to be pacified. It has been seriously questioned whether the agitation from the beginning was not simply a cleverly devised campaign on the part of the industrial competitors of the contractors to destroy the latter's advantages.[4] At all events the labor attack had no sooner been checked than the manufacturers rallied to the cause and formed their national anti-convict-contract association. Presidents of wagon factories, shoe, furniture, and stove companies, chiefly from Wisconsin, Michigan, Iowa, and Missouri—all at the time lacking anti-contract laws—gathered in Chicago in 1886 to hold their convention. Here they frankly unveiled their interest in eliminating the unfair competition of their rivals and voted to send their president, Colonel W. T. Lewis, on a lecture tour to urge their cause.

Several schemes were proposed in these years that were designed chiefly to curb prison competition. One that made considerable headway was the requirement that all products be stamped "prison made." Another proposal, revealing a curious assortment of mo-

[3] *Ibid.*, p. 295, and tables on pp. 192–99.

[4] P. Klein, *Prison Methods in New York State* (New York, 1920), p. 296.

tives, suggested that prisoners should be employed exclusively at labor with hand tools and man-power machinery. Carroll D. Wright was especially active in agitating this solution which he considered to be the secret of the success of the Cherry Hill penitentiary. At his prompting, Massachusetts adopted a modified form of the plan by forbidding the purchase of new machinery after 1887, and this remained a thorn in the side of her prison administrators for many years. New York in 1888, prohibiting all manufacture by motive power, succeeded in disjointing her entire prison system until a new law righted it. Heedless of this lesson, Pennsylvania politicians sold their state's penological birthright for labor votes in 1897 by adopting an extreme form of this scheme. This reactionary policy combined with the desire to retard prison production the more general wish to check the speed of mechanization in America and revived the old notion that the prisoner might thus learn a useful trade.

Another proposal designed to limit the competitive range of prison industries urged the prohibition of interstate traffic in such goods. The O'Neill Bill aiming at this end was introduced and almost carried through Congress in 1888. The wardens who gathered that year in Boston were greatly disturbed over the prospect and passed a resolution recommending a special convention of prison officers and state legislators to determine a just solution of the difficult problem. But this revolutionary scheme for national planning was not tested until the Richmond convention met in 1930 to face the modern crisis. The decline of the labor influence in the late eighties and the disappearance of the anti-contract association, together with the defeat of the Democrats and other factors, sufficed to stave off immediate legislation.

While the fury of the storm of labor legislation relented somewhat in most of the states toward the close of the decade, in New York it continued unabated. Situated at the center of much of labor's political agitation, this state experienced from the first the full gamut of forces playing around the problem. It devised the legislation that formed the basis for much of the discussion and practice of its neighbors in succeeding years.

The acute nature of the problem in the Empire State was due in part to its industrial environment. But the remarkable efficiency of prison industries after the creation of the all-powerful superintendent in 1877 aggravated the situation. Lewis Pilsbury's success in cutting prison costs to one-fifth of their earlier average entailed the development of extensive industries, and many competitors began to protest.[5] Governor Alonzo B. Cornell expressed this growing hostility in his message of 1880, and in the following year the legislature sent a committee to investigate industrial conditions at Sing Sing. The report favored the contract system, but the legislature hesitated to meddle with the ticklish problem and referred it to the people. Amid a confusion of issues the contract system was condemned by a small majority. Again the Republican legislature refused to act, but that astute politician, David B. Hill, who succeeded Cleveland as governor, attacked the problem with energy, insisting that the popular will be respected and that "unnecessary interference with outside industrial interests" be eliminated.[6] The amendment prohibited new contracts but failed to provide an alternative system. Fortunately for the prisons, as well as for the state treasury, most of the contracts extended ahead several years, but gradually, as they expired, the situation became critical. Finally the legislature created the Prison Labor Reform Commission to plan a new system and authorized, in the meantime, temporary piece-price agreements. These measures came none too soon, for unemployment at Auburn was desperate, and Brockway at Elmira was almost at his wit's end. The commission made a careful study and concluded in 1887 that the piece-price system was highly admirable, but, as popular opposition must be met, a special effort to diversify the industry would be necessary, and arrangements should be made for sale to public and charitable institutions. This last suggestion, an early expression of the idea that later developed into the public-use system, appeared at the time as an effort to dodge the issue. Disregarding this moderate advice, the legislature adopted the Yates Law prohibiting contracts of any kind and abolishing all manufacture that used motive-power machinery. Only production by hand labor was allowed, and then only for the use of state institutions. Immediately the recent surpluses were exchanged for enormous deficits, and the superintendent protested

---

[5] *Ibid.*, pp. 336–68; N.Y. Supt. Prisons, *Report* (1879). The cost was reduced from $317,000 in 1876 to $67,800 in 1878.

[6] *N.Y. Governors' Messages*, ed. by C. Z. Lincoln (Albany, 1909), VIII, 12, 165.

against this destruction not only of the industries but of the whole prison discipline. Only in Elmira was the industrial stoppage made an occasion for constructive measures.

The state finally realized that the problem could not be left in the hands of greedy interests. Professor Charles V. Collin of Cornell, formerly associated with Brockway at Elmira, drafted the bill which was introduced by Fassett in 1889 to become the high-water mark of prison labor legislation of the century. The new law sanctioned both the piece-price and state-account systems, but provided that no industry should employ more than 5 per cent of the number working at that occupation in the state; a few industries were further restricted to one hundred laborers and required to produce for state use only. Of larger significance, the law definitely abandoned the idea that industry should be organized primarily for self-support and accepted the reformatory motive. The convicts were to be divided into three classes: those with good prospects of reformation were to be instructed in trade schools and employed at these trades with no idea of state profit; the repeaters who were at least good prisoners and possibly reformable were to be assigned to industries at which they could find a living after discharge and in the meantime earn their keep; the desperate criminals were to be rewarded with all the drudgery and menial labor rather than the choice jobs which their long terms and professional standing had formerly secured them. In addition, a wage not to exceed one-tenth of the earnings was to be paid to meritorious prisoners.

Unfortunately the state and its officers were poorly prepared to administer so good a law. Neither the abilities of the officers nor the structural equipment of the prisons permitted the genuine classification called for. Meanwhile many industries lobbied for the protection granted to shoes and stove hollow ware at which trades only one hundred prisoners could be employed. Impatient with the persistence of the problem, and possibly stimulated by the rigors of the depression of 1893, the constitutional convention of 1894 advanced an amendment which was shortly adopted fixing 1897 for the end of all forms of contract labor. A prison commission was created to organize a new system on the state-use principle, already partially applied, and its jurisdiction was extended over the county penitentiaries which had so long escaped state interference. A law of 1896 carried out these constitutional provisions and required the several state departments to purchase from the prisons as long as their needs could adequately be supplied.

The Empire State thus finally evolved a system with great possibilities. It excluded the prisons from the haggling of the market place but opened a rich, if unexplored, field for their enterprise. Yet it was no fool-proof device, and in succeeding years, while the state prisons were able to carry on, for the time at least, fairly satisfactory industrial programs, the county penitentiaries, with their former industrial efficiency blasted and with no law giving them a pre-emption on any market, fell back into the class of mammoth city jails, condemning their inmates to noxious idleness. When the New York Prison Association made a comprehensive survey in 1900, it found a discouraging industrial lassitude, incompatible with any purpose of reformation, permeating the entire prison system of the state; and only the adult reformatory was avoiding its vicious results by other devices.

New York's pioneer legislation had been observed with interest by her neighbors, but only Massachusetts was ready to follow the new lead. The developments in the Bay State were less complex in their political aspects but hardly less so as far as the prisons were concerned. After repeated reverses the anti-contract forces finally secured a law in 1887 creating a superintendent of prisons to administer the industries at state account. Unfortunately, by failing to provide the necessary credit and by prohibiting the acquisition of new machinery, the law prevented efficient reorganization and at the same time, by banning contractors, wiped out their overtime payments which had been such an important incentive to efficient labor in the old days. Several of these mistakes were corrected in the following year as a new law permitted each prison to make piece-price agreements, but this in turn undermined the authority of the superintendent and made central management difficult. Unemployment was gradually eliminated, but repeated recommendations for a wage system to revive the interest of the convicts in their labor roused no response.

After several more or less unsatisfactory years with this system the general court was again persuaded to follow the example of New York. All contracts were abolished in 1897, and a state-use system was organized by the superintendent, now given larger powers. An efficient administration was begun and, while Massachusetts never adopted an elaborate system of labor classification, her prison equipment was such that she achieved its object more nearly than did New York. The three-year minimum for state prison commitment generally excluded all but the hardened convicts from Charlestown; the likely candidates for reformation were sent to Concord, and, when the existing piece-price agreements expired, they were given trade instruction; the county houses of correction took care of the remainder and provided fair labor conditions. At the close of the century the authorities were looking ahead to large developments of outdoor labor, and while Pettigrove's proposal that prison labor be used to build a canal across Cape Cod was not followed, the companion proposal that a state camp for inebriates be opened on a large tract of waste land was carried into effect in 1902.

When in 1883 the Democrats captured the Republican stronghold in Pennsylvania, they hastened to reward their labor allies with an anti-contract law. In this state, where the district assemblies of the Knights were so strong, no politician could propose to dodge the law by piece-price agreements, but, as the Eastern penitentiary had long depended on handicraft industry at state account and as the Western prison had long-term contracts, the effect was not immediately disastrous. A complex system of wage payments was instituted to make the best of the existing industry, and the Democrats, again in power in 1891, demonstrated their liberalism by enacting an eight-hour limit for the convict laborer. Two parties could play this game, and in 1897 some Republicans paid for their mess of pottage by pushing through the devastating Muehlbronner Act abolishing the use of power machinery in the manufacture of goods produced elsewhere in the state and seriously limiting the number of men employed at any one industry in each prison. This crippled the industry in the Eastern as well as in the Western penitentiary and only the reformatory, already turning to trade schools and farming, escaped serious injury. The act made a farce of prison labor in Pennsylvania for the next thirty years and did more than any other factor to degrade the two great penitentiaries of the Keystone State from the first rank of American prisons.

The other states did not find it necessary to follow these leaders until the beginning of the next century. New Jersey, Ohio, and Illinois had all abolished contracts in the early eighties, but the administrative authorities had almost immediately turned to the piece-price compromise and were able to continue their fairly prosperous industries. In Illinois it was not until the radical Democrat, John P. Altgeld, became governor that conscientious effort was made to put into effect the intent of the amendment of 1886. State-account industries were introduced, and by the end of his term over half of the prisoners were laboring at these. Nevertheless, his Republican successor reversed the policy, charged the enormous outlays for machinery to Democratic graft, and returned to piece-price agreements. Gradually the labor forces regained their influence, both here and in Ohio, and with the aid of outside merchants they were able, in the early years of the next century, to exclude prison products from the open market. Indiana, in part owing to the inefficiency of her prison industries, escaped the labor attack of the eighties. Accordingly in 1888, when for the first time her prisons reported self-support, it was an occasion for public congratulation, and it was not until the last year of the century that a law was finally passed calling for the gradual abolition of contracts.

That Michigan, rapidly becoming industrialized, escaped the fury of labor legislation was partially a result of the fact that her major prisons were already operating largely on public account. The Detroit house of correction continued to pay its full expenses under Superintendent Nicholson, but as in the days of Brockway it operated all its industries without any outside interference. Meanwhile Jackson prison was extending its mining activities into additional state-owned coal lands and experimenting with hog-raising and trucking on its sixty-five acre lot. When in the nineties an attack was again made on the contractors, Warden Otis Fuller was able to report to the National Prison Congress that he had successfully defended the industries of Ionia against the assault of outside companies, making no mention of labor unions.

The anti-contract agitation did not affect the labor of prisoners in all parts of the country, although it had some surprising reverberations. In the South efforts to restrict and even to abolish the lease system and to substitute farming and road labor were coincident with but entirely independent of the northern agitation; yet there were serious labor troubles in Kentucky and especially in Tennessee over prison labor, and in the latter violent outbreaks persuaded the state to terminate its coal lease in the early nineties. Meanwhile in the West the anti-contract law of the federal government, prohibiting such employment for federal convicts, practically eliminated industry from the territorial prisons. When new states were formed here, this provision was usually imbedded in their constitutions, and indeed hardly a prison in the Rocky Mountain area provided any organized labor for its inmates, aside from a little stone-quarrying, until the development of the honor road camps in the present century.

Labor problems, however, were rife in three western prisons. The lease of Nebraska's prison in 1877 was bitterly assailed until replaced by contracts in the nineties. Oregon, on the other hand, abandoned state-account industries and in 1895 leased its penitentiary. California's earlier action prohibiting new contracts after 1882 was more to be expected in view of its active labor forces, and it affords a clear example of the speed with which an organized force can get results in a young state. This wide-spreading activity of the anti-contract agitation suggested the expanding horizon of the north-eastern prison system, but it was not until the next century that the development became significant.

A few protests occurred in such border states as West Virginia, Missouri, and Kansas, but on the whole their prisons as they developed profitable industries were praised rather than criticized. In fact practically everybody in Missouri and Kansas rejoiced when their respective prisons began in the early eighties to operate nearby coal mines, thus gradually becoming sources of profit to their states. Protests that arose were brushed aside by the authorities. Similarly in West Virginia the governor pointed out that if labor should insist that the profitable contracts at the prison be abandoned, the alternative would be either work on the public highways or some lease system as in the South.

Meanwhile Minnesota was doing some constructive experimenting of its own. When its law of 1889 made one-half of the prisoners available to contractors an agreement was made with the recently organized Minnesota Thresher Company to produce its binder twine. It was a new thing for a state prison to get in on the ground floor of an expanding industry with a great market in the community. Whatever labor problems might have developed were forestalled as the state took over this industry in the early nineties and established the model state-account system of the nation. Producing and selling cheap in an almost unlimited market to the benefit of the chief portion of its electorate, and at the same time paying its prison expenses, Minnesota had an unassailable system.

The non-industrial states of the North largely escaped this problem. Wisconsin gave it no attention until the depression of 1893 caused the contractor to lay off most of his laborers and roused the authorities to the danger of dependence on such a system. An investigation was made and a change to the New York system proposed, but returning prosperity solved the problem, and it was not until 1907 that a new system was adopted, patterned after Minnesota. In Iowa, except for the successful action of button companies to secure protection from prison competition, little attempt was made to regulate the use of prison labor. Aside from Massachusetts none of the New England prisons experienced any hardships due to the anti-contract agitation. Maine, however, seriously hampered her prison industry, carried on for many years at state account, by limiting the number to be employed at any one trade to 20 per cent of the convicts. The sole industry, a wagon factory, was seriously handicapped until the warden hit upon the trick of dividing the industry into several trades; but the prison never regained its old prosperity for, symbolical of most prisons, it was putting its money on the horse in a railroad era.

The controlling factors in the convict labor problem of the nineties were thus local rather than national in character. Only in such states as New York, Pennsylvania, and Massachusetts, were the interests sufficiently organized to secure their full desires, and it was fortunate that these states were able to bear the burdens of nonproductive prisons. The neat penological rationalization of the legislation in these states attracted both the interests and the reformers throughout the country, and gradually the old American tradition of prisons supported by the labor of their inmates gave place to a new standard of convicts working to learn trades but avoiding the public markets. If its negative aspects were most prominent, both in the causes and in the results, the new industrial program nevertheless contributed much to the spread of the reformatory function of labor.

Organized labor, strong throughout the North in the mid-eighties, lost much of its political influence after the decline of the Knights. Whatever its defects for the economic struggle, this national body exerted through its state and district assemblies a powerful influence on state politicians. It not only claimed to fight the whole cause of labor but was quick in this instance to defend the welfare of a small portion of its members. When the strength of the Knights declined, this plank of their platform was eagerly taken over by the rising Federation of Labor, but the cautious political activity of the subsidiary state federations prevented them from attaining the influence of their predecessors over prison developments. Nevertheless, the continued growth of the power of the national federation, and its unswerving adherence to the attack on penal servitude, did much to prepare public opinion and especially the politicians for the new function of prison industry.

The Republicans as well as the Democrats began to see the light toward the end of the century. Carroll D. Wright, as Commissioner of Labor under Cleveland in 1886, had defended the contractor, but by 1896 he had become aware of the existence of unfair competition. The final crystallization of the new attitude appeared in the recommendations of the United States Industrial Commission of 1900, created by a Republican House. Its report strongly indorsed New York's recently elaborated state-use system; in fact, twelve out of thirteen resolutions urged the superiority of this system over all others. A considerable array of statistics revealed greater profits from the contracts, but the commission took higher ground, asserting: "The most desirable system for employing convicts is one which provides primarily for the punishment and reformation of the prisoners and the least competition with free labor, and, secondarily, for the revenue of the State."[7] Both of these reports justified rather

---

[7] House of Representatives Industrial Commission, *Prison Labor* (56th Cong., 1st sess., Doc. 476), Part III, p. 11 and *passim.* See also U.S. Department of Labor, *Special Bulletin No. 5 of . . . . on Contract Labor* (1896), p. 446 and *passim;* p. 446: "The total income in forty-one states in 1885 had been $24,271,078 and this fell to such an extent that they reported only $19,042,472 in 1895, while at the same time the number of convicts increased from 41,877 to 54,244 between these dates. The problem of comparison is complicated because the sum is the value of the goods, not of the work."

than complained of the decline in the earning capacities of the prisons, and they rejoiced in the comparative expansion of the public-
account industry; in the later of these investigations even the piece-
price system was frowned upon.

The new theories did not always have clear sailing. The national
reports showed an irresponsibility for state budgets that stood in
sharp contrast with several state investigations. An Illinois commission, originally favorable to the New York plan, was frightened
from it by a discovery of the failure of even the well-organized administrative agencies of that state to secure employment for more
than one-third of the state prisoners and for but few of those in the
counties; it was especially cautioned by the discouraging financial
results. Nevertheless, the day of self-supporting prisons was passing,
and the states were at the same time becoming accustomed to larger
budgets. The recommendations of the Industrial Commission were
to be widely quoted in succeeding years.

The one resolution of this commission which proposed definite
action by Congress revived the old agitation for the restraint of
interstate traffic in prison-made goods. The old O'Neill Bill had
been repeatedly agitated, but it had always been tabled. Several of
the states had undertaken to secure the same end by laws regulating
the importation of prison products from other states, requiring
branding or an importer's license, or some such restraint.[8] Congress
itself forbade the importation of such goods from foreign countries.
But the state laws were being attacked in the courts, and already the
more extreme New York and Ohio laws had been set aside.[9] The
problem had a clear affinity with the regulation of the interstate
liquor traffic, and the Industrial Commission favored a Wilson Act
for prison labor instead of the complete federal prohibition of such
commerce proposed by the O'Neill Bill. Three decades were to pass
before Congress passed the Hawes-Cooper Bill, which was in effect
a response to this earlier recommendation.

The prison labor problem had arrived at the zenith of its influence by the close of the century. While the aggressive activity of

[8] House Indus. Com., *op. cit.*, pp. 141–66, a complete summary of convict labor laws.
New York and Ohio were the first in 1894, but Kentucky, Indiana, and Wisconsin followed in rapid succession, and Colorado shortly adopted a moderate law.

[9] Ohio law set aside in *Arnold* v. *Yanders* (1897), 47 *N.E. Reports*, p. 50; and New
York law in *People* v. *Hawkins* (1898), 51 *N. E. Reports*, p. 257.

organized labor had turned to the economic field, politicians eager
to attract votes still campaigned, and competing industrial interests
were gaining a hearing. Only a few of the states had carried their
legislation far enough to gain political stability, but already their
measures were the center of agitation in many of the other states.
Even the federal government had mounted the band wagon and was
considering taking the driver's seat with a questionable federal police
power.

The larger significance of the problem was just beginning to appear. Most of the states, escaping the rigors of the agitation, had
been able by one means or another to provide employment for the
large majority of their convicts, and, in spite of brief crises, the old
system had been able to hold its own in their prisons. In Pennsylvania, New York, and to a lesser degree in Massachusetts a new
situation had developed; the major reliance of the disciplinarians
could no longer be a good day's hard labor. This was fortunate for
the reformatories, in that they were encouraged to develop to the
full their trade schools, their military organizations, and all the other
features of their discipline which, in an earlier era, might have been
abandoned as needs for economy urged self-support. The regular
prisons in these states were in a quandary. The labor system in
Pennsylvania had become a farce; in New York the lax administration supplied scarcely one-third of the convicts with work; in Massachusetts the prisoners were idling about antiquated machinery, and
no officer pretended to maintain the old silent system. Should the
prison adopt the reformatory methods and strive to provide a constructive associate life; should they study to provide conditions that
would keep the convicts fairly contented and orderly; could they
maintain obedience in the face of idleness by a return to brutal punishments—these were some of the questions that labor legislation
was forcing on the attention of the authorities in 1900. These questions were destined to become more insistent as organized labor
grew in strength and saw more clearly its place in a competitive
capitalistic society that faced frequent periods of contraction.

THE EARLY DEVELOPMENT OF ADULT REFORMATORIES

Fortunately the young men's reformatory, child of the imagination and the housing problem of the seventies, was already making

a creditable development when the labor problem became the dominant consideration in prison affairs. Brockway had successfully established a reformatory discipline at Elmira before the anti-contract laws effectively attacked prison industry, and he was able to take advantage of the new emergency to transform Elmira into an industrial training school, free from the responsibility of self-support. The anti-contract movement joined with the population problem in strengthening the campaign for reformatories in other states, and additional institutions were established, several of them on the now well-integrated pattern of the industrial reformatory at Elmira.

Louis Dwight and Enoch Wines had dominated their eras by organizing the propaganda for reform; Zebulon Brockway won his laurels by service in the ranks. Amos Pilsbury and Gideon Haynes before him and at least a half-dozen wardens in his day and later fully equaled Brockway in administrative ability, and a few officers have revealed similar capacities for experimentation, but no other man has so successfully united all these qualities with a long life of practical service. Although not as widely famed as the elder Wines, Brockway during at least twenty of his fifty years of service was the most significant laborer in the prison field.

After his conversion in the late fifties Brockway retained a strong religious faith. He wanted religion to help him reform convicts, but, if not always as serviceable in this respect as he desired, it did strengthen Brockway's zest for his job and provided him with an armor of righteousness that made him, in his later years, impervious to the darts of wise as well as foolish critics. His dominant personality and strong conviction earned for him by the close of his career the reputation of a tyrant, but by that time the venerable superintendent was able to bear the distinction with dignity, along with many another graduate of the school of hard knocks. Quite different features were prominent during the long years of his labors. Eagerness to confer with other reformers and to give their ideas a trial, readiness to enlist and work with men of various specialties and to adapt their programs to his needs, brilliant ingenuity in devising solutions for critical situations, practical ability in handling men and in winning their loyalty, scrupulous honesty in the administration of public funds—such were the qualities that persuaded the New York reformers to trust their new reformatory to his care.

Brockway was no Captain Ahab stubbornly chasing an illusive ideal through a half-century; rather he was a determined commander ever scanning the horizon for the blowing of a new idea that might help to put character into his young men in their cells.[10]

When he assumed his new duties at Elmira in 1876, Brockway prepared the bill which became the controlling act of the institution. Indeterminate sentences were provided for all commitments, and the board of managers was empowered to release the inmates on parole as soon as a grading system or some similar device indicated their reformation. The sole amendment added by the legislature provided that no one should be detained longer than the maximum sentence provided in the criminal code for his crime, thus fortunately safe-guarding against the danger that a few excessive terms served by unruly or feeble-minded prisoners might rouse the public to abolish the experiment before it should have a fair trial. The age limits for commitments were fixed at sixteen and thirty, and only men convicted of their first felony were to be received.

The major task remained—that of developing a system of grades and marks that would maintain discipline, encourage reformation, and determine the date of its accomplishment. This latter was the crucial point and neither Maconochie nor Crofton was an adequate guide; Brockway had to devise his own program. Accordingly, as soon as the buildings were sufficiently completed to provide separate quarters, the rapidly increasing population was divided into three grades. The first was the honor grade to which a man had to earn his way by securing a specified number of marks in the second, or reception, grade. These marks were to be earned by satisfactory performance in school and shop and by good conduct; a perfect record during six months would accumulate sufficient marks for promotion, and a similar performance in the first grade made the young man eligible for parole at the end of his first year. Very few proved able to demonstrate such an immediate reformation, and any serious misconduct or aggravated loss of marks demoted the inmate to a lower grade from which he had to earn his promotion if he desired parole. Brockway hoped to retreat behind his marking system and to substitute for the customary hostility between prisoners and officers the

[10] Zebulon Reed Brockway, *Fifty Years of Prison Service* (New York, 1912). Brockway began as a guard at Wethersfield in 1848 under Amos Pilsbury.

atmosphere of a school in which the instructor encourages the pupils to grapple with their records. In addition to developing self-control by marking the performance of the daily activities, Brockway sought to cultivate the inmate's self-respect by grading the privileges and accommodations so as to make the man in the first grade proud of his standing.

The reformatory was happily situated in a college neighborhood, and in developing his educational department Brockway soon disclosed a penchant for working with specialists. In 1878 selected inmates were placed in charge of elementary classes meeting six evenings a week, and Dr. D. R. Ford of the Elmira Women's College was engaged to conduct courses in physical geography and natural science for the more advanced young men. The next year Dr. Ford was given charge of the entire department, and six public-school principals and three lawyers were secured as instructors for the elementary classes while the advanced section was enlarged to include classes in "inventional geometry, book-keeping . . . . human physiology and sanitary science."[11] A third educational division was soon added when D. P. Mayhew was brought from the Michigan State Normal School as moral director to conduct classes in biblical teachings, ethics, and psychology. Marks were awarded for successful work in these classes, but no artificial relation existed between the three grades and the three educational divisions; the stimulus to advance to the higher division came from the popularity of those courses. This incentive was especially strong in the early eighties when Charles A. Collin took charge of the ethics and economic courses and Professor J. R. Monks lectured on history and literature. Possibly stimulated by the fame of the Chautauqua summer schools, Brockway and his educational co-workers organized a summer session in 1882 with such gratifying results that it was made a regular feature.

But it was becoming evident that all the young men did not benefit equally from these classes, and in the summer of 1883 Brockway brought Professor N. A. Wells from Syracuse University to conduct a class in industrial arts for the dullards. Fifty backward students were selected for the experiment, and ten capable inmates were appointed as monitors to aid Wells supervise a course in terra-cotta

[11] Elmira State Reformatory, *Report* (1880), p. 27.

modeling. The results were so encouraging that the thirteen weeks' course was repeated during the following summer on an enlarged scale, including classes in plumbing, tailor-cutting, telegraphy, and printing. Another year saw the experiment grow into a year-round department, one of the pioneer trade schools of the country, and in 1886 a special building was provided for this activity. The purchase of a printing press in 1883 for the more economical publication of institutional reports quickly attracted some of the ablest inmates to this trade, and a plan was hit upon of printing a weekly leaflet to digest the news of the daily papers that were excluded from the reformatory. Thus the *Summary*, the first and for several decades the best of a long line of prison papers, grew out of a desire to train selected inmates in a useful trade and at the same time to keep the rest informed of the developments of the world into which they were shortly to be released.

Brockway's ready experimentation with new ideas was further illustrated in 1886 when Dr. Hamilton D. Wey, visiting physician, was encouraged to organize a special class of twelve low-grade, intractable convicts for intensive physical training along the lines of the recently imported Swedish technique. The training included carefully planned and measured diets, steam or hot-water baths with rubbing and kneading of muscles by an expert trainer, and extended drills in calisthenics. A special early-morning school period rounded out the program for the selected men and supplied a gauge for judging results. When the treatment was discontinued after several months owing to the loss of the trainer, both Dr. Wey and Brockway were gratified to find that ten of the twelve patients were ready to take an active part in the normal institutional life.

Amid such experiments it was no wonder that both inmates and officers thrived. Brockway had early dispensed with the services of a regular chaplain and was entertaining a succession of prominent and able Sunday speakers. These visitors, numbering thirty-six in 1885, were a fruitful source of stimulation to the officers as well as to the prisoners, but, what was more important for American penology, they carried away with them a most favorable impression of the new reformatory. Champions were sorely needed, for many critics were protesting against the new-fangled methods of pandering criminals. Brockway, on one occasion, responded that he was trying to give his boys "something to pull at," something hard to do that would call into use their best faculties.[12] Charles Dudley Warner, a frequent visitor, proclaimed Brockway's work to be a remarkable demonstration of the educational theories of Froebel. In 1884 he declared that

the rose-water method, the reward and punishment method, the sanitary method, are alike and all united inadequate to touch the great criminal mass. . . . I firmly believe there is a way. . . . That way is education. . . . And by education I do not mean the teaching of knowledge, the imparting of information, learning from books or other source. I mean . . . . a training and bringing out of all the powers and faculties that go to make up a man, sound in mind, in morals, in body.[13]

It is the fundamental thing in Froebel's system of education [Warner added more than a decade later] that the only way to awake power is by creating activity . . . . that makes something, that does something. . . . The whole Elmira system is based on that ability to form and change habits.[14]

Thus Brockway and his co-workers developed the educational provisions of Elmira far beyond those of any other prison. The reformatory was well established before the tornado of labor laws hit the state, upsetting the industrial systems so laboriously developed in the prisons. A quite unexpected result of these laws was the new prominence forced upon the educational activities at Elmira. Compelled to shift from one to another of five different industrial systems during the first twelve years, only the most versatile of administrators could have maintained a distinct institutional character; Brockway, by emphasizing the educational features, succeeded in establishing a co-ordinated industrial reformatory.

The industrial program had been a major feature of the reformatory from the beginning. Brockway, with a reputation for making his institutions pay their way, had organized the first industries with borrowed money, operating them himself, as was his custom. But the legislature refused to back this system with the necessary credit and in 1881 directed the managers to make suitable contracts. Regulations were adopted limiting the hours of labor to eight on each week day and providing for an overtask bonus in cash and marks for the grading system. Brockway, however, soon became dissatis-

---

[12] N.P.A., *Proceedings* (1887), pp. 281–82.

[13] *Ibid.* (1884–85), pp. 232, 233.   [14] *Ibid.* (1898), pp. 261–63.

fied with the contractors and, as the agitation against that system was coming to a head in the legislature, proposed the piece-price system as a means for eliminating their interference and satisfying the amendment of 1884. Support for this scheme grew and it was partially introduced in 1887, only to be terminated by the Yates Law in the following year. Responsible men recognized that this last measure offered no real solution, but, while Charles A. Collin was drafting the excellent Fassett Law, Brockway was busy working out his own solution. Fourteen hours after the sudden cessation of all industries in 1888 he had a military-training department in operation, and within a month all the inmates were organized into companies and were drilling several hours each day. Meanwhile the trade-school activity was shifted from its two evening sessions to fill the six mornings of the week; the literary school was convened every evening except Sunday; and the physical education department, formerly handling only a few abnormals, was expanded so as to provide calisthenic exercises to the entire population. A touch of drama was added to this remarkable transformation when the fife and drum corps was enlarged into a brass band. Because of the emergency, these pioneer developments of the penal curriculum were safeguarded from attack, and when the Fassett Law freed Elmira from the necessity of self-support the few productive industries permitted to the institution were readily co-ordinated with the trade-school department. The erection of a gymnasium in 1890 established the physical culture and military departments as all-year-round features and gave them, together with the evening school, a co-ordinate place with the trades department in the now completely evolved reformatory technique.

Unfortunately Brockway's remarkable success in these administrative details was prompting judges in all parts of the state to inundate Elmira with new commitments. Additions to the original 504 cells were made in 1886 and again in 1892, raising the total to 1,296 cells but without adequately accommodating the growing population. Overcrowding continued to harass the institution until a branch reformatory was built to relieve Elmira in the next century, and this situation, more than any other factor, served to plague and darken the latter days of the great superintendent.

It was difficult to check Elmira's hardy development, and new innovations were made in its technique during the nineties. A succession of able inmate editors of the *Summary* made some pioneer efforts at penological research. One of them in 1893 made the first scientific study of prison diets, and his report, with its consideration of the calories and grams of the various types of nourishment and its comparison of the rations at Elmira with those of the American and German armies, contrasts sharply with the usual pound-and-quart analysis, chiefly concerned with economy. But the most important disciplinary development of the decade was the introduction in 1896, following Concord's example, of organized sport. Games had been organized spontaneously in a few prisons at earlier dates when the prisoners had been given the freedom of the yard on special occasions, but no prison, not even the Massachusetts reformatory, developed this feature to the point that Brockway now carried it in his endeavor to foster self-control and team spirit at Elmira. This feature was to prove one of the most popular of the reformatory's contributions to prison discipline in the next century, although few institutions were able to secure more than its entertainment value.

The industrial reformatory at Elmira was now successfully established, attracting sometimes the praise and sometimes the ridicule of prison administrators, aspiring politicians, newspaper alarmists, and foreign critics, who may or may not have walked in the shade of its late-Victorian turrets. Its well co-ordinated discipline, centering around the grading and marking system, was animated by an honest application of the indeterminate sentence. With an industrial activity subordinated to trade and academic schools, and a military organization and calisthenic exercises supplemented by intensive physical culture for the defectives, keeping the men fully employed; with the weekly *Summary* for the world's news, an extensive library, and the frequent Sunday lectures by prominent visitors, all prodding the fagging intellect; and above all with the stimulation and kindly encouragement of Professors Monks, Ford, Collin, and Wells, of Dr. Wey, and, last but not least, of Zebulon Brockway—Elmira, "College on the Hill," was surely supplying its inmates with something more to pull on than their own bootstraps when they wished to lift themselves out of the gutter. A large percentage of success was reasonably to be expected as long as society afforded the released men ample opportunities for constructive citizenship.

There was in the atmosphere of Elmira something vital, and yet so intangible as to escape many a scribe and copyist. It may have been the power of faith or the force of inspiration which came to Brockway because he believed in the reformatory value of his methods. Whatever it was, he passed it on to his co-workers and to the boys under his care. It created the will to pull, which is the one thing that no reformatory discipline can dispense with, and which is a lost art with so many of the later-day penologists with all their clinical classifications and numbering of the reformed. It was one of those realities which later generations discredit because they cannot reproduce them. It made all the difference in the world between the reformatories, such as Elmira at its high tide in the early nineties, and their disillusioned remnants which parade the youth of a new era down the ruts of tradition. While vital statistics frequently achieve little better than a consummate jest, considerable credence is due the investigation in 1888 which reported 78.5 per cent of the 1,125 men already paroled to be reformed and laboring as good citizens for the support of themselves and their families.[15] The more favorable economic opportunities in the years before 1893 further increased the percentage of success.

By the nineties Elmira had become the model for other reformatories, demanding imitation rather than originality; but the institutions already established did not quickly conform to its pattern. Thus the Ionia house of correction and reformatory, especially during the long years of Otis Fuller's administration, made no attempt to introduce what Fuller regarded as Brockway's reformatory frills. Elementary instruction was provided and the lock step was abandoned, but the traditional rules of silence were retained and the institution in both theory and practice placed its major reliance on good hard labor as the best method of reformation. Meanwhile at Sherborn, in spite of the determination of Mrs. Ellen C. Johnson, superintendent for many years after 1884, the presence of both major and minor offenders made the application of a system of grades and marks difficult. The poorly co-ordinated provisions for the release on permit, indenture, and parole of the various types of cases further

---

[15] Elmira, *Report* (1888), p. 26. Modern skeptics should not overlook the fact that the probation system had not yet come in to exclude from the reformatories the most likely candidates for reformation.

complicated the situation, while the failure to develop industrial activities limited the educational possibilities of the institution. The one real accomplishment was the development of a farm with its opportunities for both exhausting labor and varied occupations, including the privilege of caring for pets and flowers. The planting of a mulberry grove, although it failed to provide the intended silk industry, supplied an attractive setting for Sunday-afternoon lectures; and many visitors were to become entranced by the quaint scene as they spoke or sang to rows of primly dressed women seated in the shade. The undesirable overcrowding of the first years resulted in measures shunting more and more cases into local institutions, and Sherborn's population dwindled far below its accommodations, making the general court reluctant to answer appeals for appropriations for new developments. Nevertheless, in an unobtrusive way Massachusetts continued to give a large portion of its female prisoners a friendly care that greatly excelled the treatment of women in all other states until New York took a fresh lead at the end of the century.

The Bay Commonwealth was in these years developing a much more successful institution in its young men's reformatory. The designation of the new Concord prison as a reformatory was made possible by the decision to renovate the old Charlestown prison prompted by the decline in the commercial value of the old site in the early eighties. When the reformatory was first organized in 1884, no age limits were fixed on commitments and both major and certain minor offenders were admitted. The Elmira pattern was already gaining repute, and a new law of 1886 provided for indeterminate sentences with two-year maximums for misdemeanants, five-year maximums for major offenders, and a grading system to determine the date of parole. But Concord was prevented, by the mixed character of its population, from adhering strictly to the Elmira pattern, and the ingenuity of its officers made it in some respects an additional experiment station.

The reformatory was fortunate in securing as its first superintendent Colonel Gardiner Tufts,[16] and equally fortunate in his young

[16] N.P.A., *Proceedings* (1891), Appendix I. Tuft's teaching career ended when he secured an appointment under Secretary Stanton; in 1869 he became visiting agent under the board of charities, and when Sherborn was opened Tufts was made treasurer in order to keep a male eye on affairs without offending the women.

assistant, Joseph Scott. Both were educators with a strong religious bent, and they secured the faithful co-operation of Chaplain William J. Batt in making this force a major feature of the discipline. The grading system and many of the educational features of Elmira were introduced, and *Our Paper* followed the *Summary*, although it gave a larger space to original composition by the inmates. Industrial and manual training departments and physical exercises were introduced after their value had been demonstrated in New York, but this was also after the slightly tardy labor laws of Massachusetts had made it necessary to find a substitute for productive industries. Concord authorities were the first to develop a program of organized sports but failed to supply a roof to cover the open-air gymnasium, while Elmira was enabled by its better equipment to profit from this activity throughout the year. The most original achievement at Concord was the organization of several societies or clubs to one of which all convicts who had advanced to the first grade were eligible for election. Little restraint was placed on the activities of these organizations at their weekly meetings, and in many cases the club members and the institution reaped many of the advantages to be derived from the self-government schemes that were to arouse so much controversy two decades later.[17]

When Colonel Tufts died in 1891 his able assistant, Joseph F. Scott, succeeded to control and continued with even greater success the reformatory policies of the institution. After the example of Mrs. Johnson at Sherborn, farming activities were extended, and a 200-acre farm was put under the plow. Among other improvements an up-to-date hospital was erected in 1900. The establishment of a state farm for misdemeanants relieved the reformatory of many commitments for drunkenness, but hundreds of these charges continued to crowd the cells at Concord, and their two-year-maximum sentences occasioned the rapid turnover that released 2,465 between 1885 and 1889 in contrast with the 2,674 parolees from the larger

---

[17] Massachusetts Prison Commission, *Concord Report* (1887), pp. 19–28, 61–72. The societies included a Reformatory Prayer Meeting with 30 members, a Y.M.C.A. with 187 members, a Catholic Debating Society with 225, a Saturday Scientific and Literary Club with 75, a Baseball and Literary Society with 45, and a Chautauqua Club with 15 members. The Saturday-afternoon games included baseball, football, wrestling, and leaping; neighboring towns frequently sent teams to play against the reformatory on special days.

Elmira during its first thirteen years. Although the fullest realization of the reformatory influences was thus prevented, Concord had become a most creditable addition to the institutional equipment of Massachusetts by the end of the century.

The further extension of the reformatory pattern was in large part the work of the revived National Prison Association. Its sessions provided a parade ground for the various disciplines, and Elmira invariably carried off the blue ribbon. Even the strong self-righteousness of the eastern Pennsylvanians could not resist this influence, and the proposed middle penitentiary of that state, patterned after Cherry Hill in 1878, was transformed, while still on paper, into a young men's reformatory. Huntingdon was slowly built during the eighties on the Elmira model, adding the farming activities of Sherborn and Concord as a major feature, and when Major R. W. McClaughry was called from his rich experience at Joliet to take charge, an efficient reformatory discipline was organized. A half-dozen additional states took steps toward the establishment of young men's reformatories before the end of the century, and, although their programs were in many cases delayed, the Elmira model had gained full recognition as the correct penitentiary pattern. Thus in place of the generous dreams and ambitious resolutions of the earlier generation, a practical interest in Brockway's achievements had become the chief growing point of penology.

THE REVIVAL OF THE NATIONAL MOVEMENT

The success of Elmira and the rising clamor of the labor forces, occurring together in the early eighties, were large factors in the revival of the National Prison Association. The passing of the earlier generation had not put an end to the general agitation for prison reform, for the National Conference of Charities had voted in 1879 to enlarge its scope so as to include problems of correction; but the secretaries of state boards of charities and other interested reformers who had gathered to these conferences failed to enlist the collaboration of prison officers, and their sessions had little practical effect. It was at Brockway's suggestion that W. M. F. Round, secretary of the New York Prison Association, and Franklin Sanborn, president of the American Social Science Association, joined in calling the preliminary gathering at Saratoga in 1883 of those interested in reviving the National Association. In spite of the imminent danger of anti-contract legislation, prompting the wardens to gather together to work out a solution for threatening unemployment, it proved to be a difficult task to weld the various elements together into a united association. The wardens, usually hard-headed Civil War veterans with some political connections, were not eager "to sit at the feet of the Gamaliels who were running the machine." But the reformers were not the kind of men to take back seats, and Sanborn, Brinkerhoff, the younger Wines, Round, Byers, and Francis Wayland of Connecticut quickly monopolized the platform. Brockway was an old comrade, but most of the other wardens did not feel at home in this company, and the first regular congress in 1884 had scarcely closed before a group of prison officers gathered separately at Chicago. William Round, secretary of the revised Association, hurried to Chicago and was greatly relieved when he learned that they were not bolting from the reform movement.

Possibly the factor that did more than anything else to hold the Association together was the personality of its president, Rutherford B. Hayes. A record of faithful co-operation in the earlier period combined with the prestige of a former President of the United States to prompt his annual re-election until his death in 1892 brought to an end the first phase of the revived movement. But, while the Association might have held together, it would have accomplished little had not a number of able wardens been so situated that they enjoyed unusually long terms of service. Such officers as Brockway at Elmira, Joseph Nicholson who had succeeded him at Detroit, Charles E. Felton at the Chicago house of correction, Ellen Johnson and Gardiner Tufts at the two reformatories of Massachusetts, and Michael Cassidy and Edward Wright at the two Pennsylvania penitentiaries, were in charge of institutions never subjected to politics. At least one warden, Major R. W. McClaughry, enjoyed a long career in several institutions as a result of distinguished ability. A. A. Brush, whose eleven years at Sing Sing created a record for that political football not broken until the arrival of Lewis E. Lawes, and H. F. Hatch and E. C. Coffin at Jackson and Columbus helped to provide the successive congresses with an atmosphere of realism that kept their speculations within the bounds of practical affairs. A few outstanding chaplains, notably George Hickox at

Jackson, John Milligan at Pittsburgh, and William Batt at Concord, served to keep the religious tradition alive although it no longer stood forth as the dominant inspiration. The annual deliberations of these men as they traveled from city to city helped to co-ordinate prison developments throughout an expanding section of the country and supplied instruction for the new officers—wardens for a year or two—thus preventing the anarchy of politics from swamping the few achievements already made in the field of penology.

Preoccupation with practical affairs was an outstanding feature of most of the earlier congresses. The term "reform" gained a genuine disrepute as the crusading zeal of the leaders of the seventies was disclaimed, at least among a group of self-styled practical wardens led by Michael Cassidy of Cherry Hill. Although the sessions usually opened with a large popular assembly on Saturday evening at which visiting and local dignitaries lectured on the public's responsibility for the criminal, and although a symphony of sermons filled the next day as chaplains and local pastors celebrated prison reform throughout the convention city, the real work of the congress did not begin until Monday brought the wardens out in full force, airing the soiled garments of the prison system. Strange alignments developed during the debates over various issues. Brockway defended the "rod' against Cassidy, Brush, and others who maintained that a solitary cell with bread and water was the best way of taming the intractable. When Judge Wayland urged that the moral welfare of prisoners should be safeguarded to the extent of denying the use of tobacco, Warden Brush was quick to retort that he was not striving to make angels out of his charges. When Brockway urged that prisons be limited to six hundred inmates as against Brush's contention that they should be prepared to house one thousand, the delegates supported Brockway, but the states, here as in so many cases, continued to build as economy and population dictated, exceeding even Brush's standard in a dozen institutions by 1900.

The Association undertook to stimulate federal action in the collection of penal statistics and in behalf of federal prisoners. Frederick Wines, as criminal statistician for the census bureau, complained of the irregularity of prison records. Every warden appreciated the difficulties in the way of statistical comparisons, and Joseph Nicholson introduced a resolution in 1890 calling upon the federal government to establish a bureau to gather annual statistics—a practice already established in several European countries but not to be adopted in America for several decades. Meanwhile the makeshift arrangement of boarding the federal prisoners in the various state and local prisons without supervision or adequate records of their whereabouts was still more reprehensible. General Roeliff Brinkerhoff's agitation on this point, beginning in 1885, continued for a decade before a faltering start was made toward the development of a federal penal system.

Lively discussions occurred at the congresses on most aspects of the penal problem. The care of the discharged, the influence of education, and of course the power of religion were considered in an attempt to evaluate their aid to reformation. Occasional reports were made on the nature of developments in Europe, praising the centralization achieved there or attempting to account for the remarkable decline of crime in England.[18] But the two subjects which received most attention were the convict labor problem and the challenge of reformatory technique. Only death could silence such critics of Elmira as Michael Cassidy, but, as the number of reformatories and the experiments with release on parole increased, sterile objections to the new procedure were pushed aside, and discussion centered on the respective merits and defects of the various adaptations of the technique.

The wardens, never quite content with their place in the Association, organized a subsidiary body in 1886 to take charge of the sessions at which their special problems were considered. Joseph Nicholson of Detroit was chosen president and McClaughry of Joliet, secretary. The latter was charged by his fellows to find a scheme for identifying prisoners in order to settle the old argument as to the number of allegedly reformed men released from one institution only to be gathered into another.

McClaughry received his commission at an opportune time.

[18] N.P.A., *Proceedings* (1891), pp. 80–106, 237–49. Warden Cassidy, after a visit to England, attributed her enviable record to the migration of discharged convicts to America. Captain Massie of Canada credited the achievement to the large amount of Christian work among the poor and middle classes. C. E. Coffin gathered statistics to show that the reduction in commitments was largely due to a substitution of fines for prison sentences.

Alphonse Bertillon had recently elaborated a scheme for the identification of recidivists, or "back-sliders" as F. H. Wines translated the term, based on the theory that while the bone structure of the body does not change after reaching maturity, individual variations are so elaborate that a series of minute measurements provides an infallible identification. The city of Paris had adopted the scheme in 1883 in order to aid in classifying its unwieldy file of criminal photographs, and four other French cities were introducing the system when McClaughry ordered instruments from Bertillon. The demonstration of the novel scheme before the Association at its Toronto session attracted keen interest. Skepticism was soon allayed but feelings were aroused, and A. A. Brush, the hard-fisted warden of Sing Sing, joined with the sentimentalists who considered the convict's past his own affair. Nevertheless, the Bertillon system gained wide approval, and in the course of two years a central bureau was set up at Joliet under the direction of the wardens' association with fourteen prisons pledged to co-operate. Unfortunately only a few states provided funds to purchase instruments, and no assistance was given to the central bureau, thus forcing its abandonment. The scheme was saved from complete discard only in 1896 when New York established a bureau of identification at Sing Sing staffed to supply service to any prison officer in the country, and when the association of chiefs of police opened a similar clearinghouse at Chicago. By the end of the century seventeen states and Canada were co-operating more or less efficiently through these two agencies, and the wardens' association was content to see its self-appointed task in more capable hands.

Meanwhile the chaplains had likewise formed a subsidiary organization in order to maintain their position in the movement. The Rev. George Hickox of Jackson was chosen president, and the association undertook to secure general observance of the third Sabbath in October as Prison Sunday, a special occasion for chaplains and Christian wardens to invade the public pulpits and for ministers far and wide to try their hands at prison reform. But while this campaign was winning much success, the chaplains were under fire within the profession, where the old faith in the conversion of convicts was rapidly waning. Brockway dispensed with the services of a chaplain and even moderate-tempered Hastings H. Hart of Minnesota urged that "no convict ought to be allowed to feel for a minute that he can make a gain of godliness."[19] Some chaplains felt constrained to justify their calling before the congresses by lengthy perorations on "The Ideal Chaplain," but many were content to perform their kindly functions in an unobstrusive fashion among the friendless men behind the bars.

A fundamental transformation occurred in the national movement during the early nineties. New vistas were appearing, and the redirection of attention became especially evident at the St. Paul congress in 1894 where a host of professors and doctors almost pushed the practical wardens off the platform. Professor Charles R. Henderson of the new University of Chicago presented his first paper, debating the existence of a criminal type and introducing his audience to the contemporary European speculations on that subject.[20] Professor Carlton T. Lewis of New York analyzed the theoretical and practical implications of the indeterminate sentence, while Charles A. Collin, now a professor of law at Cornell, described the recent achievements of Elmira. Eugene Smith, Esq., presented a paper on criminal-law reform, and Charles H. Reeve again attacked the problem of a national standard for criminal statistics. Dr. J. B. Ransom, physician at Clinton, and Dr. M. V. Ball of Cherry Hill reported the results of experiments in the care of tubercular prisoners which revealed that they were taking advantage of the most recent scientific discoveries concerning that troublesome malady.

A changing social landscape was favorable to the leadership of the professors. The development of departments of sociology in the colleges brought into action a new group of specialists, among whom Henderson of Chicago was the most active. The flood of laws regulating convict labor took the problem of determining the proper industrial policy for prisons out of the hands of the wardens and made occasion for comprehensive studies of the situation by such national authorities as Carroll D. Wright. A growing attention to the care of the discharged rendered especially timely the information Barrows in 1895 gathered from Europe's longer experience in this field. The

[19] *The Reformation of Criminals* (Oberlin, 1890), p. 23.

[20] Only Dr. Wey of Elmira had made a previous reference to the theories of Lombroso before the national congresses.

appointment of Samuel June Barrows as the United States Commissioner on the International Prison Commission in 1895 marked a revival of federal interest, dormant since the days of Enoch Wines, and paved the way for the visit of the International Association to America fourteen years later. All these activities were a bit beyond the range of busy wardens.

Meanwhile the accumulating mass of statistics was adding fuel to many old controversies. The mounting criminal ratios called forth again from "Easy Street" hoarse cries against the "collegiate and hotel prisons."[21] The dispute over the percentages of the reformed and the broader rivalry between institutions which attempted to make much of education and those which still clung to the cleansing influence of hard labor gained in feeling as labor laws threatened the latter. The debate over indeterminate sentence and parole laws took on a new aspect as statistics convinced the reformers that they had either to secure mandatory laws or to awaken the proper officials to a fuller appreciation of those already on the statute books. In justifying their programs to the general public the leaders continued to rely upon appeals to humanitarian sentiments and to the state's interest in deflecting as many individuals as possible from criminal activities —justifications which were possibly as reasonable as could be made in a society which had not undertaken the responsibility of securing to every citizen the opportunity to realize the fullest development of his capacities.

The Association was becoming conscious of a larger audience. The lecturers were preparing their addresses for the judges, legislators, and editors of popular journals—authorities who wielded the real power in prison affairs. The warden's annual seminar was developing into a migrating chautauqua and responded to more than one appeal to come over into Macedonia. Such were the visits to Denver and Austin, but the new spirit was most dramatically expressed when an extra session was convened in New Orleans in response to an earnest call from Michael Heymann for aid in his fight for reform in Louisiana. These wide-ranging travels extended the influence of the northern movement into the relatively foreign Southland and the virgin West. In the process new and promising methods of farm and

---

[21] The Forum, October, 1891; Howard Association of London, The Collegiate and Hotel Prisons of America (London, 1891).

road labor were uncovered and introduced into the North. At the turn of the century the isolation of the sections was only in part broken down, and the South continued to maintain a characteristic system of its own. The Association did not gain a truly national character until the first decade of the new century when it helped to round out the growth of the pedagogical penology it had nurtured so long.

BIBLIOGRAPHICAL NOTE

The revived National Prison Association, *Proceedings* (1884——) are of primary importance, as are the New York Reformatory, Elmira, *Reports* (1876——) and the official reports of the other early reformatories. The Special Commission of the State of Connecticut on Convict Labor, *Report* (1880) provides a convenient summary of the reports of similar commissions in other states. United States Commissioner of Labor, "Convict Labor," *Report* (1886); *ibid.* (1905). United States Department of Labor, *Convict Labor* (1896). House of Representatives Industrial Commission, *Prison Labor* (1900). Massachusetts Superintendent of Prisons, *Report on the Various Methods of Employing Prisoners* (1898). Carroll D. Wright, *Hand Labor in Prisons* (Boston, 1887). National Anti-convict Contract Association, *Proceedings of the Chicago Convention* (1886). The Brockway Collection in the Russell Sage Library in New York City is of considerable interest.

In addition to Z. Brockway, *Fifty Years of Prison Service* (New York, 1912), Frederick C. Allen, *Hand Book of New York State Reformatory* (Elmira, 1927) and Alexander Winter, *The New York State Reformatory in Elmira* (London, 1891) shed light on this subject. Hastings H. Hart, *Reformation of Criminals* (Oberlin, 1890), presents an excellent summary of prison reform. E. R. Beckner, *A History of Labor Legislation in Illinois* (Chicago, 1929); Mollie R. Carroll, *Labor and Politics* (Boston, 1923); T. V. Powderley, *Thirty Years of Labor* (Columbus, 1890); and E. T. Hiller, "Labor Unionism and Convict Labor," *Journal of Criminal Law and Criminology*, V, 851–79—all supply important materials on this crucial problem.

CHAPTER VI

THE PROGRESS OF REFORM IN THE NORTHEASTERN STATES

Although the revival and increasing strength of the national movement were important aspects of prison history, it was up to the states to determine the success or failure of the reform programs. The outstanding problem facing prison officials in the last decades of the century was the labor dilemma; but the two controlling factors of the previous era, population growth and the struggle to develop non-partisan agencies for central control, continued to influence developments. Meanwhile the remarkable growth of the country with its improved living conditions was raising the standard of decency considered proper for prisons. Propelled by these forces, many northern states made reasonable progress toward introducing reformatory technique into the strongholds of the earlier penology of Louis Dwight, but the total effect on the mass of the prisoners remained obscure.

THE STRUGGLE FOR CENTRALIZATION

The efforts of the states to develop more satisfactory administrative agencies in the correctional field persisted in the directions suggested during the seventies. Experience continued to demonstrate the folly of trusting prisons to the control of transient politicians. The attempt to secure candid reports led to an extension of the spheres of the existing non-political boards of charities and to the creation of such boards in additional states. The move to give genuine powers of control to these boards or to other central agencies made considerable headway in at least a half-dozen northern states.

Massachusetts and New York had played the pioneer rôles in this field during the seventies and now continued to reveal abilities for leadership. As before, it was the former that made the greater progress toward stable centralization. Although its prison commission, organized in 1879, was second only to the Rhode Island board of charities in the extent of its control, the Bay Commonwealth found, with changing conditions, that many of its features were unsatisfac-

tory and that other functions had to be added. Thus, when the indeterminate sentence was adopted for Concord reformatory in 1886,
the commissioners were given the responsibility of releasing on permits such prisoners as were reformed. The habitual criminal act
of the following year conferred on them the discretion of releasing
men sentenced under its provisions after they had served at least
five out of their twenty-five years; again in 1895 the general parole
and indeterminate-sentence act unwisely placed this same function
on their overburdened shoulders. It was no wonder that the proposal was frequently made that these volunteer servants be made
full-time, salaried officers.

The struggle for central control was unexpectedly aided when labor laws upset the prison industrial system. A superintendent of
prison industries was provided in 1887, following the New York
precedent, to organize state-account trades in all the penal institutions in the state. The decision in the following year to permit piece-
price contracts lopped off the major functions of the new officer, but
a decade later a new act abolished all forms of contract labor and
re-established his responsibility for the organization—this time—of
state-use industries. The appointment of the able secretary of the
prison commission, Frederick G. Pettigrove, as superintendent in
1898 brought harmony between the two authorities, but it was not
until 1901 that a new reorganization combined these authorities into
one commission with full authority to appoint and remove officers of
state institutions, to order transfers or new construction in both
state and local institutions, and to manage industries. With Pettigrove as chairman and each of the members receiving a full-time salary, this board became the most efficient correctional authority in
the country.

The throttling hold of politics was much tighter in New York, but
rivalry between the parties in the end carried centralization to a
point not far behind that of Massachuetts. The successive superintendents of state prison industry made notable financial records, but
political considerations limited most of them to a single five-year
term. The New York Prison Association, experiencing a revival of
activity in the nineties similar to that of Enoch Wine's day, continued its services as semiofficial inspector of the prisons of the state
until 1896. A political upheaval in the previous year and the result-

ing investigation of prison management had disclosed considerable corruption.[1] The legislature was finally persuaded to adopt the old proposal of Enoch Wines, and a prison commission with eight non-salaried members was created and given authority to inspect all state and local prisons, to recommend changes, and to enforce its recommendations in local institutions by court orders. Unfortunately the superintendent of industries was left independent of this body which in practice did not prove to be as effective as the Massachusetts commission in controlling either the state or local institutions.

The drive toward central control was making greater progress in the states of the Upper Mississippi Valley. The simpler problems of young states enabled them to gather all their charitable and correctional institutions under one authority. With the example of the Kansas board of charitable institutions in mind, the authorities of Wisconsin in 1880 abolished all its separate boards of directors and created one board of supervision, going beyond Kansas by including the prison under the board's control. The older board of charities continued its annual inspections, until in 1891 the friction between the two authorities was eliminated by joining them into one board of control with full powers over state institutions and duties of inspection in the case of county jails. Wisconsin thus completed an organization that should have secured her leadership in penal developments.

But other factors intervened, and Minnesota stepped foward as the real leader in this section. The state was fully equipped with institutions by 1883 when it first considered the necessity for centralization, and the problem did not appear to call for more than a board of charities. Fortunately the board secured the services of the young Rev. Hastings Hornell Hart, and his persistent labors not only laid the basis for a distinguished public career but directed the development of correctional and charitable institutions along sound and progressive lines. The reorganization of these activities under a board of control in 1901 merely institutionalized an influence that

[1] Subcommittee on Investigation of State Prisons, *Report* (New York Assembly Document No. 76, 1895), pp. 1–27. The Democratic boss of the city of Auburn had supplied the prison with meat during the terms of the last two wardens at excessive prices, and the evidence indicated that he had secured the appointment for one of these men.

had long been dominant. Iowa, after considering the rival procedures of its neighbors for at least a decade, chose the more authoritative instrument of government when it created a board of control in 1896; but here, as in the other states of the plains where similar authorities were established after the turn of the century, the organizational advantage did not offset Minnesota's gain from Hart's leadership.

Of the remaining states of the North not previously equipped with some such form of central supervision, only Indiana took effective action in the right direction. The old boards of charities continued to make annual inspections and offer helpful suggestions on all correctional matters in Connecticut, Pennsylvania, Michigan, and Ohio. The governors in Maryland and the northern New England states undertook to perform this function. But in New Jersey, Illinois, and Kansas existing state boards were not responsible for the state prisons, and, except for emergency investigations, the public was dependent on the reports and the policies of the political authorities. Missouri alone took no steps toward freeing its correctional activities from political dominance. Indiana was roused to action only by a scandal in its southern prison under Warden Howard in the late eighties; nevertheless, its board of charities, created in 1889 under the leadership of Timothy Nicholson, assumed an aggressive policy and supplied enlightened leadership in correctional affairs for several decades.

These boards provided a permanent body of recruits for the national movement. Even in states where they were not effectively in control, they helped to propagate the theories and programs discussed at the congresses. One interesting device developed by several of these boards was the annual state conference of charities and correction, into which the many officers of state and local institutions were gathered for mutual discussion of their problems in the light of the more advanced theories of the day. Michigan, where the first of these conferences was staged in 1881, and neighboring North Central states into which the scheme quickly spread, profited greatly from these educational gatherings. The boards, relatively free from partisan control, struggled to remove the blight of politics from prison administration, and while their success in this direction was very limited they deserve much credit for the improvements made in the prison system.

REFORMS APPROVED BY THE LEGISLATURES

The last quarter of the nineteenth century witnessed a steady drift of opinion toward the conclusion that "a prison without reformatory influence is but a nursery of crime."[2] Much that was said on this subject in innumerable reports was little better than official cant, but the advantages offered by the new methods and the disruptive effects of the labor laws were compelling many officers to take the new theories seriously. When critics complained that it was distorted philanthropy if not sheer injustice to "take money from honest labor to make dishonest idlers comfortable, teach them trades, furnish them books, papers, and teachers," Charles H. Reeve responded that it was not philanthropy but sound public policy to redeem rather than to damn offenders.[3] While many of the theoretical reformers attempted to clothe their proposals in the terms of practical policies, some of the wardens did not hesitate to speak out boldly for the claims of sentiment and Christian brotherhood, thus dodging the demand that these public welfare measures be sacrificed to the dominant philosophy of individualism. The reform doctrine was aptly phrased in 1890 by the new board of charities of hitherto backward Indiana when it declared: "It is the criminal and not the crime that justice must consider. . . . . Not what the man has done, but what he will do, should determine the length of his imprisonment."

The indeterminate sentence had long since become a familiar principle, and its successful application at Elmira had dispelled many doubts as to its practicability, but it was a political upheaval in Ohio that first brought the principle into the realm of major prisons. When the Democrats captured the state in 1883, they not only redeemed their pledge to the labor forces by abolishing prison contracts but undertook in one fell swoop to apply the whole reformatory technique to the penitentiary. They created a new board of directors and appointed new and inexperienced officers to introduce a grading and marking system and administer paroles at the prison. The board of charities was overwhelmed by this sudden adoption of its principles, and its fears that the reform program would be discredited seemed to be well grounded as the $50,000 annual income of

[2] Indiana Prison North, *Report* (1886), p. 15.

[3] *The Prison Question* (Chicago, 1890), p. 148.

the prison was turned into a deficit of $150,000. Fortunately the Republicans, who recaptured control at the next election, were persuaded by General Brinkerhoff to improve rather than to abolish the new system. A fresh set of officials was placed in control, and piece-price contracts were negotiated, but the only changes in the parole law were directed at its obvious defects. Under the new law only those serving sentences for their first felony, in case it was not first-degree murder, were eligible for parole after the minimum sentence for the crime had been completed; questions of guilt and arguments by attorneys were barred from consideration by the board of directors charged with issuing paroles; and the applicant was required to have reached the top grade in the prison and to show the promise of a job awaiting his discharge. Many were surprised at the approval which greeted these measures. Criticism was more freely showered upon a companion law that provided life sentences for habitual criminals, those sentenced for their third felony, and popular sentiment supported the courts in their failure except in rare cases to prosecute such offenders, even after the introduction of the Bertillon system at the penitentiary made identification possible.

Meanwhile difficulties were being encountered in the attempt to convert an old disjointed prison, overcrowded with 1,600 felons, into a reformatory. The officers and guards were poorly selected for the task of applying the marking system, and attainment of the first grade was not always made a prerequisite for parole. The requirement that a job be available was working to the advantage of a favored few with influential friends on the outside. At the same time the irregular application of the habitual-criminal act was creating an atmosphere of resentment inimical to the reformatory aspirations of the prison. These handicaps were accentuated by the repeated changes in management at Columbus, resulting in turn from the continued seesaw of politics in Ohio.

The admitted limitations to Ohio's success did not restrain other states from following her lead. The distinction between indeterminate-sentence laws and parole laws was not yet clearly appreciated, and their constitutionality was still in doubt. The two sentiments—to "sock" the repeater and to succor the first offender—were inconveniently confused, and when, as in Ohio, they were drafted into law at the same time and the enforcement of both attempted in one prison, the difficulties were indeed multiplied. Few wardens suspected the obstacles that would have to be overcome before they could report that the Elmira technique was functioning smoothly in their old prisons. Not only the traditional-minded judges and lawyers but a large section of the public and most of the criminals were still blind to the justice of the new correctional philosophy that concerned itself with the criminal rather than with the crime. European visitors were amazed at the hardihood with which the Americans ventured to experiment in spite of these unsettled issues.

The first batch of laws applying the principle of the reformatory sentence to the mass of criminals came to grief in one way or another. The attorney-general of New Jersey advised against the use of the state's 1889 parole law on the grounds that the legislature could not tamper with the authority of the courts to fix sentences. Michigan's indeterminate-sentence law of the same year was held invalid by the court as an infringement of the governor's power to pardon. Optional indeterminate-sentence laws in New York and Wisconsin were but seldom applied, as the judges hesitated to surrender to the prison officers the power of determining the length of sentences which they themselves had so long been accustomed to mete out with judicial poise. Legislative affirmation in Kansas and Vermont of the governor's power to grant conditional pardons had some effect on the pardoning procedure of the latter state where the small population made possible such direct executive supervision.

Meanwhile Massachusetts, already busy with plans for the reformatory treatment of its less vicious men and women, took up the attack on the repeaters. A habitual-criminal act was adopted in 1887, providing twenty-five-year sentences for men convicted of a third felony but permitting parole after five years provided their reformation was evident to the commission. The ancestry of these laws goes back at least to Edward Livingston; Virginia, Louisiana, and New York had adopted such laws before the Civil War, although only that of Louisiana had been given effect. Europe's more extensive use of the principle was now attracting the attention of American travelers. Encouraged by the promise of accurate identifications through the use of the Bertillon technique, Wisconsin and California quickly adopted the measure. But events soon demonstrated the un-

willingness of attorneys and judges to apply these laws. Massachusetts, by far the most conscientious in its enforcement, had convicted
only twenty-five under this law by 1895, the majority of them as a
result of a special drive against criminals in 1894.

In spite of these early discouragements the advocates of the reformatory sentence returned to the attack with renewed determination
in the mid-nineties. A succession of court decisions upheld several
of the older laws and removed barriers to new ones. Under the inspiration of Hastings H. Hart, Governor William R. Merriam and
Warden Henry Wolfer successfully applied the reformatory technique at the Stillwater prison in Minnesota in 1892, granting conditional pardons, with restraint, to the worthy men in the top grade.
A parole law passed by the legislature in the following year was so
efficiently administered as to attract the interested attention of the
delegates at the St. Paul congress of the National Prison Association
in 1894.

Massachusetts and Illinois made additional improvements in the
application of these principles to the mass of their criminals in the
mid-nineties. A law of the former state in 1894, authorizing the commissioners to parole any reformed first offender after two-thirds of
his fixed sentence had expired, was followed the next year by a mandatory indeterminate-sentence law requiring the courts to give maximum and minimum sentences to all except the habitual criminals
already provided for. A survey in 1896 discovered that the average
leeway between the maximum and the minimum sentences was three
years and six months, thus revealing that many judges were ready to
give the principle a fair trial. Governor John P. Altgeld secured the
adoption of a parole law in Illinois and directed the introduction of
a grading system at Joliet. A conservative parole policy saved the
reform from discredit, and the returning Republicans were prompted
by Major McClaughry, rich with reformatory experience, to extend
the principle. An indeterminate-sentence law was passed in 1897,
patterned after that of Massachusetts but taking a step forward by
creating a special board of pardons to administer paroles.

Encouraged by these examples several additional states indorsed
the reformatory sentence in the late nineties. Backward Indiana
awoke with a start in 1897, led by its new board, and adopted sweep-
ing reforms. Among other things provision was made for the parole

of first offenders in each of the men's prisons, and two years later this was extended to the women's prison as well. Even before Indiana took these rapid strides forward to the front rank of penal reformers her northern neighbor had discovered that she could quietly dodge her court decision by extending to the prison officers the power to release the reformed men on licenses to be at large. While this was by no means satisfactory, it sufficed until replaced by a comprehensive parole law in 1903. Connecticut, another leader of the earlier days, failed to respond to the petitions of its prison association until 1897, and the parole law adopted at that time was poorly drafted and seldom applied. Vermont went further, adopting both indeterminate-sentence and parole laws in 1898 and applying them to all at the state prison and at the house of correction. Although the state court shortly declared the parole law unconstitutional, the governor stepped forward and granted conditional pardons to all deserving them under the unchallenged indeterminate sentences.

The influence of this profuse legislative activity was not as far-reaching as might have been expected. Aside from those fortunate enough to be committed to one of the better reformatories, the great majority of prisoners gained little of value from the laws. The courts neglected to give the indeterminate sentences in New York and Wisconsin; the boards rarely used their parole authority in New Jersey, Michigan, and Connecticut; none of the new principles applied to any of the convicts of Pennsylvania outside of Huntingdon reformatory. Finally in Massachusetts, where the reformers had achieved their most complete successes, new legislation in 1898 directed that release be granted automatically at the expiration of the minimum term if the prisoner's record showed no black marks, thus changing the admirable law of 1895 from a reformatory to a disciplinary measure. It was no wonder that the courts steadily increased their minimum sentences, greatly reducing the margin that was to serve as an incentive to reform. In a similar fashion the courts of Illinois fixed the maximum and minimum sentences so close together that a new law was necessary in 1899 taking this power completely out of their hands. Ohio, Indiana, and Minnesota were developing stable parole policies, but at least in the first two of these the great majority of the prisoners were not kept awake nights by prospects of parole, largely because the requirement that applicants for release show the promise of a job was not always easily met.

If the entire penal system had not been revolutionized, it was not due to the inactivity of the legislatures. The reformatory sentence had at least won its way into the statutory law. Twenty-five states had some form of à parole law in operation in 1898, and these scattered all the way from Massachusetts and Vermont in the Northeast to California in the West and Alabama in the South. If the administration was almost everywhere unsatisfactory, a few enlightened experiments were being made, and the courts and the public as well as the prisons were having an opportunity to adjust to the new theory.

Massachusetts, prize laboratory of nineteenth-century reformers, was pioneering in still another direction, making discoveries that were destined not only to contribute much to the technique of reformatory penology but also to revolutionize the entire prison problem. The custom of releasing individuals on probation, when circumstances suggested that they might be saved from a life of crime without a term in prison, had a wide, extra-legal practice throughout the world, especially in juvenile and minor cases. It was in Boston that this early practice was most extensively applied under the kindly efforts of the venerable shoemaker, John Augusutus, in the forties and "Uncle" Rufus W. Cook in the seventies. Massachusetts was likewise the first to organize and grant legislative recognition to this practice when in 1869 it directed the state board of charities to investigate the cases of children under seventeen years, to have an agent present at their trials, and, further, if circumstances warranted, to care for them in homes. Another law in 1878 authorized the mayor of Boston to appoint an officer to probate both juveniles and adults; two years later this authority was extended to all other mayors in the state. Boston, at least, gave it a fair trial when Captain E. H. Savage, a former chief of police, was placed in charge; in the course of fourteen months bonds were provided for 536 persons, only 43 of whom failed their trust and had to be committed to prison. As experience brought confidence in this treatment, its application was expanded. In 1890 the cases totaled 2,050 in greater Boston and 196 in the rest of the state; already 1,000 of these cases involved persons over twenty-five years of age.

England in her Probation and First Offenders Act of 1887 began to explore the possibilities of this treatment; Australia, New Zealand, and finally, in 1891, France adopted somewhat the same idea.

Massachusetts, however, maintained her leadership by developing a well-organized administration for the new treatment. A few months before the French legislation went into effect the Bay State reorganized its system, taking the function from the local executives and making it mandatory for county courts to appoint probation officers. These agents were directed to investigate not only the juvenile cases but all those involving drunkenness as well. They found themselves nearly swamped in this inexhaustible social problem but were able to demonstrate so many advantages of outside treatment that the state extended the system to major offenders and directed the superior courts to provide themselves with probation officers. In 1890 the prison commission, securing the power of central supervision over this activity, assembled the scattered officers into the first annual conference and worked out schemes for co-operation in locating straying probationers. The superiority of this method of supervising outside treatment to the plan of requiring the men to report by letter recommended itself to parole administrators and prepared the way for the appointment of parole officers in several states in the next century.

Reformers in other states were watching the Massachusetts experiment. As early as 1880 R. L. Dugdale had recommended that New York adopt the scheme, but no action was taken until 1893 when the legislature affirmed the common-law power of the judges to suspend sentences. An increasing use of this power was made in an informal fashion in co-operation with the charity organizations of several large cities, and by 1898 agents of the Philadelphia and Baltimore prison societies, an officer of the Woman's Club of Chicago, and volunteers in each county under the direction of the board of charities in Minnesota, were all functioning as active if unofficial probation officers. This new feature of the correctional system was destined for extensive use in later years.

NEW REFORMATORIES AND SPECIAL INSTITUTIONS

Some of the states were indorsing the reformatory theories by more substantial action. The unceasing growth of the criminal class, outstripping population growth in many states, was forcing the construction of new prisons, and the remarkable success of Elmira and the example of Sherborn, Concord, and Huntingdon encouraged

imitation. Already in the nineties it was no longer a matter of experimenting with new devices, for Elmira was the unchallenged
model. The establishment and satisfactory organization of a half-
dozen such institutions were the largest practical achievements of
the states in penal reform during this decade. But the peculiar problems presented by certain classes of misdemeanants were likewise
demanding state attention, and several special institutions were provided for their care, partly but not entirely on the reformatory model. Meanwhile the wider application of the elaborate reformatory
technique was having the unexpected result of emphasizing the in-
ability of demented and insane criminals to adjust themselves to the
normal institutional activity, and several states undertook to establish special institutions for their proper care, thus advancing a step
further the classification of institutions that had originally helped to
differentiate the reformatory from the penitentiary.

The reformatories established during the seventies and eighties
continued their development in the nineties. A fairly stable character had already been attained at Elmira, Ionia, Sherborn, and
Concord, and their problems were now essentially those of continued
administration, although Elmira was faced with the additional problem of accommodating a steadily growing population. Pennsylvania,
on the other hand, was busily engaged in organizing its recently
opened reformatory at Huntingdon, a task beset by difficulties since
the adoption of the indeterminate sentence had aroused opposition
in the eastern part of the state. Fortunately Major McClaughry remained in charge long enough to commit the institution thoroughly
to the reformatory doctrine, and T. B. Patton, a former inspector,
beginning a long term of service in 1891, continued his predecessor's
program, minus his inspiration. Restricted by the drastic labor laws
of Pennsylvania, the idyllic prison on the banks of the blue Juniata
turned to farming and non-productive trade schools and became the
penal show place of the Quaker State in the industrial era.

Minnesota was one of those states where prisons and almost everything else were built ahead of traffic. The aspiring community at
St. Cloud was determined that it should have a state institution, but
all it could secure was the promise of the second prison when one
should be built. With the small population exhausting neither the
accommodations nor the possibilities at Stillwater prison this was a

chimerical prospect even in a boom state. The reformers saw an opportunity to enlist the local interest in their programs and in 1887 persuaded the legislature, with the help of an appeal to state pride, to vote $100,000 to erect a reformatory at St. Cloud. Albert Garvin, trained under McClaughry at Joliet, opened the institution with its 128 up-to-date cells in 1890. The 139 young men who first moved in had already received indeterminate sentences; and they were soon organized into grades under a system of marks based on educational, labor, and disciplinary activities. Within a short period other features of the Elmira system were added, such as a military organization in 1892, a course of lectures in ethics two years later, and a trade-school department built around the institutional activities. A 446-acre farm was purchased and became an important adjunct. The one great drawback to the development of this institution was the reluctance with which the people of the state turned to crime.

Few indeed were the states that faced this handicap! Overcrowding had long been most serious in Illinois. When McClaughry returned from Huntingdon in 1891, full of enthusiasm for reformatories, he found Governor Joseph W. Fifer and others eager to join in his agitation. Together they persuaded the state to convert Pontiac "boys' prison," as the court had termed it, into a young men's reformatory. The transition was started under the direction of General F. B. Sheets, but when Governor John P. Altgeld came to power McClaughry was persuaded to take charge. Again the veteran warden introduced the reformatory system with all its trappings— literary and trade schools, military organization, inmate paper, band, farm, and, of course, grades and marks with which to determine the date of release. The speedy construction of the first large cell block to accommodate five hundred was beggared by the rapid growth of the population; even the five hundred additional cells completed by 1897 were inadequate for the 1,200 youths confined there at the end of that year. Pontiac reformatory was unique in that it was forced to receive boys as young as ten years of age. While these boys were always in the minority, the problem of keeping them separate from the young men was a serious handicap to the development of the proper treatment for each class, and the difficulty was not solved until the next century. Nevertheless, Pontiac was securely established—the only major institution in the Great Valley to be fully geared to reformatory penology during this era.

Ohio had every reason to be among the first states to build a reformatory. Second only to New York in seriously considering the proposal back in the sixties, its able board of charities and successive wardens and directors had persistently emphasized this measure as the proper solution for congestion at the overgrown penitentiary in Columbus. The legislature did provide in 1884 for a commission to plan and locate a young men's reformatory at Mansfield, but in the close contest for political supremacy neither party dared add to the tax burden by appropriating for the construction of a "dude factory." Finally in 1896, when the 1,600 antiquated cells at Columbus were crowded with 2,100 men, temporary buildings were opened at Mansfield, and some two hundred young men were transferred there. The permanent buildings were not sufficiently completed to permit a thorough organization of the institution on a reformatory basis until J. A. Leonard took charge in 1901.

The establishment of a young men's reformatory did not receive responsible consideration in Indiana until the newly triumphant Republicans decided to give the penal system a thorough overhauling in 1897. The two prisons were seriously overcrowded, but economy ruled that the aged prison at Jeffersonville should be transformed into a reformatory; transfers were made, and soon its 536 wretched cells were crowded with over nine hundred men under thirty years of age; the building program to provide proper housing did not make progress until the next century. Fortunately the appointment of a prominent politician as superintendent was counteracted by the selection of Albert Garvin of Minnesota as deputy, and genuine reformatory measures were rapidly introduced, encouraged by the expiration of industrial contracts and the restrictions against new ones.

Several additional reformatories were provided for in the last years of the century although their satisfactory organization was delayed a few years. Kansas had taken the first step in 1885, accepting the donation of a 640-acre farm near Hutchinson for the site of its reformatory; but the opening of profitable mines at the state prison had discouraged a division of the labor supply, and it was not until the prison became excessively overcrowded in 1895 that thirty young men were transferred to Hutchinson to start the development of the reformatory. Neither here nor at Green Bay reformatory, established by Wisconsin in 1897, was a reformatory discipline developed until the opening years of the next century. While these states were using their young men to build reformatories, New Jersey turned the job over to contractors in 1895, but the urgent need for relief at Trenton prison did not prevent delays, and Rahway reformatory was not opened until 1901. Meanwhile the reputation of Elmira was spreading into the South and West. Kentucky, Texas, and California each made legislative gestures in the reformatory direction, but obstacles intervened, and Buena Vista reformatory in Colorado, opened in temporary buildings in 1891, was the only genuine adult reformatory established outside the northeastern state in the nineteenth century.

All these reformatories received major offenders and some of them, following Ionia and Concord, opened their doors to special classes of misdemeanants as well. In the meantime additional cities were developing houses of correction to relieve their overcrowded jails, and most of these institutions were able to supply their short-term inmates with some form of occupation. Three New England states went further and established state workhouses that provided many genuinely reformatory features to these classes. New York established some excellent institutions for women misdemeanants that pioneered in new fields of correctional activity, but their full significance was not realized until major offenders were admitted at the turn of the century. The same state provided some special institutions for another class of criminals, the insane, a development which represented a significant modification of the trend to make all prisons into reformatories of the same type. Other states, following this lead, helped to prepare the way for the emphasis on classification that was to become the dominant characteristic of penology in the early twentieth century.

Massachusetts, Vermont, and Rhode Island had each created its house of correction during the seventies, but little use was made of them until this period. The Bay State first took its workhouse seriously in the late eighties when it was casting about for a solution of the problem presented by the increasing number of drunkards before the courts. A law of 1889 renamed the workhouse at Bridgewater the state farm and directed that a hospital for inebriates be erected there. Delays ensued, and the hospital was not opened until 1894 and not provided with a special indeterminate-sentence law until 1898 when the elaboration of a special treatment was making headway. Vermont's efforts to develop correctional activities at its house of correction were repeatedly obstructed by the many tramps that crowded the institution in the winter months, but the use of this labor to erect a new cell house in 1895 and the visit of the officers in that year to Elmira provided new inspiration. Military drill, calisthenics, educational features, and a liberal discipline were introduced, and the institution was opened to young felons with indeterminate sentences at the discretion of the courts, thus giving it a more genuine reformatory character.

The most significant development in connection with the minor offenders of New York State was made in behalf of a small number of its females. Reformatory penology had almost overlooked the women during the last decades of the nineteenth century, possibly because their number in most states seemed too insignificant to demand special care and they fitted readily into the household economy of both jails and prisons. This was, however, not the case in New York, and the agitation of Mrs. Josephine Shaw Lowell finally roused the state to establish the Hudson house of refuge for women convicted of certain misdemeanors, chiefly those involving sex morality. Hudson and a similar institution opened at Albion in 1893 adopted the Elmira discipline. The inmates here were the first women to receive the complete reformatory treatment—indeterminate sentences, grades and marks, literary and trade instruction, and wholesome farm labor—and the provision of separate cottages for the accommodation of those of the top grade added a significant feature to the environment of adult reformatories. Although antedated by the institutions at Detroit, Indianapolis, and Sherborn, if they are to be regarded as women's reformatories, the New York institutions, when opened in 1900 to women committed on indeterminate sentences for major offenses, rapidly took rank as pioneers in reformatory discipline. They not only heralded a new day for female prisoners but led the next generation in its attempts to improve on the Elmira technique.

The recognition of a public responsibility for the care of the defective and the insane was one of the humanitarian achievements of the mid-nineteenth century, but it was several decades before many states came to recognize a special responsibility for those both afflicted with insanity and convicted of crime. New York, driven to action by her expanding prison populations in the late fifties, had erected an asylum for insane convicts outside the walls of Auburn prison. This institution, equipped with the latest methods for ward treatment, had been placed under the independent control of an able physician in 1876, but it was soon overcrowded, and in 1892 under the guidance of William P. Letchworth a new penal insane asylum with adequate provision for security was built at Mattewan. Mattewan, in turn, became so popular with wardens desiring to rid themselves of unbalanced inmates and with judges wishing to avoid passing sentence on demented prisoners at the bar that the state was persuaded to erect a second institution at Dannemora in order to provide adequate and separate accommodation for these two distinct groups. When the latter institution was opened in 1899 to receive transfers from the prisons, New York was able to achieve an advanced standard of classification in penal treatment.

Only a few states followed this lead at the time. Frederick Wines persuaded Illinois that the twenty-four solitary-punishment cells at Joliet were unsatisfactory accommodations for the insane, but the 150-man hospital started in the early eighties near the prison at Chester was not ready for occupation by the criminal insane until the mid-nineties. Michigan provided a similar though less satisfactory institution near the Ionia house of correction in 1885. Massachusetts gave up its practice of transferring insane prisoners to the regular asylums in 1895 when it converted the asylum on the state farm at Bridgewater into an institution for the criminal insane; by the end of the century over three hundred were securely housed there. Makeshift ward arrangements were provided at the prisons of Ohio, Indiana, Iowa, and Kansas, but only the separate ward for the insane at Wethersfield in Connecticut provided the competent medical attendance necessary to free these departments from the prison atmosphere. In spite of the provisions for transfer to the asylums, most of the insane prisoners of the remaining states continued to blunder through the prison routine, to the injury of themselves and the disruption of institutional discipline.

Several factors were involved in the campaign for special asylums for insane criminals. As prison discipline became more complex with the introduction of grades and marks, the demented found themselves less able to make adjustments. On the other hand, desperate criminals were frequently attempting the ruse of insanity in order to take advantage of the laws providing for transfer to the insecure asylums from which they might effect their escape. Hard-fisted wardens, naturally reluctant to see their worst prisoners put something over, frequently attempted by means of the strap or other device to take the idea out of the wrong man's head. Meanwhile serious overcrowding at both the prisons and the asylums was the most influential factor in forcing the construction of the new institutions. But there was, in addition, a very significant theoretical aspect to the problem. The debate as to how far insanity exonerated a criminal had long been of interest to the medical and legal professions, but the public did not begin to show concern until new theories were imported from Europe suggesting the inherent insanity of a large portion of the criminals. Richard Dugdale's study of the Jukes in the seventies stood practically alone in America as a consideration of criminal heredity, without, however, establishing any clear conclusions along this line. The dominant belief that all men were reformable presented a stubborn opposition to the Lombrosian theories and admitted only the moderate concession that the violent insane should be given special attention.

The close of the century found reformatory penology triumphant. Not only had its chief tenets been accepted by the responsible leaders of the many official and semiofficial bodies concerned with prisons but they had been widely recognized in the statute law of the North. If this had not yet greatly transformed the outlook of the common run of prisoners, substantial gains had been made in the struggle to bring correctional treatment closer to the lives of the convicts. Ten or more special institutions had been erected in the last quarter of the century and dedicated to the methods and purposes of the pedagogical penology worked out by Brockway at Elmira. This system had been actively applied for at least a decade in several places, and the faith of its advocates was still strong—so strong, indeed, that its introduction elsewhere was being rapidly advanced.

But the first stage of the application of reformatory penology was drawing to a close. Zebulon Brockway, the one vital genius of this development, retired from his post in the closing year of the century. Elmira, product of his labors, had grown unwieldy owing to forced expansion to more than twice its intended size and was now inadequate for its charges, so rapid had been their increase. Brockway's technique, ingeniously elaborated and integrated according to the best knowledge of the day, was helping to regenerate prison discipline, but at the same time it was failing to transform the lives of all the young men under its charge. Critics, some sentimental and some statistical but all incapable of understanding his problems, gathered to heckle the old man, now gray with fifty years of service. Stangely enough, he was accused of cruelty; the founder of the reformatory was paddling young misfits who could not or, as he thought, would not profit from the more subtle persuasion of the best grading system in the country. A thorough investigation more than vindicated Brockway, but he had become tired of breasting the criminal problems of an ungrateful world and was glad to hand his job over to younger men. The several universities that were assuming the responsibility of recognizing exceptional merit in the community missed an opportunity to prove themselves superior to the common understanding, and no honorary degrees were conferred on the creator of pedagogical penology. Nevertheless, Brockway stands without rival as the greatest warden America has produced.[4]

The first stage of reformatory penology was closing in other respects as well. Younger wardens were taking charge in several of the institutions, and their jobs as well as their abilities were largely administrative in character. At the same time social statesmen with a scientific turn of mind were displacing the experimenting wardens as the spearhead of reform. Suggestions of a special treatment for inebriates, for women, and for the insane and new methods of outside supervision were opening larger horizons for reformatory activity. The extension of the movement into the outlying sections of the country and the application of the new discipline in the old penitentiaries were drawing men outside the reformatory field into action. While the task of pressing these varied activities to their logical fruition was to be left to the next generation, considerable effort was already being devoted to the rejuvenation of state prisons.[5]

[4] An examination of the collection of manuscripts in the Brockway Collection in the Russell Sage Library discloses the fact that he had earned the respect of leading European criminologists, for here are typed manuscripts, some with sketchy translations attached, of works by Tarde, Sailles, Kraepelin, Proal, and several others, many of them evidently examined by Brockway in the early nineties.

[5] See the Bibliographical Note to chap. vii.

CHAPTER VII

THE STATE OF PRISONS IN THE NINETIES

American prisons have developed through a succession of fairly clearly defined eras, much like a great unfolding pageant, and the central theme has been the evolution of penological realism. Each era has had its special set of actors, its peculiar stage properties, and its dominating problems, but in an important sense the underlying plot can be detected only by observing closely the relation of these factors to the changing background. Stocks, whipping posts, and grim gallows cluttered the background during the eighteenth-century prologue; the scenes of the first act, running through several decades of the early nineteenth century, were staged in front of the massive walls of rival prisons; now in the second act the walls have been pushed aside, and we watch the officers and reformers debating before the open face of towering cell blocks in which the figures of convicts can be seen crouching silently behind the bars; in the next era the convicts will file out onto the front stage and take a major part in the drama; finally, in an epilogue an individual convict will remain standing in center stage while keepers, teachers, doctors, psychologists, divines, and judges will make up a speechless background. Neither the sentimental persecution stories of tortured convicts nor the record of boodling activities by officers and contractors but rather the persistent quest by society for penological realism has been the central drama of the penitentiary.

All the earnest argumentation and recital of experience, the dickering for office and its spoils, the agitation against the competition of convict labor, the diversified law-making and formulation of discipline—all the complicated activities which occupied center stage in the last quarter of the nineteenth century took place in the imminent presence of great tiers of overcrowded cells. So tumultuous was the babble of the actors in the foreground that the setting was too frequently obscured. The curious citizen could have examined the extended tables of standard symbols that were annually presented to the legislatures, reporting the numbers of convicts and cells, the receipts from the labor contracts, the pennies in the daily budgets, and the pounds of food distributed; he might have taken account of the wild stories that constantly leaked out *sub rosa* from the wretches behind the bars; but it was to be many years before anybody in America became much interested in reporting the nature of the convicts. The second phase of penological realism was coming to a close in the nineties, but still the curious citizen, as well as the prison authorities, believed loyally, if vaguely, in the equality of men and was confident that most criminals, if given a fair chance, would reform; therefore he inspected the prisons.

The numerous books and pamphlets written by convicts during this era lacked the candor of several of the better ones of the next century. They were chiefly concerned over the injustice of their trials or with the coarseness, corruption, and brutality of their keepers, but by this very preoccupation they reveal much concerning the atmosphere of the great walled cages called penitentiaries. The reforms and improvements that occupied such a large place in official reports were seldom noted by convict annalists. Instead a long procession of wretched beings shuffled past in close step, a large portion of them still in stripes, all of them dreary with long days of sullen waiting, too frequently in stupid idleness. In place of the paternal indulgence so loudly condemned by the public press, these accounts revealed a reign of fear and deceit—soft-footed guards sneaking along the cell range to catch men talking through the pipes and to hurl them into the dungeon for a day or two; treacherous "stools" or trusties goading the new arrivals and carrying tales to the deputies; overtaxed doctors gruffly dosing the daily sick list, fakers and diseased alike, or giving the dread hospital assignment from which few were reputed to return alive; the ever present "shyster" ready to fleece the guileless with hopes of pardon or parole; above all, fear of the "cracked ward" to which so many unlucky comrades had graduated after a siege in the dungeon with straight jacket or repeated cuffings. In place of the achievements in reformation these stories were loaded with incidents of "bootleg" activities involving opium, liquor, and tobacco; here were also morbid accounts of the "kid business," implicating both officers and prisoners, and occasional birth

notices in the many prisons where the female convicts were imperfectly segregated.[1]

More or less aware of the vicious evils which these accounts displayed, the reformers could discover no simple method of routing
them. They continued, however, to beat around the bush in the best
fashion of the day. They strove to eliminate political influences and
to secure impartial supervision in order to assure the public that the
prisoners were enjoying the primary decencies for which it was paying. They even undertook to apply to all convicts the positive disciplinary measures of the reformatories. Finally in a few places enlightened attempts were made to deal with specific problem groups,
thus foreshadowing some of the major concerns of the next century.

POLITICS IN PRISON MANAGEMENT

It was one thing to create impartial boards of non-salaried inspectors and quite another thing to keep politics out of prison. Not only
did the one or two well-paying jobs attract spoilsmen, but the large
and expanding institutions had many lucrative contracts to dis-
tribute, and patronage is apparently indispensable to party solidar-
ity. The continued dominance of one party, as in Minnesota and
northern New England, and the presence of successful wardens there
and in a few other prisons, especially those with excellent financial
records, safeguarded their institutions from the disturbing effects of
political upheavals. Pennsylvania, however, was the only state with
a well-established tradition of prisons free from politics, but Massachusetts and Connecticut succeeded in organizing their prison man-

---

[1] Alexander Berkman, *Prison Memoirs of an Anarchist* (New York, 1912), especially
pp. 240–62, 304–7. Berkman, aided by other convicts, gathered evidence to present to
the board of charities at Riverside penitentiary in the nineties but was prevented from
doing so when his plan was reported by a "stool" and he was placed in the dungeon. His
evidence included (a) dope, dice, cards, cigarettes, and knives—proving smuggling;
(b) prison-made beer—proving theft of potatoes and yeast supposedly used for the
prisoners' food; (c) names and numbers of men engaged in the "kid business"; (d) graft,
specific instances of which included the disappearance over a term of ten years of all the
fees collected from visitors for the library fund; (e) favoritism, "stool" and trusty
espionage—all contrary to law; (f) "basket," dungeon, cuffing, chaining up by the
wrists, punishment of the insane. Whether this indictment of Warden E. S. Wright,
generally considered a reformer, and the Riverside penitentiary, frequently listed
among the best in the country, was accurate or not, it was probably not a very extreme
picture of the seamy side of prisons in general.

agement on this principle by the end of the era. Elsewhere the state prisons suffered considerably from the rack of politics.

After the retirement of her great reform warden under a cloud of scandal in the seventies, Charlestown prison saw a succession of five wardens come and go as their political support dictated. Warden E. J. Russell complained in 1890 against the chicanery of the investigations which were regularly made the excuse for political dismissals and which at the same time undermined even the best efforts at discipline. The Massachusetts prison commission, long a critic of the situation, finally, in 1891 gained the authority to appoint the wardens, and Benjamin F. Bridges, the last of the political appointees, was retained in control, thus at least nominally ridding Charlestown of politics—as the two reformatories had been from the start.

Strictly speaking, the Connecticut state prison had never been a political plum. From Moses Pilsbury down, its wardens had been able officers, many of them called from other states. Changes had, nevertheless, frequently occurred when political supremacy passed from one party to the other. Thus the Democrats in 1893 conducted an investigation and removed S. E. Chamberlain, formerly at Charlestown, appointing in his stead J. L. Woodbridge of the Rhode Island state farm; the quick recovery of the Republicans prompted a new investigation with the inevitable discovery of graft. Although the warden this time was cleared of responsibility his discipline had been undermined, and he soon resigned. Fortunately one of the ablest wardens of the day, Albert Garvin, was called from the West, and Wethersfield was soon enjoying a stable administration and renewed fame.

Politicians elsewhere were not so circumspect, nor were they so easily eliminated. It was an era of sharp political rivalry, and from New York west to the Rockies only Missouri experienced the unbroken sway of one party throughout the period, although Illinois, Iowa, Minnesota, and Wisconsin approached that record. Even the creation of central authorities in New York State merely concentrated control over patronage. Individual wardens, such as A. A. Brush at Sing Sing and Isaiah Fuller at Dannemora, retained office under successive superintendents as a result of their efficient administrations, but they had become, in fact, little more than disciplinarians. The managing authority changed practically every five years in response to political shifts, and with it went the important contracts and other advantages of control.

In Ohio, scarred battleground of politics, the penitentiary suffered probably more than any other institution from repeated pillaging. The loud rejoicing on the part of the reformers over the law of 1874, with its provision for a board of five directors, one to be chosen every year, was hardly justified by results. An ingenious method of defeating its purpose was discovered in 1884 when the Democrats passed this law a second time with slight changes, thus creating the occasion to appoint an entirely new board. This procedure was repeated four times within the next twelve years, and the only warden able to win even a second appointment when his own party returned to power was E. C. Coffin.

No other state quite equaled Ohio's record, although several were not far behind. Indiana's boards of directors served only two-year terms, but the fact that they appointed the wardens for four years added something to the stability of their administrations. The state board of charities secured the passage of a bill in 1895 for the removal of public institutions from politics, but at the last moment the prisons were excluded from its jurisdiction. The five-year terms of wardens in New Jersey and Maryland were considerable assets to their prisons, and John H. Patterson and John F. Weyler could each boast ten years of unusually successful administration when the Republicans captured both states in 1896. Although Weyler was retained at his post for fifteen more years to gain international fame for his industrial achievements at Baltimore prison, the politicians of New Jersey decided that they could easily afford to lose a good warden, and the interests of party were satisfied. Similarly, although Republican control in Michigan and Kansas was shaken only for short periods in the mid-eighties and again in the mid-nineties, each of their prisons suffered a double change of wardens on these occasions, and the resulting instability was a major factor in depriving these states of the leadership in penal development which their institutional equipment might have earned for them.

The states where party rivalry was not so close enjoyed an initial advantage over their neighbors but made varied use of it. Minnesota alone maintained a stable and progressive administration, importing two of McClaughry's ablest officers, Albert Garvin and Henry Wolfer, to manage her prison and reformatory, and it was no coincidence that Stillwater was the best state prison in the country throughout the era. On the other hand, the prison at Jefferson City carried off the honors at the bottom of the list in spite of Missouri's lack of political upheavals. In Illinois Major McClaughry served the state well, making Joliet for a time a model prison in spite of serious overcrowding; but opportunity called the Major and his best officers elsewhere, and when the Democrat, John P. Altgeld, carried the state, he found and removed from control a lesser grade of Republican politicians. Altgeld proceeded to demonstrate that his motives for reform were not entirely Jacksonian by appointing McClaughry superintendent of the recently established reformatory at Pontiac. When the party of the full dinner pail recaptured the state, the prisons were taken over as part of the reward; fortunately McClaughry was persuaded to take charge again at Joliet.

Real stability depended upon non-partisan control. Thus while Iowa and West Virginia enjoyed considerable political stability, the administrations of their prisons changed as rapidly as that of any Methodist church. The successive wardens at Moundsville remained at the beck and call of their party, but Iowa took steps to correct a similar situation by creating its board of control in 1898. Wisconsin had led off in this direction in 1891, although the Democrats, who created the first board, secured most of the advantages for their supporters, and the Republicans, returning to power, appointed an entirely new board in 1895 and secured a new distribution of benefits. Nevertheless, these boards, slowly gaining prestige, freed themselves from political entanglements, and in the next century several of them provided able leadership in public welfare developments, particularly in the mid-western states.

Civil service reformers were making another attack on the spoils system, and their measures were already affecting the prisons of the more progressive states. New York and Massachusetts each had laws dating from the eighties which covered the minor prison officers. The Wisconsin board of control adopted merit tests for many of its employees, and after 1897 the authorities of the Indiana reformatory required its guards to pass certain tests of fitness. Unfortunately these laws did little more, in practical operation, than to guarantee the tenure of office of aged Civil War veterans long after their efficiency as guards had become doubtful.

Indeed the evil influences of politics were inherent in the type of democracy current in America at the time. The principle that any man who helped build the political strength of a party was able to fill and had a right to demand any administrative post he chose largely controlled the selection of wardens, and as long as this principle was maintained elaborate reformatory programs were doomed.

PRISON STANDARDS OF LIVING

Americans in these years were making considerable improvement over the makeshift living arrangements of their frontier days. They were building more spacious homes in which plumbing fixtures and other conveniences were receiving attention. But this was the work of an individualistic materialism, and it was some time before the new standards began to influence the discussions of prison housing conditions. Nevertheless, the growing size of the institutions forced attention to sewage disposal, sanitary bathing, ventilation, and standardized diets. As growing populations compelled new construction, better provision was made for these accessory features of the housing problem.

The building programs of the seventies had considerably relieved the desperate crowding in most of the prisons, but the rapid growth of the population in the tier of states reaching from Massachusetts to Kansas kept this problem in the foreground. Only a few states were able to provide separate cells for every prisoner throughout this era, and for long periods several states continued to crowd two into a cell, thus becoming inured to the evils of the practice and preparing the way for a break from the Auburn traditions in other respects as well.

The New England states were the most assiduous adherents to the old standards. In its struggle to provide for a growing convict population, Massachusetts not only built new institutions at Sherborn, Concord, and Bridgewater but remodeled Charlestown prison and raised their total cell capacity to over 2300 by 1896. Serious consideration of plans for another prison was delayed only as the Spanish-American War checked commitments for a year or two. The prisons of Maine, New Hampshire, and Vermont adequately met the demands of these languishing communities, but Rhode Island had to

erect barracks in 1893 to house the overflow from its 126-cell prison
at the state farm. Connecticut disregarded the advice of Charles
Dudley Warner, chairman of its special investigating committee in
1885, and erected a new cell house at Wethersfield instead of a totally new prison; however, even an additional expansion in 1898
brought the total up to only 550 cells, which fortunately proved
adequate for the time. The close of the century thus found all the
states of New England living up to the old standards of Louis
Dwight.

Wisconsin and especially Minnesota had a surplus of cells, and the
critics failed to explain why the model 573 cells at Stillwater could
not attract sufficient lodgers from the less considerate states. Maryland, Michigan, and Iowa were the only other states outside of New
England able to approach this standard. When the old Baltimore
prison became crowded in the mid-nineties, John Weyler was already
building a model addition, and the completion of the new building
with its 820 steel cells, each 9 by $5\frac{1}{2}$ and 8 feet high and equipped
with a basin, toilet, ventilating shaft, and sliding door, enabled the
state in 1899 to boast of one of the best prisons in the world. In
Michigan, when Ionia failed to relieve congestion at Jackson in the
eighties, the temporary expedient of stringing a row of cots in the
corridor was first applied in order to avoid confining two in a cell; but
continued growth of population persuaded the authorities to erect a
branch prison at Marquette, thus increasing the state's cell capacity
to 1,774 by 1896. The cell capacity at Waupun was increased to
500, adequately meeting the needs of Wisconsin until the end of the
period when the reformatory was made ready to supply necessary
relief. Anamosa prison was completed in Iowa during the eighties,
and, together with the older prison at Fort Madison, supplied sufficient cells until the prisoners approached the thousand mark in the
late nineties.

New York could have approximated the old standard if its convicts had been satisfactorily distributed between its three major
prisons and its reformatory, for each had by the end of the period
over 1,000 cells, and the total was near 5,000. Unfortunately Sing
Sing's location near New York made it the destination of a dispro-
portionate number of commitments, and large transfers from there
and from Elmira failed to relieve their congestion. Agitation developed at the turn of the century for a new prison to replace Sing Sing

and a new reformatory to relieve Elmira. In sharp contrast Ohio was unable to decide on a site for even a second prison, and continued to add new buildings at Columbus until the cells totaled 1,800, greatly exceeding any other prison in the world. Many of these cells were too cold in winter, and others were too hot in summer, but the authorities did not begin to transfer batches of the younger men to the unfinished reformatory at Mansfield until the main population had exceeded the two thousand mark in 1896, and the continued development of Mansfield did not relieve congestion at Columbus.

Pennsylvania built more extensively than any other state during this era but failed to keep pace with its needs. The 732 "solitary" cells at Cherry Hill were forced to house an average of 1,100 prisoners during these years, thus finally defeating the old tradition, although Warden Cassidy and Inspector Richard Vaux stubbornly refused to recognize the fact. The expansion of Pittsburgh compelled the abandonment of its old penitentiary and the construction of a new one at Riverside during the eighties, but its 1,160 modern cells, each 8 by 5 and 8 feet high, were soon filled to capacity. The abandonment of the plan for a new prison in the center of the state and the construction in its stead of the Huntingdon reformatory, although providing an additional 500 cells, delayed for several decades the relief of the Eastern Penitentiary. But, if two convicts were to be housed in a cell, certainly they could live more comfortably under such an arrangement at Cherry Hill than anywhere else in the country.

Several other states made attempts to provide the accommodations required by their laws but were defeated by the steady growth of their populations. New Jersey frequently enlarged the prison at Trenton, but the population persistently registered 200 ahead of capacity. West Virginia made good progress with the construction of Moundsville during the eighties, but when the original plan for 404 cells was completed in 1894, the population already stood at 500 and continued to grow unchecked. Indiana built 760 Joliet-sized cells at its Michigan City prison and 200 fine new ones at Jeffersonville, but, as the prisoners multiplied more rapidly, the authorities determined to admit the inevitable and announced that the new cells were double ones.

But Illinois was more responsible than any other state for shattering the Auburn tradition. The imposing structure at Joliet, together with the growing reputation of its able warden, made it a model for many western prisons; but since its 1,024 cells, each 7 by 4 and 7 feet high, were continually crowded with around 1,500 prisoners, many of them eagerly admitted as lodgers from the federal government and western territories, the example was not in the Auburn tradition. When in 1882 the first 400 cells were completed at Chester in the southern part of the state, the authorities announced the capacity to be 800, and even this limit was exceeded before the close of the century. The construction of 1,000 cells at the young men's reformatory at Pontiac in the nineties failed to relieve the situation, and in 1898 the prison commissioners finally expressed strong condemnation of its evils:[2]

When one thinks of two men spending never less than fourteen hours each day during six days of the week and on the seventh day nearly twenty-one hours in a space so reduced, and with a slop bucket in the cell for their use . . . . he is compelled to ask what excuse the great State of Illinois can offer for compelling men . . . . (to) eat, rest and sleep in quarters so repellent, so utterly unfit for the purpose that their very existence is a disgrace to the State that permits it.

Kansas, likewise, whether prompted by the Illinois example or the zest for profits, crowded lodgers from outside the state into its already overcrowded 688-cell prison at Lansing and failed to relieve the situation by the tardy construction of 200 cells at Hutchinson in the nineties. But Missouri was the state that maintained the most wretched prison in the country, rivaled only at times by Virginia, Kentucky, and California. The prison at Jefferson City, already crowding 1,200 convicts into 500 old cells in 1880, permitted the population to reach 2,300 before 236 small "congregate rooms" were added in 1898. It had become, as one governor described it, "the largest school of crime" in America.

Thus the last quarter of the century witnessed the constant expansion of prison accommodations. The adult reformatory had become a major factor in the situation, and eleven institutions of this type, more or less fully constructed, were housing around 6,000 inmates by 1900. By the same date a dozen prisons in the northern states were confining in excess of 1,000 prisoners each, two of them

[2] Illinois State Penitentiary, Joliet *Report* (1898), p. 14.

over 2,000, and the old ideal of the 500-cell prison was forgotten. Not only had the solitary system of Pennsylvania finally passed out of existence in practice, but several mid-western states were regularly confining two men in a cell with complete equanimity, thus heralding the end of the Auburn tradition as well.

An interest in the equipment of prisons was taking the place of concern over the number of cells. Thirty or so years after the "floating palaces" of America's western waters began to advertise wash basins in their staterooms, prison officers started an agitation for such conveniences for their grimy lodgers. Very little, however, was accomplished in this direction until after the growing popular interest in sanitation had produced laws requiring minimum health standards in the tenements of the larger cities. Meanwhile industry was equipping itself to meet the new demands, and the J. S. Mott Iron Works issued a catalogue in 1881 announcing a simple and efficient plumbing device ready for installation in prison cells. The new prison cell was gradually transformed into an efficient cubicle during this era as iron and steel became the materials of construction, but prisons are substantial structures, and once built even industrial revolutions do not readily alter them. Thousands of prisoners continued to drowse away the hours in musty old brick or stone cells heavy with layer on layer of whitewash.

Bathing requirements had long been among the most unpopular features of prison discipline. It was with a touch of irony that one of the most severe of prison punishments was nicknamed the "shower bath." Tub bathing was almost as fearful and certainly much more vile than the punishment. Joliet's announcement in 1884 that sixty wooden tubs had been installed in a new bathroom gave it the right to boast the best equipment for bathing convicts in the country. The fourteen hundred men could now each have a tub to himself once a week, a great luxury when compared with the prisoners forced to jump into a large tank with a hundred of their fellows once or twice a month. Other prisons followed Joliet's example, until in 1892 Clinton prison set a new standard by introducing the first equipment for shower bathing. The physician reported that the men now enjoyed bathing, and other prisons became interested; when Baltimore opened its model cell house in 1899, it was the sixth prison to provide showers. Meanwhile the more difficult job of introducing running water into each cell had been accomplished by several prisons. The Riverside penitentiary, built by Pennsylvania in the eighties, was the first Auburn structure to provide this convenience, and most new construction followed its example. There was one very considerable problem that had to be solved before any of these sanitary devices were possible, and that was the provision of an adequate water supply. The ideal site of the early days had been a high spot near a town with possibly a stream flowing by a corner of the plot. But the rapid expansion of most institutions had soon outgrown the services of the first wells, which in many cases were abandoned only after their waters had been contaminated owing to the imperfect disposal of the prison sewage. The struggle to solve this problem demanded repeated attention from many prisons.

The night bucket maintained its disagreeable place in most of the cells. Efforts to correct some of its evils led to the substitution of enameled iron for wooden buckets, as the former could be more easily and thoroughly cleansed. Illinois was the first to provide bucket chambers, and these enclosures in the cells at Chester were connected by air ducts to the ventilators in the roof. Maryland's new cell house in 1899 was the first Auburn prison to introduce toilets with running water into each cell. Although most of these devices were adopted by later builders, only the most costly reconstruction could instal them in the old structures. When J. B. Ransom made a study of prison conditions responsible for the spread of tuberculosis, a visit to seventy-seven prisons in the early part of the next century revealed that the great majority were still using the old bucket system.

Similarly in the closely related problem of ventilation most of the prisons continued to rely on the old "law of the diffusion of gases." Charlestown prison converted every pair of its small cells into one, thus securing for each cell a door and a window as well as greater air space. Open grated doors of steel were gradually substituted for the heavy iron or wooden ones of the past, and the new cells were built on larger patterns than the first Auburn standard, although this fact encouraged the doubling-up that more than offset the advantage in increased air space. Fans were frequently installed to drive the bad air that gathered at the top of the cell house out through ventilators in the roof. Most new prisons provided air ducts leading from each cell to the fans and ventilators, but the convicts were quickly arrayed against this system, preferring foul air to the armies of crawlers that constantly campaigned through these highways. Many a warden installed and gave generous praise to a new ventilating system, but his successor a year or two later usually discovered the fan to be out of commission and the pipes stuffed shut by the convicts. Ventilation was proving to be about as difficult a problem in prison as in the large city tenements of the day.

The coal stoves and kerosene lamps in the corridors aggravated the problem by polluting the atmosphere without fulfilling their own functions. The wide introduction of steam and hot-air systems during the early part of the era was a considerable improvement. When electric lighting gained a commercial basis, Elmira was quick to instal an expensive equipment of incandescent bulbs, thus becoming in 1892 the first adequately lighted prison. Nevertheless, for many years even such a well-equipped prison as Riverside continued to depend on candles.

In most of these matters the prisons were slowly improving their living conditions, but in the dining arrangements there was a decided regression. Enoch Wines had found dining-rooms in almost all state prisons in his day, but several factors had contrived to close most of them. Population growth rendered the old rooms inadequate at the same time that it demanded their space for new cells or shops. The occasional prison outbreaks usually occurred when the men were all gathered together in these halls, thus prejudicing wardens against them. Even the economy of the dining-room failed to prevent prisons from returning to cell feeding. When the directors of Joliet made an investigation in 1900, they found only about a dozen major prisons equipped with dining-halls, and most of these served the evening meal in the cells. This additional use of the cells gave increased significance to the problems of overcrowding and sanitation.

Meanwhile the standard of prison diets was slowly rising. Scurvy and other forms of undernourishment were practically eliminated, and yet the science of dietetics received almost no attention from prison authorities. Diets were frequently compared, but the outstanding conclusion was that a reasonable budget was ten cents for each man each day. Mush, milk, bread, potatoes, vegetables, pork, beef, apples, beans, and coffee, made chiefly of bread crusts, were the staple foods. There was constant complaint against the condition of the bread and particularly of the meat. Prisoners were usually drafted as chefs, and their concoctions did not always display skill. These facts, combined with the absence of fruits, sugars, and fats, made the meals anything but pleasant or wholesome. Possibly however, the convicts missed their liquor and, in many prisons where it was prohibited, their tobacco more than they suffered from the meals.

A western convict recorded an instructive sample of prison humor, which now began to find its way into these bastilles as the silent system was relaxed. According to the story a young farm hand on his arrival at prison received his equipment and was heading for his cell when an old "con" asked if he had not been cheated of his sheets; the youth took the hint and went to the officer with his complaint; the tale further has it that he got sheets. If the story may be relied upon, these were about the only sheets ever distributed in prison during the era. Towels and soap were not so rare, but they were expected to last. Few prisons followed Elmira's policy of supplying a comb, toothbrush, and fresh mattress to each new arrival.[3]

The newspapers and politicians who cried out against luxurious penal hotels were sadly misinformed. The prisons were tardily following the general rise in the standards of sanitation, but only in the new buildings were any real improvements made. The critics would have had a genuine issue had they condemned the single standard of security, which was the major cause of the enormous expenditures, or had they stressed the state of idleness resulting from the labor laws. It was this latter factor rather than the number of the cells or their alleged sumptuousness that dominated the life of the prisoner in this era.

SCHEMES FOR DISCIPLINE AND REFORMATION

Overcrowded prisons threatened with the cessation of their industrial activities presented their officers with a problem that the Auburn tradition could not solve, and they were thus prompted to turn

[3] J. B. Ransom, *Tuberculosis in Penal Institutions* (Washington, 1904), p. 14: "The straw ticks or mattresses of many institutions are seldom disinfected, are not protected by sheets or pillow covers. The bedding . . . . is left in the cell to be occupied by another. . . . ."

to the Elmira technique for assistance. The older educational and religious activities were not overlooked, but the newer features were given greater emphasis. The extension of the parole system to the state prisons joined with the disciplinary problem to encourage the introduction of grades and marks but without supplanting the older devices for maintaining order. A new atmosphere took the place of the traditional restraint in many prisons, but only one or two wardens succeeded in developing the spirit as well as the technique of Elmira at their institutions.

Most of the prisons maintained some sort of an evening school during the winter months, but none of them attained the standards achieved at Charlestown in the days of Warden Haynes. Warden Hatch developed a comprehensive program at Jackson in the eighties, but it was not continued by his successor. Jackson and a half-dozen other prisons provided school buildings and laid in a stock of children's textbooks, and these frequently proved serviceable to new wardens wishing to inaugurate their administrations with a generous flourish. The slowly accumulating stocks of the libraries, aided in an increasing number of prisons by modest annual grants, provided greater comfort to a few lonely intellectuals, and Joliet was able to boast at the turn of the century that its library of 16,271 volumes was the largest prison library in the world, but no librarian or chaplain was prompted to congratulate his prison on the nature of these collections.

Book learning was not, after all the chief need of the convict, and a few officers found occasion to note that Victor Hugo's dictum "that he who opens a school closes a prison" was not verified by American experience. But there was in these years an increasing appreciation of the broader aspects of education, and wardens began to refer to their industrial establishments as trade schools. The fact that Lynn, Massachusetts, gained local notoriety as the home of discharged prisoners because of the number of its laborers who learned their trade in prison shoe shops helps to substantiate the claim in one instance, but prison industries had never been selected with this object in view. Indeed, further to obstruct this possibility, many of the laws regulating prison labor undertook to ban those industries in which a convict might find employment in his state after discharge. Industries were not all excluded, however, for the prison officers succeeded in circumventing the regulations in most cases, and the increasing number of reformatories usually developed some trade-school departments. As at Elmira printing presses were acquired by many prisons, providing valuable trades to a few selected inmates and prompting the publication of prison journals in four prisons and four reformatories during the early nineties.

Sunday continued to serve as a day of rest in prison. The libraries afforded about the only relief from the boredom of the long hours spent in the cells from Sunday dinner to Monday breakfast. The Sunday-morning service was not a regular feature, and many of the prisoners were at least grateful for its diversion. A few of the chaplains attempted to make the day more congenial for a portion of their flock by organizing special societies which were in some cases permitted to meet in the afternoon hours. Such were the Christian Endeavor groups at the prisons in Wisconsin and Indiana, the Chautauqua circles in four or five prisons, and the Mutual Aid League at Jackson. In most of the institutions, however, even the favored trusties could not be permitted out of their cells on Sunday afternoon, for this was the one time when the guards received a respite from their long hours of thankless vigil.

A new tone was added to many of the chapel services during this era as additional instruments were introduced to support the traditional prison choir and organ. Several orchestras were developed, and these, together with the bands of the reformatories, added a feature that was to become more prominent in the next century. Chapel services were generally under the direction of full-time, Protestant chaplains, but Catholic priests were permitted to minister to inmates of their faith, and by the end of the period some of the states with increasing Catholic populations were officially naming Catholics as assistant chaplains.

In the late nineties Mrs. Maud Ballington Booth strode into the midst of this prosaic clericalism waving the banner of evangelism. Mrs. Booth came to America under the auspices of the Salvation Army and gained her first interest in convicts during visits to its prison-gate missions. After her break with the Army in 1896 she formed the Volunteers of America with a subsidiary branch, the Volunteer Prison League. Her labors began in Sing Sing and spread rapidly to many of the major prisons. Stirring emotional appeals were the foundation of her strength, but Mrs. Booth followed her first success in each prison by gathering her converts into permanent League units. Each member pledged to pray and read his Bible daily, to use clean language, form cheerful habits, and obey the prison rules; for this he was given a badge, and the League's paper, the *Volunteer Gazette*, was sent to him weekly. Mrs. Booth undertook to answer all letters the prisoners wrote to her, and Hope Halls were opened in New York, Chicago, and San Francisco to which the members were invited to come for aid after their discharge. The League units in nine of the largest prisons numbered a total of 2,679 Volunteers by the end of the century.

But the abler prison officers were pinning their reformatory hopes on disciplinary rather than on emotional methods. The progressive grading system became the favorite nostrum of the day. When Warden E. S. Wright moved his prisoners into the new penitentiary at Riverside in the eighties, he reorganized an earlier grade system after that of Elmira, and a similar system was introduced at Columbus along with the parole and labor reforms of those years. Grades were provided at Charlestown when Concord was being reorganized as a reformatory, and Warden Hatch developed a similar device at Jackson. But, except at Elmira and Concord, these first experiments were not coupled with an indeterminate-sentence system, and, deprived of the vital function of determining the date of discharge, they were soon abandoned or permitted to degenerate into meaningless routine. The revival of the agitation for parole systems in the nineties was accompanied with a more effective development of the grading system, first at Stillwater in 1891 and then in quick succession at Charlestown, Jackson, Joliet, Columbus, Jeffersonville, and Wethersfield. Grades were introduced in other prisons as well as in the new reformatories but without the elaborate agitation that accompanied the programs in the above institutions.

Here was such a widespread stampede to their ideas that veteran reformers began to rub their eyes and soon discovered that their prize reformatory device was degenerating into a shield for lax discipline. The Indiana state prison was the first to make open recognition of this fact by providing that all new arrivals should enter the top grade and only lose the privileges it accorded them when they were detected in some offense. By the late nineties the reports of most prisons showed fully nine-tenths of their inmates as members of the top grade, enjoying the full privilege of talking, playing games, reading newspapers, and engaging in whatever additional activities the warden had seen fit to develop. Brockway, whose reports showed that the majority of his boys still had much to do before they could be considered reformed and accorded full privileges, had become a cruel disciplinarian in the eyes of many of his associates and finally retired in disgust. Only Stillwater prison under Henry Wolfer and Wethersfield under Albert Garvin were able to maintain grading systems on the genuine reformatory basis that encouraged the men through self-control to earn privileges of freedom and responsibility. Elsewhere, except in the reformatories, the grading system not only lost its capacity for stimulating individual development but failed to afford the parole authorities any real assistance in selecting men for conditional release. Nevertheless, it performed one real service— that of civilizing prison customs by restricting the use of striped suits, head-shaving, lock-step marching, and such old practices to the punishment grades in most prisons.

Everywhere the principles of Louis Dwight and the discipline of Amos Pilsbury were losing ground. Wethersfield, long the most stubborn stronghold of these traditions, led the revolt in the mid-nineties by devoting one hour each day to calisthenic exercise and granting the members of the top grade the privilege of organizing literary societies and enjoying free association one hour each fortnight. At about the same time Michigan permitted conversation at mealtimes in its prisons and gave the inmates in the top grade a daily recess in the yard, while Indiana permitted conversation in the cell houses for two hours each evening. The public did not always approve of these concessions, and the people of New Hampshire decided at the polls that the old rules requiring downcast eyes and silence should not be abandoned. Nevertheless, Warden Hunter was applauded when he announced at one of the Iowa quarterly conferences of superintendents in 1899 that his experience in granting freedom of the yard on public holidays encouraged him to follow the example of Joliet, Columbus, Jackson, and Wethersfield and grant the privilege once a week. But the extensive developments of organized sports on these occasions did not take place except in a few reformatories until well into the next century.

The abandonment of the old rules of silence greatly simplified the job of discipline in one respect but opened the way for favoritism and intrigue and encouraged the development of espionage. The barriers which the Auburn system had erected against mutual corruption were let down and neither the prisoners nor the officers made a very good use of their greater freedom of intercourse. Many wardens declared that if given enough rope most criminals would hang themselves, and these wardens then proceeded to let the rope slip through their fingers.

The legislators frequently tried their hands at prison discipline, filling the statute books with laws abolishing all sorts of punishments, but the legal rights of prisoners had long served as the stock joke among cynical convicts. A few years after New York abolished corporal punishment in prison an investigation at Clinton revealed the frequent use of paddling, tying up by the wrists so that the toes barely touched the floor, confinement in dark cells, and the like. Warden Howard was dismissed in Indiana when evidence leaked out proving that he had made frequent and sometimes cruel use of the "cat" although it had been abolished six years earlier. When Ohio prohibited the lash and the "shower bath," the authorities invented the "humming bird," a device for administering electric shocks, which was even more fearful than the former tortures. The correct punishment was not, in fact, a simple matter to be determined by a legislative majority. Thus it frequently happened that riots and fires broke out, and old grudges were settled in bloody frays in which officers were sometimes killed when the prisoners learned of the abolition of punishments they had feared. Naturally the officers on such occasions, remembering that the legislative and administrative branches had distinct responsibilities under the American system, proceeded to re-establish and to maintain discipline by the use of their own judgment.

Public opinion, sometimes acting through the legislature, had its influence, but so did the particular conditions of each prison. When the industrial activity was sluggish and there was no great demand for the labor of each convict, the bread and water, or "Pennsylvania diet," sometimes combined with confinement to a dark cell, was the mainstay for serious cases; or an intractable convict might be hand-cuffed to the door of his cell and forced to stand through the day looking at a gray wall while his fellows idled in the shop. On the other hand, the model prison in Baltimore, with more use for its labor, retained the "cat" until 1905 when the physician discovered that the blood of one victim remaining on the cords of the lash in-fected succeeding victims with syphilis. Meanwhile greed for profits in Kansas invented another deviltry designed to bring the prisoner to terms quickly. The culprit's hands and feet were all bound to-gether in a knot behind his back, and he was then deposited, face down, on a stone floor with his feet held above him by a wooden "crib," and here he remained until he fainted or made a convincing cry for mercy.

In the midst of viciousness, brutality, repression, and varied out-croppings of insanity it would have been surprising if personalities and techniques had not frequently become mixed up in tragic epi-sodes. Rare investigations and more frequent reports by former convicts told appalling tales of prisoners who were relentlessly driven down the entire gauntlet of punishments until with broken health they landed in the "cracked ward," possibly with, and possibly with-out, shattered intellects. Penology still had a considerable distance to go before it could boast that it encouraged as well as permitted every inmate and every officer to develop only the better faculties of his manhood.

These were the extraordinary punishments that seemed indispens-able to many of the men in charge of prisons, no matter what grading system they might maintain. Nevertheless, in spite of the funda-mental flaws that these exceptions revealed, the rigid regulations of the past were giving place to the technique of the reformatory, and, although the spirit and the motivation that animated Elmira in its best days were sadly lacking, new privileges and customs had trans-formed the activities of many prisons and had made them much more tolerable places in which to live.

THE CARE GIVEN SPECIAL GROUPS

With the major forms of pedagogical penology more or less clearly worked out and widely indorsed, a greater attention was given to the peculiar problems of special groups within the criminal classes. The movement had enlisted the support of diverse elements of the population, and several of its new programs grew out of the special interests of some of these allied groups. Prison physicians took the initiative in projecting new treatments for the tubercular as well as for the insane. Local philanthropic societies helped to provide more generous aid to the discharged. The federal government was at last aroused to undertake the care of some of its own prisoners. Only the city and county authorities, except in rare instances, continued to shirk their responsibilities.

The prisons were profiting along with the country at large from the gains made for the science of medicine in these years. Resident doctors had for some time been on the staffs of the larger and more progressive institutions, but the visiting physician was still the mainstay elsewhere. The periodic examination of the sick list remained hopelessly inadequate in most prisons and disheartened many an unfortunate criminal with a genuine ailment. The influence of these doctors on the development of higher standards of sanitation and dietetics was not as great as it might well have been, nor did they take an independent stand in connection with their responsibility for safeguarding the health of prisoners receiving corporal punishment. Their most significant service was performed in connection with the campaign for the proper care of special groups, such as the tubercular and the insane; in time they were to assume large responsibilities in the study of the individual criminal.

Several prison physicians were fully abreast of the medical profession in its attack on tuberculosis. When the doctor in attendance at Wethersfield prison reported in 1881 that only one prisoner had died during the preceding year from pulmonary consumption and congratulated himself that only a few of these cases had developed, "due to the grace of God," he was, for his day, no old fogy. Gradually, as discoveries were made in Europe and America concerning the nature of this malady, a new interest in its treatment developed among prison physicians. In 1888, shortly after the first tuberculosis congress gathered in Paris, McClaughry's physician at Joliet segregated thirty-odd consumptives of that prison into an idle shop where they were employed at light tasks during the day and where they slept in an airy dormitory at night. But it was Dr. J. B. Ransom, physician at Clinton prison, who made the first permanent contribution to the treatment of tuberculosis in prison. Possibly stimulated by Dr. Trudeau's success at Saranac Lake. Dr. Ransom conducted experiments with the care of selected cases in dormitories near the prison and demonstrated that the high altitude and pure air of this choice site in the Adirondacks were admirably fitted for the treatment of tubercular prisoners. The superintendent was persuaded to transfer convicts suffering from this malady from the other prisons to Clinton, and special fresh-air wards were constructed for their accommodation. Since a study of the reports of a dozen major prisons revealed that about 45 per cent of the deaths in prison were attributable to this disease, the successful development of a treatment at Clinton in the early nineties provided a pattern for other prisons, but the general provision of real hospital wards and of open-air wards on the roof did not come until the next century.

The spread of the parole laws attracted public interest to the problems of the discharged prisoners. The strongest prison-aid societies of the earlier period, notably those in New York, Philadelphia, Maryland, and Connecticut, continued to perform their valuable services. About the only truly active organizations to join this group were the society and home of Agnes d'Arcambal in Detroit and the new Massachusetts Prison Association, both started in the late eighties. Additional homes were founded in Chicago and Providence, and societies existed in several other states, but none of these performed much service. The state agents in New York and Pennsylvania continued to function, and most of the reformatories appointed special officers to perform the similar service of finding jobs and homes; the reformatory agents frequently tried, in addition, to maintain a friendly contact with their boys. Practically all the states supplied their released prisoners with a few dollars, a ticket home, and a suit of clothes, While these added up to considerable sums in the eyes of the taxpayers, they were as necessary a part of justice as the meager meals fed to the prisoners; unfortunately this last "handout" aroused about as little gratitude from the friendless derelicts as had the daily meals; the self-conscious former convict always tried to scrap the suit as soon as possible.

A few new friends rallied to the cause of the "down-and-outer" during this period. The Salvation Army prison-gate movement started in the mid-nineties, and the Volunteers of America and the Central Howard Association commenced activities not long afterward, although these bodies did not become fully effective until the next period. Indeed, little real work had yet been done in any of the states or by any agency toward helping the criminal at the most critical point in his entire career—a failure which contrasted sharply with the record of England and parts of the Continent.

If the Americans were falling down at the close of their penal treatment, they were making diabolical blunders at its beginning. European critics who found American democracy most rotten at the bottom certainly could not have been parried off by any indignant local patriot who knew anything about his county jail. The hundreds of thousands who paid forced visits to these institutions, year after year, almost without exception returned the worse for their experience. Here one could find inadequate separation of sexes, ages, diseases, and experience; here the inmates continually idled about the inclosures with almost no disciplinary restrictions except occasionally those of the insidious "kangaroo courts" under which guise the old-timers preyed upon the new arrivals until all illusions about public justice were shattered.

The reformers of the day did not leave it to visiting Europeans or to the students of a later generation to condemn this situation. A half-dozen of them surveyed the problem on successive years before the national gatherings, exposing the evils with caustic remarks; nevertheless, their major interests were in other matters. No sheriff's association appeared to rank with that of the wardens, chaplains, and physicians; in fact, practically none of this class of officers appeared at the congresses. Their tenure was too short and insecure to permit many of them to develop professional interests, since the sheriff's job remained one of the most lucrative spoils of local party victory. The fee system still reigned supreme, permitting a thrifty man to extract a large profit between the sum paid by the county for the support of each "head" and the pittance paid out for food; well-to-do inmates added to these profits by renting the more comfortable cells and buying their own food and clothing. Boarders were naturally in demand, and, as profits were large enough to permit their division into several shares, it was not unknown for constables to "run men in for revenue only." The wheels of justice appeared always to be clogged.

Efforts to correct these evils were not lacking. Possibly Massachusetts made the most effective reforms by centralizing its jail system under the prison commission and by authorizing that body to determine institutional standards, thus creating an authority to remove undesirable officers, to transfer from one jail to another, and even to close an unsatisfactory institution. Meanwhile the Minnesota board of charities planned a model jail and directed the erection of forty of these institutions, and the Ohio board almost equaled that achievement. A few new houses of correction were erected, notably that in Milwaukee, but none of these did much more than provide an opportunity for labor and possibly a smattering of schooling—none came up to the Detroit house of the old days. Unfortunately New York's labor laws, by destroying the fine industry and discipline of its county penitentiaries, condemned their thousands of inmates to desultory idleness, offsetting any gains the generation may have made in the field elsewhere. Wherever a good system did develop, the jail was almost immediately crowded beyond capacity by neighboring cities or counties eager to house their criminals as safely as possible—a procedure which the fortunate sheriff was usually glad to encourage. These evils were everywhere obvious, and inspections repeatedly brought them to the attention of the legislatures, usually holding up England and Scotland as the shining examples of how the job should be handled.[4] But it was not until the next century that Hastings H. Hart and Joseph Fishman were to force this problem before the public with a fanatical persistence that produced some results.

The difficulties presented by the task of moving the decentralized local authorities to effective reform were not as surprising as those

---

[4] Wisconsin Board of Charities, *Report* (1890), pp. 10–11: "We have found a very large part of the jails of the state at one time or another in a deplorable condition, filthy, swarming with vermin, without bathing facilities, with foul bedding, and with disgusting and disease breeding privies right in the jail. . . . . We have found women and men given the liberty of the same corridor, and we have frequently found boys in unrestricted intercourse with hardened criminals. Even in those jails built for classification we have frequently found all the inner doors thrown open and indiscriminate association of all prisoners allowed."

encountered by the reformers in their attempt to persuade the federal government to assume its obvious responsibilities. General R. B. Brinkerhoff's attempt to get a report of the number of federal prisoners had at first been blocked, but finally an appeal to President Cleveland produced results, and information was given out showing a total of 1,027 federal prisoners lodged in state prisons and about 10,000 in county jails in 1885. A steady increase in the number of these prisoners, reaching 2,516 and about 15,000 respectively by 1895, aided the agitation for a federal penal program, led by Brinkerhoff and Congressman Samuel June Barrows. A law was passed in 1891 directing the purchase of three sites for federal prisons. But no funds were supplied, and nothing was done until Congress in 1894 provided for the temporary conversion of the military prison at Fort Leavenworth into a civil prison and directed that a new prison be erected near that site. Cleveland placed Warden J. W. French, formerly at Michigan City prison, in charge at the Fort, and 500 federal prisoners were shortly gathered there. When McKinley and the Republicans took over the government, they cast about and selected the best Republican warden in the country—the veteran of Joliet. Under Major McClaughry's able direction a model penitentiary on the Joliet pattern was slowly erected at Leavenworth, but the second institution, planned for the site selected at Atlanta, was delayed until the next era.

As the nineteenth century was drawing to a close, the movement for prison reform was girding itself for a more effective realization of its principles and programs. The northern states had finally recognized the reformation of criminals to be a part of their responsibility for maintaining public safety. Laws, institutions, and customs had been provided, and it was hoped that they would all work together toward the desired end. The old compulsion for self-support had been widely relaxed as a result of the labor laws, and a more liberal discipline was being applied in an attempt to handle the problem of increasing idleness. Everywhere the continued growth of the country had forced and made possible the erection of new institutions, usually on a grander scale. Better living conditions and an abandonment of old traditions were, it is true, more in evidence than a genuine application of the pedagogical penology of the reformatory, but the wide introduction of the forms of Brockway's technique at least indicated the aspirations of the younger generation that was taking over the task of prison management for the next era.

Professional penologists were coming to the fore, and they were challenging the authority of politicians in prison control. But if the political place-men who still manned the majority of the prisons were piteously incapable of carrying forward the high aspirations of the positive features of the reformatory discipline, the august members of the well-schooled bar showed little better understanding of the significance of the indeterminate-sentence laws they were applying. Most attorneys and judges continued to play the part of old Shylock, demanding the exact pound of flesh that the old contract theory of society considered the prisoner to have forfeited when he committed his crime. The law schools, with their newly perfected case method of instruction, were failing to consider the most important factor in the criminal case—the criminal, and their emphasis was accordingly on the standardization rather than on the individualization of criminal law. Penal reformers were not to make much headway against this rival educational trend until the development of a science of criminology in the next century enabled a few of its experts to invade the schools.

Thus stupidity and the lack of imagination were not only the chief sources of cruelty in prison, as Oscar Wilde had discovered, but the chief obstacles to a full realization of the positive values of reformatory penology. Yet these obstacles did not appear insurmountable to the new generation coming forward at the turn of the century. Zealous advocates, such as Samuel June Barrows and Hastings H. Hart, and thorough analysts, such as Charles R. Henderson, were assuming leadership. The application of pedagogical penology and the extension of its influence into the West were to be the dominant features of their program for at least the first decade of the new century.

BIBLIOGRAPHICAL NOTE

The official reports of the institutions, of the state boards of charities and correction or the state boards of control, of the prison commissions, and, where these are not adequate, the messages of the governors supply the main source of information on this period. The National Prison Association, *Proceedings*, and the New York Prison Association, *Reports*, are of exceptional value during these years. The two volumes of F. H. Wines, *Report on Crime, Pauperism and*

Benevolence in the United States at the Eleventh Census: 1890 (Washington, 1895–96), provide statistical analyses of correctional trends.

In addition to the works of H. E. Barnes on Pennsylvania and New Jersey, and Philip Klein on New York, Frank W. Blackmar, "Penology in Kansas," *Kansas University Quarterly* (1893); J. E. Briggs, *Social Legislation in Iowa* (Iowa City, 1914); Harry H. Jackson, *The Michigan State Prison* (Jackson, 1928); and Frederick G. Pettigrove, *Prisons of Massachusetts* (Boston, 1904), supply historical treatments of developments in individual states. Other volumes of special interest are: John P. Altgeld, *Our Penal Machinery and Its Victims* (Chicago, 1884); Samuel June Barrows, *The Criminal Insane in the United States and Foreign Countries* (Washington, 1898), and, among others, his *Prison Systems of the United States* (Washington, 1900); Alexander Berkman, *Prison Memoirs of an Anarchist* (New York, 1912); Mrs. Maud B. Booth, *After Prison —What?* (New York, 1903); R. B. Brinkerhoff, *Recollections of a Lifetime* (Cincinnati, 1900); F. R. Johnson, *Probation for Juveniles and Adults* (New York, 1928); M. M. Hurd (ed.), *Institutional Care of the Insane* (4 vols.; Baltimore, 1916); E. C. Lekkerkerker, *Reformatories for Women in the United States* (The Hague, 1931); A. R. Macdonald, *Prison Secrets* (New York, 1893); D. J. Morgan, *Historical Lights and Shadows of the Ohio Penitentiary* (Columbus, 1893); Charles K. Reeve, *The Prison Question* (Chicago, 1890); J. B. Ransom, *Tuberculosis in Penal Institutions* (Washington, 1904); L. V. Rule, *The City of Dead Souls* (Louisville, 1920); Salvation Army, *Broken Souls* (New York, 1929); W. R. Stewart, *The Philanthropic Work of Josephine Shaw Lowell* (New York, 1911).

CHAPTER VIII

SOUTHERN PENAL DEVELOPMENTS[1]

The southern states from a penological point of view never really belonged to the Union. Their halting developments looking toward a penitentiary system had been cut short by the Civil War, and the turmoil of reconstruction created social and economic problems and standards of cruelty that have since continued to vilify the penal practices of the South. While the northern prisoner may have grown pale and anemic gazing through the bars in the pale dusk of towering cell blocks, his southern brother dragged his chains through long years of hard labor, driven by brutal physical torture, oftentimes to his grave. A half-century was not sufficient to efface this institutional estrangement.

Practically all the forces and conditions controlling northern developments were absent in the South. Men and women, preoccupied with the task of rebuilding their homes and communities, did not organize to carry on the patient humanitarian labors that blossomed so fruitfully in prison societies and boards of charities in the North. The incessant lash of increasing convict populations that drove the northern states to build new and better institutions was certainly not lacking here, but the South had no Auburn tradition of one man to a cell to compel sober consideration of new plans at each overflowing; the authorities simply lengthened the chains binding man to man, and the railroads and other companies that leased such labor gladly pushed their construction camps farther into the mountains, the swamps, or the mining regions. No strong unionism raised its voice to order the convicts out of the construction field, and in the few cases where violent struggles did occur, as in the Tennessee coal fields, the stable political situation of the South forestalled effective legislation.

Indeed the penal developments south of the Potomac were dominated by fairly unique problems. Evidence that reconstruction

[1] The author is grateful to the publishers of *Social Forces* and the *Journal of Negro History* for permission to use portions of his articles appearing in those journals.

helped to aggravate the race conflicts was graphically presented by
the rapid increase in the number of Negroes in the criminal population. They soon exceeded 90 per cent of the total, making the traditions and methods of the old slave system seem more logical patterns
for southern penology than the costly methods of the North. The
prostrate South had to rebuild its railroads as well as its prisons,
both considerably demolished by northern troops, and the tax-laden
citizens were only too eager to hear of large profits coming to the
state from convicts busy constructing the highways of commerce
and the foundations of industry. When good people believed that
the end justified the means, it was not surprising either that simple
Negroes, facing long sentences for unlucky escapades, should make
desperate breaks for freedom or that their guards should adopt brutal measures to curb them. Thus race hatreds, slave-driving traditions, necessities for economy, public ignorance of the facts, and
desperation among the convicts—all combined during the first trying years of reconstruction to saddle a damnable lease system on the
southern states.

Rare criers in the wilderness protested, and, although their idealism failed to turn the tide, the lease system gradually receded of its
own accord. Several of the forces, such as the railroad boom, spent
themselves, and, when the agrarians captured political control in the
nineties, a more wholesome plantation life became a major feature
of a still distinctively southern penal system. But while these latter
developments were taking place in the Lower South, the border
states had detached themselves and were adapting many northern
methods to their peculiar needs, thus further demonstrating the
sectional character of southern penal developments.

DARK DAYS IN THE BLACK BELT

The defeat and surrender of its armies opened an era of partial
chaos in the governmental functions of the South. Several of the
prisons, such as they were, had been dismantled by northern troops,
and something had to be done to provide for the punishment of the
increasing number of vagrant and sometimes desperate freedmen.
Something had to be done quickly, whether the government was
temporarily in the hands of a faction of southern patriots, southern
unionists, or northern army officers. Accordingly an adaptation of

the old lease system of Joel Scott and his imitators was devised in several places, and with the exception of Alabama and Texas all the Gulf states quickly turned unreservedly to this system. When the Democrats regained control during the seventies, their determination to cut the tax burden prompted them to exhange corrupt leases for others more favorable to the state treasuries. The exploitation of convict labor thus became an established tradition, with the lease system as its first standard pattern.

Georgia's penal developments were typical of the section. When in 1868 General T. H. Ruger took over the state government, he found a hundred convicts on his hands with the old prison in ruins and promptly leased them to an enterprising railroad builder. The first carpetbag governor, Rufus Bullock, was easily persuaded to continue the policy to the benefit of the railroads of his associate, H. I. Kimball. When Bullock lost control in 1870, a Democratic investigation revealed, among other shocking facts, that only 380 of the 496 convicts could be located. Nevertheless, as the major concern was economy, the legislature hastened to indorse the lease system, and 500 prisoners were soon contracted to seven different lessees. A permanent policy was finally worked out in 1876 when the prisoners, now numbering 1,100, were distributed among three leasing companies on twenty-year contracts, each company agreeing to pay the state $25,000 a year for the labor. Governor J. M. Smith congratulated the state in 1877 upon its happy solution of a perplexing problem.

Penal developments in Mississippi followed practically the same course. The military government leased the convicts in 1867 for three years, and the carpetbaggers extended the term. A partial reorganization of the government in 1872 brought to power some critics of the lessee who was receiving $20,000 a year from the state, and an attempt was made to return to the old penitentiary system with a superintendent in charge. But the superintendent, noting that the dilapidated state of the prison, with its locks and machinery demolished by the troops, could be corrected only at great expense, determined to keep only the young, the infirm, and the sick at the "Walls" and leased the able-bodied to a railroad on favorable terms to the state. When the Democrats gained full control in 1876, a proposal for a new penitentiary was quickly voted down, and the entire population was leased to the Hamilton and Hebron Company on what appeared to be favorable terms; the company, however, soon discovered that it could sublease the convicts at even higher rates, and no check was maintained over the cruel fate of the penal slaves.

In a similar fashion Louisiana, with the prison at Baton Rouge sufficiently dismantled to discourage its repair, created a board of control to supervise the leasing of the convicts. A twenty-year contract was negotiated, providing for increasing returns to the state and requiring the lessee to enforce any regulations which the board should adopt for the discipline of the prisoners. But this slight improvement over the other leases proved of little value, for the board found that it could neither enforce its regulations nor collect the annual payments, and the political backing of the lessee, coupled with popular indifference, preserved the system from attack for many years.

Arkansas and Tennessee likewise turned their prisons over to lessees at the close of the war, but, as the first contracts required that the convicts be employed within the walls, the companies maintained prisons comparable to those of Kentucky and Missouri. Arkansas not only paid a small fee for the support of each prisoner but permitted the lessee to incur a huge state debt for the construction of additional cells which he then proceeded to fill with federal prisoners to the advantage of his own profits. The Democrats, finally gaining control, compelled the lessee to pay an annual rental of $25,000 but permitted him to employ the convicts as he chose. Tennessee, finding its old 356-cell Nashville prison overcrowded in the early seventies leased the excess in batches to various companies, but the unsatisfactory nature of this arrangement was soon evident, especially as the population was growing by leaps and bounds. In 1884 the Tennessee Coal and Iron Railway secured a lease of the entire convict population, then numbering around a thousand, and agreed to pay the state $100,000 a year for the privilege of using this labor in its mining camps.

But Florida took the prize for corruption and cruelty in penal affairs during this period. The federal government had loaned the arsenal at Chattahoochee for a state prison, and during the eight years of reconstruction the boodlers in charge housed an average of eighty-two convicts there at a total cost of $234,473. When the federal troops were withdrawn, the Democrats quickly cut expenses by leasing the prisoners to a construction company for the nominal sum of $100 a year. Succeeding years saw a shift of leases almost every year as the state sought to improve its bargain thus, shuttling the convicts about in a haphazard fashion, with never any permanent quarters. The prisoners were held together only by a barbarous discipline enforced at the point of the gun, and the system was aptly described as "the American Siberia."

Neither Alabama nor Texas had suffered so cruelly from war or reconstruction, and their earlier traditions resisted the new trends for a time. The first reconstruction government in Alabama had leased the prison at Wetumpka for six years, but when the state recovered the institution in 1872, a warden was placed in full control. The buildings were unfortunately in a wretched state of repair, and, as the legislature provided only a small appropriation for maintenance, the warden found it desirable to hire out the able-bodied in order to meet expenses. The legislature agreed to sanction the policy but required the warden to station an officer at each camp to supervise discipline. A little experience revealed that the lessees were shirking all responsibility for guarding the convicts, thus permitting many to escape and prompting Alabama to follow its neighbors in placing full responsibility upon the lessees. A striking hint as to the origin of the technique of the lease system appeared in 1880 when the warden advertised three grades of prisoners for contract, asking $5.00 per month for the "full-hands," $2.50 for "medium-hands," and nothing but their keep for "dead-hands," thus borrowing some well-known terms from slave traditions. A move toward the abandonment of this system during the eighties was blocked by financial considerations. The best the state could do was to secure the construction of some model log camps at the Pratt mines where 400 of the prisoners were employed.

Texas with its great area and rapidly growing population found the 225 cells at the Huntsville prison hopelessly inadequate during the first years after the war. The first expedient of employing the overflow on state railroads was terminated when the railroads were sold to private interests, and the entire prison was leased. But the first lessee soon defaulted and, herding all the convicts into the small prison, turned it over to the state. A new lessee was found who agreed to build a second prison with 400 cells at Rusk and to equip it with a foundary to develop the product of nearby mines. When the lease expired in 1880, this structure was finished and 50 additional cells were available at Huntsville, but the total of 675 cells could not accommodate the 2,000 convicts who were at the time scattered over a wide area, laboring at railroad and bridge construction, iron-blasting, and plantation-farming. The state superintendent was accordingly compelled to contract out the majority of his charges but succeeded in maintaining efficient inspection and regulation, thus eliminating many of the worst evils of the lease system.

PENAL SYSTEMS IN THE BORDER STATES

Institutional developments in America have had their sectional variations but never any sharp boundary lines. The sectional variations are particularly noticeable in penal history, possibly because prisons have been more closely tied to state political affairs than have been the educational and charitable institutions. Thus there was a belt of states stretching from Virginia and the Carolinas to Missouri that scarcely fell in with the general penological trends of either the North or the South. In the Carolinas, where before the war the administration of justice had been entirely in the hands of the counties, the state authorities now built penitentiaries, but events soon converted them into little more than penal hospitals while the majority of the convicts were placed out in the hands of lessees. The prisons of Virginia, Kentucky, and Missouri were maintained as the center of the penal systems of these states, but they did not react to the reform movement rampant north of the Mason and Dixon line. West Virginia alone, and only for a time, turned its back resolutely on the southern influences.

The reconstruction government in North Carolina decided in 1868 to build a penitentiary on the Auburn pattern. After a scandal occasioned by the disappearance of the first commissioners with $100,000 paid them for eight thousand acres of worthless pine barrens,[2] a second commission chose a 22-acre site near Raleigh and hired an archi-

[2] North Carolina Commission of Inquiry, *Report* (N.C. Senate Documents, 1868-69), pp. 1-9.

tect from Ohio to build a prison on the model of the new construction at Pittsburgh. When the Democrats captured the state and appointed still a third commission, the plan was enlarged to include 1,000 cells, and temporary wooden huts were provided to house the prisoners while construction slowly proceeded. But the number of convicts increased rapidly, and as funds were not provided for rapid construction the authorities were forced to turn to the lease system, placing out 500 on various railroads by 1877. In 1882 the wall and the first 500-cell house was completed, but the early failure of a half-hearted experiment with a shoe factory discouraged the full use of the prison, and it soon gained the status of a hospital for the mistfits whose labor the railroad lessees did not desire. In 1883, when 800 of the able-bodied were scattered in camps on six railroad systems and living under such conditions that 100 escaped during the year in spite of the fact that 11 others were shot down in such attempts, the directors were able to congratulate the state that its convicts had earned a surplus of $678 above the combined cost of their keep, the construction work at the prison, and the officers' salaries.

South Carolina made an equally poor start in the development of its penitentiary. A small structure was built and equipped with 200 small cells in the late sixties, but, although nearly half a million had been spent for construction and maintenance before Theodore Parmele took charge in 1875, even the practice of pardoning about 200 a year had not kept the population within the capacity of the prison, and a few had been leased in 1873. Governor Chamberlain attempted to correct this situation by renting a farm for the use of the prisoners, but his successor, Wade Hampton, was pledged to a reduction of state taxes, and Parmele was forced against his protests in 1877 to lease 200 of the able-bodied to railroad and canal companies. Parmele's protests led to his displacement, but his successor continued to complain of the methods of the lessee over whom he had no control. The prison continued to function as an asylum for the young and the infirm, but in other respects the penal system of South as well as North Carolina approximated that of the Lower South by the mid-eighties.

The Virginia and Kentucky prisons, fairly in line with northern penal standards before the war, soon became desperately overcrowded after that conflict and were compelled to adapt many southern traditions to their needs. Responsibility for the introduction of outside labor for Virginia convicts rests with the northern or "restored" government. While struggling to establish order in the war-torn state, this government had been forced to gather large numbers of vagrant Negroes into the penal net, and the state's interests in several railroads prompted the loan of the convicts to help reconstruct their lines. When the legislature began in 1870 to dispose of the state's railroad interests, the authorities continued to loan the convicts to the private companies as a sort of subsidy, even providing guards at state expense, and justified the policy on the ground that the 170 cells at Richmond were inadequate to house the 600-odd state convicts. But the development of a prosperous shoe factory at the prison prompted the concentration of 700 men there in 1876 and the erection of a women's building near enough to the prison to facilitate the use of their labor in the shops. Thus the interests of the prosperous contractor at the prison checked Virginia from turning to the lease system. The legislature in 1889 directed the authorities to lease the surplus prisoners to companies that would pay the entire cost of their maintenance, hoping thus to relieve congestion at the prison, but the contractor had the pick of the lot, and only a few hundred were employed outside during succeeding years.

Lessees continued to manage Kentucky's prison at Frankfort for many years after the war. An increasing population compelled the construction of additional cells in the seventies, but the new total of 700 failed to accommodate the convicts who numbered 1,000 by the end of the decade, while the increase was clogging the narrow confines of the hemp factory. Disturbing rumors of cruelty roused Governor Luke P. Blackburn to cancel the lease and place a warden in full charge at Frankfort and to project a second institution on the Elmira pattern at Eddyville. But as the state was not prepared to operate prison industries, contracts were let for this purpose, one of them to a railroad company permitting the use of 250 men in its construction camps. The railroad soon acquired the other contracts and increased the numbers at its prison camps to 650 by 1885. But this action roused popular indignation, and, when free labor stormed one of the camps and released the convicts, the state was again prompted to assume control. Many were sent to Eddyville to speed construction of the new prison, but the remainder so seriously crowded the old prison that a disastrous uprising among the idle convicts discouraged the state authorities and the prison was again turned over to a lessee in 1889. Not until the second prison was completed in the early nineties did Kentucky finally assume full responsibility for the management of its penal system.

By 1880 all the former Confederate states and Kentucky as well had surrendered a major portion of their criminal populations into the hands of lessees. Alabama and Texas were attempting to supervise the lease camps, while Virginia, Kentucky, and the Carolinas were maintaining prisons for a portion of the prisoners; but in each of these states, and in Missouri as well, the dictates of economy had given rise to a wretched system of penal slavery that was little better than that of the Black Belt. Occasionally the voice of a reformer was heard above the sound of the money-changers, but the taxpayers soon reasserted their interests. Although the most critical years of poverty in the South were over by 1878, the convicts continued to pay retribution, not only for their own sins, at a time when that old principle was losing force in the North, but also for the public crimes of Civil War and reconstruction. Many thousands of happy-go-lucky Negroes awoke from rosy dreams of freedom and forty acres and a mule to find themselves shackled to the task of rebuilding the wealth of the South in hopeless penal slavery.

CONVICT LIFE IN THE SOUTHLAND

Sentimental proposals for the reformation of criminals found little support during the years when the New South was in process of formation. The struggle between the races and the factions was so fierce during the first years that cruel penal conditions could have aroused hardly any surprise. In the eighties George Washington Cable urged that the just treatment of the convicts be recognized as a public responsibility, but, with the public schools and charities making the best of their niggardly support, the criminal could not escape the demand that he at least earn his keep. In place of the religious and educational ideals that were inspiring the development of the adult reformatories in the North, the old slave system was supplying traditions and customs to the penology of the South. Unfortunately the lease camps never saw the development of the paternal-

ism that had been the saving grace of the old plantation system, and
no private-property interest in the life of the laborer safeguarded the
convict from injury. New laws which horrified idealists in the North
gathered the most restless and independent from among the freedmen and gave them hopelessly long sentences. The discipline which
had kept the relatively docile slaves in the fields before the war could
have no effect now; the penal slaves had to be herded about their
camps by armed guards and shackled in the "cribs" at night. The
interests of the lessee in the largest possible return from the least
outlay too frequently determined the policy of the state.

There were no standard living arrangements in the southern prison
camps. Yet one strong factor, the demand for economy, brought
them all practically to a common level—scarcely that of subsistence.
None of the lease camps ever tried to introduce any of the Auburn
traditions, and the penitentiaries that did have individual cells
seldom attempted to apply rules of silence. Wooden huts of one
story usually housed a hundred or more on crude bunks strung
around the walls. The danger of escapes frequently compelled the
authorities to shut these up tight at nightfall, and they soon became
very foul. Water was usually scarce, and bathing almost impossible;
other sanitary arrangements were invariably crude, and disease was
rampant. Food was plentiful or scarce as the economy of the lessee
determined. Heat was usually lacking although rickety stoves or
open fires sometimes added much smoke and a little warmth during
the cold nights of the winter months. The fear of escapes was the
controlling factor in discipline. Various devices for shackling the
feet were tried, and in desperate cases heavy iron balls were added
to the chains. Striped garments were everywhere in use, and the
convicts had no such picayune tastes regarding their footwear as
northern prisoners had; they were glad to get any at all. Tobacco
chewing was everywhere in evidence, but smoking was prohibited
because of the fire risk. Southern newspapers did not cry out, as in
the North, against the hotel accommodations of their prisoners, but
the criminals failed to migrate north.

Religious influences, though not absent, had little effect. It was
difficult to secure white chaplains, and it was out of the question to
hire Negroes. However, plenty of the latter turned up in the camps
by legal proceedings, and these dusky but fluent souls usually prac-

ticed their calling without restraint on the one day of rest. Sunday schools were popular among the prisoners, and occasionally outside workers added to the value of these feeble attempts at regeneration. When the religious forces did bestir themselves, they usually attacked such popular devices of the devil as card-playing. Arkansas passed a law against that vice in 1890, but the warden reported that he found it impossible to stamp out the most popular Sabbath pastime.

Such were the living conditions of the great majority of the southern convicts in the first two decades following the war. Even when Alabama determined to make the lease system as respectable as possible, the model camps constructed at the mines did little more than improve the sanitary and eating arrangements. After fourteen years' experience in charge of convict camps in Florida, Captain J.C.Powell was inspired to compare that system with the horrors of Siberia. If his information was limited to the very worst system of the South, his account certainly depicted villainy that surpassed any responsible picture of the situation in Siberia. Warden Bankhead in Alabama was more to the point when he called on local analogies:[3]

I am prepared to demonstrate that our system is a better training school for criminals than any of the dens of iniquity that exist in our large cities. . . . . The first lesson taught is that the state cares nothing for the criminal, nor his well being. . . . . You may as well expect to instill decent habits into a hog as to reform a criminal whose habits and surroundings are as filthy as a pig's. To say there are any reformatory measures at our prison, or that any regard is had to similar subjects, is to state a falsehood.

Death or escape were the only quick methods of relief available to the convicts. Before the lease system was well established, and where the convicts were let out to numerous lessees, escapes were very frequent. Both the concentration of the convicts into the hands of one lessee and the demand that the guards be held responsible for the escape of men under their supervision were measures taken to check the evil. Yet as late as 1882 a survey of the reports revealed that a total of 1,100 men had made successful breaks for freedom in the two previous years in southern states, in contrast with sixty-three escapes from among 18,300 northern convicts in one year. A similar study of convict mortality revealed that, while the average death-

[3] Alabama Penitentiary Inspectors, *Report* (1882), p. 15.

rate of twenty-eight northern prisons was 14.9 per thousand, the average in the South was 41.3 per thousand.[4] The appalling conditions which these statistics reveal were partly the cause and partly the result of the brutal practices of the lease system.

Southern discipline was not complicated by elaborate schemes for reformation. Cable described it as "such as provides for efficiency in labor, and against insurrection and escape." No rules of silence gave occasion for petty punishments as in the North; in fact, there were no written rules of any sort in many cases where complete control was intrusted to the lessee. Punishments were usually administered with the lash or the strap, but ingenious guards sometimes devised special forms of torture, such as the notorious "watering" penalty in Florida, during which a convict would be stretched on his back and a stream of water poured into his mouth until he was nearly drowned.[5] Alabama and Texas were the only states to regulate punishments by law during the period; elsewhere the only check was the interest of the lessee in seeing that punishments did not impair his labor force.

The chief reliance for security was on the chains, the dogs, and the armed guards. In the early days guards did not always shoot at escaping prisoners. Fines were accordingly assessed on the lessee for every escape, and the guard's job was made to depend on his vigilance. Scores of fugitives were shot down every year in some of the states, and yet, with conditions as they were, desperate men were always ready on the slightest occasion to "hang it on a limb" in the hope of freedom.

Cruel as was the fate of the convicts, southern courts showed no sentimental hesitancy in meting out the full penalty of the law. There were no habitual-criminal laws here; none were needed. Massachusetts courts might consider a twenty-year sentence for a third felony too harsh to be applied, but out of 1,200 convicts in Georgia in 1880 only 150 had terms as short as three years, and over 500 had terms of ten years or more. Everywhere in the South sentences were unreasonably long, and the Negroes got more than their just share. The social hatreds engendered by years of strife were still rampant, and it continued to appear a social good to take idlers

[4] George W. Cable, "The Convict Lease System," *The Silent South* (New York, 1885).

[5] J. C. Powell, *The American Siberia* (Philadelphia, 1891).

off to construction camps long after the notorious vagrancy laws were forgotten. There was no check, as in the North, where cells rapidly became crowded and compelled the construction of costly bastilles if convictions were too frequent. There were, in fact, no saving circumstances to protect the unfortunate southern convict from hopeless oblivion until the first era of large-scale construction came to a close in the early nineties.

Even more than in the North the great majority of the prisoners remained under the control of the counties. These authorities had no more adequate housing equipments than the states when the new constitutions abolished branding, whipping, and the stocks in favor of fines and imprisonment. While the states were experimenting with their leasing systems, the county sheriffs showed no lack of initiative in making use of their new labor forces.

The many responsibilities of southern counties provided them with ample use for cheap labor. The employment of convicts in cleaning the streets was introduced by many cities at the close of the war, but the construction and repair of rural wagon roads soon became the chief task for such labor. Counties in the North as well as in the South had experimented with road labor from early times, but it did not become a regular activity until the reconstruction days in the South. Carroll D. Wright found county convicts laboring on the public roads in eight southern states in 1886. Even West Virginia, striving to develop a northern penitentiary system, permitted its counties to labor 25 per cent of its total criminal population on the roads in that year.

There was seldom any clear distinction in southern law between state and county offenders. Judges usually had the discretion of committing their prisoners to the state prison or to the county chain gang, although North Carolina and a few other states limited the county sentences to ten years. The arrangement usually worked to the advantage of the counties, for in districts failing to make profitable use of this labor supply the judges handed the great majority over to the state; but when a sheriff was building roads or leasing the men to advantage, the courts kept the able-bodied at home and sent only the aged and infirm to the state prison. The state authorities, eager to meet the largest demands of their lessees, made frequent protests, but little was done until the states themselves began to take over the responsibility of road construction at a later date.

Such rivalry sometimes called forth damning indictments of the county systems. As county camps were less permanent or substantial than those of the state and as the authorities were, if possible, less responsible, the conditions were much more wretched. Many of the sheriffs, rather than superintend the labor themselves, leased their charges to private companies to work the roads, drain swamps, operate lumber camps, or perform other local functions for which free labor could not be readily secured. There was no adequate state regulation or inspection and seldom any responsible local supervision, and the scanty records at the court houses considered only the financial accounts, the convictions, escapes, deaths, and discharges. Again chains, dogs, and guns were the chief means of preserving public security, while the interests of the convicts were disregarded. The evils of this system joined with those of the state leases to supply arguments to the tardy agitators for reform in the late eighties.

NEW INFLUENCES IN THE NINETIES

After two decades of reconstruction the South began to develop a new sense of proportion. The common man with the aid of his various Populist organizations was crowding the old gentry out of politics, and, as long as the Negro accepted the inferior status to which he had been reduced, the common man in politics was willing to consider his welfare, even the welfare of those convicted of crime. But the lease system was doomed by its decreasing usefulness to the state rather than by the growth of a strong humanitarianism, and it was not abandoned until profitable substitutes were perfected. First the women, the children, and the sick were moved into separate quarters; then experiments with plantations, industrial prisons, and road camps supplied promising patterns for a new southern penal system by the close of the century.

Humanitarian and economic interests joined to intercede in behalf of the women and the boys in the later eighties. The North had made the care of juvenile delinquents a charity distinct from the penal system before the war, and the segregation of the sexes had been accepted as a principle since the days of Louis Dwight, but the South had largely escaped these problems until Negro women and boys began to appear in large numbers in the criminal line-up after the war. The slave traditions of the lease system recognized no distinctions until the practice of dividing the convicts into "full-hands," "half-hands," and "dead-hands" revealed the advantage of separate treatment for the women and the boys. Attention was at last given to the recommendations of the charitable-minded that special farms be provided by the state where these classes could earn their keep free from evil influences. Few lessees were willing to take such "dead-hands" and left them to clog the prisons. Texas, North Carolina, and Virginia, whose prisons were becoming centers of industrial activity, were the first to provide asylum farms, and Alabama soon followed their example. The interests of the Populists in the practical education of the "forgotten man" strengthened the movement, and by the close of the century only Tennessee and Louisiana had failed to provide for the removal of at least a portion of the women, the children, and the sick from the mass of the prisoners.

These experiments with small penal farms came at an opportune time for southern penology. The new political leaders were anything but partial to the large leasing companies whose political ties were usually attached to their predecessors. Sharp bargains pressed many of the lessees to the wall just as the railroad boom on which they had depended was drawing to a close. Long contracts and new opportunities in mines and swamps preserved the lessees of the southeastern states, although more abundant returns were gradually extracted from them and more careful regulations enforced, but elsewhere the lease system was gradually replaced.

The first extensive use of adult prisoners on large farms and plantations occurred in the southwestern states of this period. In Texas the criminal population was expanding rapidly beyond the capacity of the two state prisons and beyond the demands of the construction lessees, prompting the authorities in the mid-eighties to experiment with share-crop farming. By 1888 one-third of the 3,000 state prisoners were employed in this fashion on private farms, and the state was itself organizing the work on the newly purchased 2,700-acre Harlem farm. Texas continued to enlarge its penal plantations by a gradual acquisition of scattered farms, but Mississippi made a bold and complete shift to the new system. The people of the state, discouraged by the failure of the authorities to collect profits from the lessee, adopted a constitutional provision ordering the termination of all leases by 1895. Accordingly the authorities, after experimenting for a few years with share-crop farming, purchased the 15,000-acre Sunflower plantation and developed on it the model penal system of the South. Only Louisiana adopted this program wholeheartedly before the end of the decade, but most of the other southern states made farming an important accessory to their other penal activities, much as several northern states were to do a decade or so later. At the turn of the century the penal plantation appeared to be the ideal goal for southern penology.

A considerable number of northern traditions crossed the border and traveled down the Mississippi Valley in these last years of the century; unfortunately in penological matters they were chiefly the cast-off techniques of a former era. Thus the contract labor system, in the years of its expulsion from several northern prisons, received a ready welcome in the prisons of Kentucky and Tennessee and was given more intensive application in those of Virginia and Missouri. When Kentucky opened its branch prison at Eddyville in 1890, state officers took full charge at both prisons, terminating the long leasing tradition, but the original intention to make Eddyville a reformatory was forgotten, and contractors were brought in to make an active industrial program the main feature of both prisons. Similarly in Tennessee, labor and Populist agitation persuaded the legislature to abolish the old lease under which the Tennessee Iron and Coal Railway had used convicts to break strikes in its mines; the state replaced its old prison with a new one on a large plantation near Nashville, and completed its equipment of 800 cells, each 8 by 6 and 8 feet high, in 1898; but in the meantime temporary log dormitories had been erected on public coal lands at Brushy Mountain, and the major portion of the convict population continued to labor under the contractors who operated these mines for the state. The state profits from these activities were rivaled only in the other border states—Virginia, Maryland, Missouri, and Kansas.

The only genuine intrusion of current penological theory from the North occurred in New Orleans. A prominent resident of that city, Michael Heymann, had been thrown into close association with Frederick Howard Wines at the World's Fair in Chicago, and returned to New Orleans determined to organize a prison society to fight for the adoption of reformatory penology. Heymann's society succeeded in persuading the state constitutional convention, then in session, to incorporate progressive principles into its clauses providing for the abolition of the lease system, but even the assistance of a special visit from the National Prison Association failed to induce the legislature to follow up these northern leads. Lousiana rejected reformatory penology in favor of the new southern pattern evolved in Mississippi, and ten thousand acres of good land were purchased in the Angola and Hope farms to replace her abandoned lease.

But the increase of state control represented by these shifts to plantation and industrial prisons and the improved supervision of the lessees in the other states was counteracted in many localities by an increased use of the convicts on county roads. Farmers in politics were partial to this use of convict labor, and the uncertain distinction between county and state offenders permitted the courts, especially in Georgia, Alabama, and the Carolinas, to sentence an increasing proportion of the able-bodied to hard labor on the local roads. No supervision was provided, and the chain gangs on the roads, lodged in boxcar cages and surrounded by dogs and armed guards, became a notorious symbol of southern justice—a greedy heir to the technique of the lease system it helped to displace. The widely boasted reduction in the death rate of southern convicts did not take these county chain gangs into consideration, and indeed for a time their fate was entirely overlooked by the state authorities.

Thus by 1900 all the penal programs that were eventually to replace the lease system were in active operation in the South. The prospect, in spite of its darker aspects, was the most encouraging the section had envisaged or was to enjoy down to our day. But there was a total absence of men studying the problem in any thorough fashion, and there was almost as great a dearth of public-spirited citizens organized to safeguard the interests of prisoners. Public authorities never for a moment slaked their thirst for profits from convict labor, and the first three decades of the twentieth century were to witness public greed defeat the hopes of the late nineties. The penal systems, whether centering around plantations as in the southwestern part of the section, specializing in road labor as in the southeastern states, or developing contract industries as in the border states, remained strangely isolated from the vital influences active in northern penology.

BIBLIOGRAPHICAL NOTE

The printed documents of the states contain but few reports by the lessees, and, except where wardens or superintendents were appointed, the student is forced to rely on the brief comments on penal affairs in the governors' messages. The development of state control or supervision in the eighties and nineties brought with it regular official reports, usually of a statistical nature. Special legislative committees or special messages from the governor, at times when one lease was being discarded or other revision made, supply fuller detail. This situation renders the occasional address on southern conditions before the National Prison Association of great value, and the address of G. W. Cable, "The Convict Lease System," delivered before the National Conference of Charities in 1883 and reprinted in his *The Silent South* (New York, 1895), is indispensable to the student. Frances A. Kellor, *Experimental Sociology, Delinquents* (New York, 1901), is of similar value for a study of conditions in the nineties.

Volumes of special interest are: F. W. Hoffer, D. M. Mann, and F. N. House, *The Jails of Virginia* (New York, 1933); Collins Lovely, *The Abuses of Prison Labor* (1905); A. D. Oliphant, *The Evolution of the Penal System in South Carolina* (Columbia, 1916); J. C. Powell, *The American Siberia* (Philadelphia, 1891); L. V. Rule, *The City of Dead Souls* (Louisville, 1920); J. F. Steiner and R. M. Brown, *The North Carolina Chain Gang* (Chapel Hill, 1927); Elizabeth Wisner, *Public Welfare Administration in Louisiana* (Chicago, 1930).

CHAPTER IX

PENOLOGY IN THE WESTWARD MOVEMENT[1]

The Great West was the third fairly distinct section of America during the last half of the nineteenth century. The normal advance of the frontier had come to a halt at the edge of the plains, and the building of states on the Pacific coast and in the vast mountain areas was in many respects a new phase of American development. The settlers brought a large heritage of eastern culture with them, but the barrier of plains and mountains severed many of the connecting links that might have kept them in touch with new developments in the East, and they quickly revealed an easy freedom from older traditions. This freedom was particularly evident in the case of penal institutions, for neither the traditions of Louis Dwight nor the programs of Enoch Wines influenced these territories and states during their formative years. Indeed, the frolicsome cowboys and carousing miners who enjoyed their practical jokes at the expense of zealous missionaries and energetic drummers would have doubled up in boisterous laughter if a kindly spirited Easterner had appeared to urge the reformation of cattle thieves and highwaymen. The surprising fact was the speed with which these scattered settlers built their homes, schools, churches, and finally their prisons, universities, and asylums.

Thus the establishment of prisons in the Great West was a phase of the institutional conquest of the last frontier. A rough-and-ready, oftentimes desperate struggle to curb lawlessness determined the character of the early instruments of justice. The federal government, holding the territories in tutelage, was quite innocent of penal experience, and many of the officers sent west to administer its functions were political adventurers, frequently described in the territories as "carpetbaggers." Prison techniques and patterns were imported, but unfortunately the channels of influence, whether by way

[1] The author is grateful to the publishers of the *Pacific Historical Review* for permission to use portions of his article under this title published in the December, 1933, number of the *Review*.

of California or the Missouri Valley, were dominated by several of the worst prison structures in the country. Thus, as thick patches of population crept up the valleys, through the passes, and along the railroads during the last quarter of the century, permanent prisons were erected, but, except in a few cases, they were not brought into line with northeastern developments until the opening of the next century.

Unsolved problems of convict employment were major causes for the unsatisfactory conditions of western prisons. The federal anti-contract law of 1887 combined with a scarcity of local industry suitable for prisons to keep most of the convicts in idleness, thus creating a disciplinary problem that made the application of the Auburn discipline impossible. Only in the few states where an adequate industrial program was devised and where the creation of boards of charities provided leadership did a stable penal system emerge during this era.

PRISON DEVELOPMENTS IN CALIFORNIA

California, the outstanding state of the Far West, was beset by major criminal problems from the start. El Dorado of the world's adventurers, its population of 90,000 in 1850 grew tenfold by 1880, ranking it on a level with Minnesota and Kansas, but the criminals increased at an even greater rate. The old Spanish jails had become inadequate during the first turbulent prospector days, and when the San Francisco Committee of Vigilance rallied the people to the support of law and order, the legislature voted to build a penitentiary. Following frontier traditions, that task, together with the care of the convicts, was committed into the hands of a lessee. A site was selected near some clay pits on Point San Quentin, and buildings were erected and fitted with forty-eight cells and several small rooms for the accommodation of the convicts. By 1855 these quarters were crowded with over three hundred men, and reports of the large numbers of deaths and escapes and the reckless practices of armed guards prompted the state to assume control. Although a political shift turned the prison back to the lessee in the next year, continued corruption forced the state to reassert its control finally in 1858; but California's penal problems were just beginning.

Eastern traditions gained some recognition from the new authorities. The governor, lieutenant-governor, and secretary of state were constituted a board of directors; a warden was appointed and contractors were brought in to run the industries. In order to relieve congestion a contract was signed with the Natoma Company to supply convicts for the construction of its dam and canal at Folsom in return for the erection there of a second prison on the Auburn pattern. As this did not meet the needs of the prisoners at San Quentin, two cell houses were erected, adding 396 cells, each $6\frac{1}{2}$ by 4 and 8 feet high, but the population increased to 900 by 1873, a year after these were completed. Meanwhile the Rev. James Woodwurth, recently of New England, had organized a prison association and memorialized the legislature condemning the lax discipline, the corruption and the congestion permitted at San Quentin, but the authorities were content to appoint a moral instructor to organize a reading school for the young boys in the prison, and the other problems were left unsolved. The influence of eastern ideas increased considerably toward the end of the seventies, largely because of the development in California of the same conditions that had favored the success of these ideas in the East. A strong workingmen's party, outgrowth of the fight for the exclusion of Chinese labor, readily undertook the closely analogous campaign against penal contracts. The labor party upset the political equilibrium, and the opportune gathering of a consitutional convention in 1880 enabled them to secure the adoption of a constitutional provision against future contracts, excluding from the prisons all industries that competed with free labor in the state. The close political rivalry between the parties further encouraged the convention to seek a new basis for prison management. The report of Wines and Dwight had found its way into the hands of some of the delegates, and the convention was finally persuaded to adopt the rejected New York amendment providing for a long-term, nonpolitical board of managers.

But the politicians intrusted with the task of dividing the cards could not resist the temptation to favor their own hands. The Republicans, who had been able to oust the Democrats because of the presence of the labor party, proceeded to man the entire prison system with their henchmen. The new board of managers sent one of their number to visit the better prisons of the East and proceeded to formulate an advanced program in several respects, but this show of righteousness failed to appease the ousted Democrats. When the labor forces discovered that the contracts were quietly being continued, they joined with the Democrats to drive the Republicans from control. Two investigating commissions—one appointed by the Republican governor in an attempt to head off the opposition, and the other by the legislature when the Democrats regained control—made careful studies of the situation and roundly condemned the political affiliations of the board of managers. The governor's commission did not hesitate to brand the existing prisons as among the worst "colleges of crime" in the country. The commission created by the legislature was bipartisan and, when its report recommended the removal of the board of managers, the legislature readily determined to name the commission members as the new board. Democratic officers were soon installed at San Quentin, but the Republicans were left in charge at Folsom. Thus by the mid-eighties California achieved a system of bipartisan control, and, since the managers were acquainted with the most advanced theories of the day, the prospect for enlightened developments was encouraging.

The labor problems were the first to demand attention. In spite of the constitutional provision prison industries were continued under piece-price arrangements until the Federated Trades Council forced the complete abandonment of the system in 1889. A jute factory, started a decade earlier with state funds, was enlarged and made the center of a new industrial activity. There were no local competitors to oppose this industry, and the increasing demand of the farmers for burlap sacking assured the prison officials of a prosperous market. Meanwhile the convicts at Folsom labored under the old arrangement with the Natoma Company until its dam and canal were completed in 1892. The contract had pledged the company to supply the prison with power for its industrial establishments, but the location of the prison combined with the labor laws to block the development of industries. Aside from those engaged in construction work and the few employed at stone-crushing, the majority of the men here were confined in idleness until the development of highway construction in the next era provided increased demand for crushed stone.

California made considerable advance in line with eastern trends in management and industry, but here the development stopped.

The bipartisan managers failed to show the expected zeal for the solution of other problems, but it was not entirely their fault, since their frequent recommendations received scanty attention from the legislature. The fact was that no strong local interests concerned themselves with housing or other problems, as had been the case in respect to labor and management. There were no public-spirited organizations to rally popular sentiments in behalf of the reformation of the criminals.

California's worst failure was in the matter of prison accommodations. With a generous allowance for doubling-up, the authorities at San Quentin were able to report a capacity of 700, and 413 cells were provided at Folsom; but the total convict population hovered around 2,000 during the nineties, and appeals for new cells were disregarded. Statistics fail to tell the complete story, for California was gathering a much larger portion of its lesser offenders into these "colleges of crime" than was the custom in the East. Few attempts were made at intramural classification, and the suggestion that Folsom be converted into a reformatory was soon forgotten. No pretense was made of enforcing the restraints of the Auburn tradition, and no other system of correctional discipline was applied in its stead, with the result that these prisons, especially when employment was slack, became great seminars in vice and crime.

Fortunately the strength of the campaign for public education helped to bring tardy success to the agitation for a reform school. The boys' department at San Quentin, started in 1875 under the supervision of the chaplain, had been gradually disbanded as the officers became convinced of its futility. The legislature was finally persuaded in 1888 to provide for the construction of the Preston School of Industry for Boys at Ione, but it was several years before the first boys were moved there from the prison. But Preston and Whittaker, opened in 1899, were reform schools, and, when they became well established and provided a progressive curriculum in the first decade of the next century, the demand for a young men's reformatory was still unanswered.

The managers had evidently arrived at their final conclusions on penal problems at the time of their comprehensive investigation of their predecessors in the early eighties. About the only additional innovation they sponsored was the Bertillon system of identification, which was adopted in 1890 at the time of its high favor with eastern wardens. When the legislature in 1893 granted the managers limited powers of conditional discharge, these officials, having studied the problem when "tickets of leave" were still considered impracticable, declined to exercise their new powers. California, however, was facing some fairly unique criminal problems; not only was its convict population disproportionately large, but its prisons were the first to be seriously troubled by the opium traffic. The last decades of the century saw this problem attain major importance at San Quentin, and M. G. Aguirre, the new warden in 1899, was to make a considerable reputation as a prison reformer as a result of his vigorous efforts to stamp out this vice.

PRISONS IN THE NORTHWESTERN STATES

The half-dozen more or less thriving settlements in the Northwest revealed the wide assortment of influences that stem on the frontier. The first three to attain statehood contrasted in almost every respect except in their failure to develop satisfactory prisons. Nebraska, the most accessible and most populous of the group, quickly forgot the idealism of its early days when a succession of droughts and pests brought defeat and disillusionment. The trail to Oregon witnessed a motley rush of home-seekers to that distant settlement, providing the state with ninety thousand people by 1870, but in the confusion all distinctive penal traditions were lost by the way. Nevada in her boom days was prompted to undertake an ambitious penal program, but the quick disillusionment concerning the state's future relegated this program together with many other rosy dreams to the scrap heap. Colorado, Utah, and the Dakotas were more successful in developing stable penal institutions and in maintaining connections with eastern movements, although the size of the problem in Colorado made the struggle a most difficult one.

Nebraska in the early days had close ties with the Northeast, and the agitation of Enoch Wines readily attracted attention. In the early seventies a state penitentiary was established at Lancaster, and under the management of the board of public lands and buildings a 400-cell prison on the Auburn pattern was slowly erected, with the cell capacity always ahead of the requirements of the population. Unfortunately hard times diverted attention to more personal problems, and few protests were heard in 1877 when the authorities leased the prison in accordance with the old frontier tradition established by Kentucky. A warden was still nominally in charge of discipline, but, as he was forced to rely on the guards supplied by the lessee, this lone representative of the state had little real authority. When the first ten-year lease expired, a second was issued to an individual who was shortly lodged behind the bars of his own prison, then under the management of his assignees. Criticism of the situation was brought to a head in 1892 by the death of a feeble-minded inmate as a result of brutal punishment at the hands of the guards. A legislative investigation revealed shocking conditions, including the total neglect of sanitation, the improper association of women and boys as well as the insane with the rest of the population, and the use of physical torture as a penalty for failure to complete the labor tasks.

It was not so easy to correct as to condemn these evils. Two years passed before the state was able to buy out the rights of the lessee, and then the board of public lands was only prevented from contracting a new lease by the intervention of the governor through the courts. When the warden was finally secure in his control, contractors were brought in to operate the industries, and the authorities rejoiced that the prisoners were at last earning a part of their cost to the state, for the fees required of the state under the terms of the lease had added weight to the demands of the reformers. In the mist of the discussion of penal affairs in 1893 the legislature adopted a parole law, and the governor, upon whom the parole authority had been conferred, was able to work in co-operation with the warden after 1895 not only in selecting worthy parolees but in developing a better discipline within the prison. The governors, however, were busy men, and these first happy results did not continue for long. On the other hand, the wretched conditions in the old cell house remained until fire destroyed the entire structure in 1901, compelling the state to make a fresh start in penitentiary matters.

Oregon had a longer but hardly more satisfactory experience with prisons. The territory had erected a log structure in the early fifties, but rumors of corruption soon involved the officers in charge, and the legislature leased the prison to a private company. Shortly after statehood was acquired, this system was discontinued, and the governor became ex officio warden. The federal government granted the state ten sections of the public domain to aid in the development of public institutions, and when in 1871 Salem was finally chosen as the permanent site for the prison, a stone structure was erected there on the Auburn pattern. As late as 1888 H. H. Bancroft, the historian, was able to speak of the Salem prison as "the present fine structure," but it failed to maintain that reputation, and ten years later its superintendent, after a visit through the Northwest, pronounced the prison "the worst in seven states." An unsolved labor problem was the cause for the institution's decline. The state had become jealous of its expenditures, and the authorities did not seem able to earn their expenses from the labor of their charges. The booming success of the jute mill at San Quentin prompted a poorly planned experiment with this industry at Salem. Discouraged by repeated failures which threatened his political career, the governor in 1895 turned the entire responsibility over to a lessee. Protests were numerous, but practically the only improvement made before the end of the century was the removal of the juveniles to a farm several miles distant from the prison and the gradual establishment there of a reform school.

During boom days in Nevada great plans were prepared for the state institutions. The log structure erected as a territorial prison fortunately burned to the ground shortly after statehood was acquired, and the warden employed the convicts at the construction of a stone prison with 43 cells, each 8 by $4\frac{1}{2}$ and 8 feet high. But the state was thronging with desperadoes, and overcrowding forced the authorities in 1874 to plan the construction of an ambitious penitentiary on the Joliet pattern at Reno in the eastern part of the state. But Nevada boosters had overshot their mark, and the population of the prison as well as that of the state declined rapidly. Construction at Reno was halted and so rapid was the decline of the population that the old prison at Carson City soon found its accommodations practically equal to the state's needs. But the spirit was taken out of the reform element. The shoe industry provided in the seventies was abandoned, and stone-quarrying became the sole occupation, with a very dull market for its product. This activity, nevertheless, saved the day in a most unusual way; some prehistoric tracks were uncovered in the quarry, attracting thousands of visitors whose fees supported a library and a chaplain and whose presence dispelled the atmosphere of stagnation that had threatened to settle upon the institution. The warden, meanwhile, was elected by the legislature, and so important was this political plum that one man had to be removed from the post by force of arms, while another more influential politician held the titles of warden, governor, and warden successively. Nevada had not solved its penal problem, but depopulation had practically eliminated it.

Meanwhile several other settlements in the Northwest were making more creditable penal developments. The hard-times of the late seventies did not blight the development of Colorado, Utah, and the Dakotas, as had been the case in Nebraska, and fertile lands supplied a basis for permanent growth after the mining rush had spent its force. The channels of eastern influence were kept open, and before the end of the century these states were taking an active part in the National Prison Association congresses.

Colorado voted to erect a prison ten years before it attained statehood, and, although the federal authorities took charge of construction, the state thus inherited a prison equipped with 90 cells when it joined the Union in 1876. As the convicts already exceeded the capacity, new cell houses were erected on the Auburn pattern, increasing the equipment to 444 cells by the end of the century. A contractor was engaged to develop a shoe factory; rules of silence were adopted; a chaplain was appointed; and a library and school classes were organized, as Colorado attempted to match the penal standards of the East. But the problems increased too rapidly for the authorities, partially because the instable political situation in the state shifted the prison back and forth under a rapid succession of political appointees, and partially because of the desperate economic problems of the early nineties. Organized labor persuaded the legislature in 1890 to copy New York's model anti-contract law of 1888, but no provision was made for the development of state-account industries. The prison authorities soon found that the small amount of quarrying possible on the twenty-five-acre prison lot at Canon City was entirely insufficient. Experiments with the labor of convicts in small gangs on the roads near the prison and on a state irrigation canal had to be abandoned when the public protested against the use of armed guards to check escapes. The continued growth of the population had persistently exceeded the cell capacity and reached 600 by the end of the period, thus considerably aggravating the problems of idleness and discipline.

The disturbing influences of political instability were partially offset when Colorado organized a state board of charities in 1891. The board was soon advocating several of the better ideas of the East. The legislature was persuaded to give this board the authority to release prisoners on parole, and a grading system was introduced at the prison to facilitate the selection of parolees. The industrial school for delinquent boys, previously established at Golden, was developed into one of the best institutions of its kind in the West, and now, although funds were not available for permanent construction, the board persuaded the state in 1892 to open its reformatory for young men at Buena Vista in temporary buildings. When Colorado entertained the National Prison Association on its first visit to the mountain states in 1895, its leaders were able to boast not only the first adult reformatory and the first board of charities, but also the only separate building for women, the only effective parole law, and the only genuine grading system west of Kansas. The legislature was shortly to take a lead over most eastern states as well by adopting a mandatory indeterminate-sentence law applicable to all but a few exceptional offenses.

During Utah's long apprenticeship the prison was one of many points of friction between Mormon and federal authorities. In the early days the thrifty Mormons had farmed out their occasional criminals to enterprising individuals. Several of the convicts were not members of the church, and, when the federal authorities took control over the settlement, the marshal demanded that all prisoners be turned over to his care. For a time the Mormons bitterly contested this claim of jurisdiction, but the erection by the federal authorities of a fine prison with 224 cells at Salt Lake City brought them to terms. When statehood was finally granted in 1896, Utah inherited this fully ample prison and made immediate efforts to develop a stable and progressive system. A board of corrections was placed in control with full powers of parole, and under its direction a grading system was developed on the Elmira pattern. A library and school were provided, and diversified industries were organized to produce for state use and to provide trade instruction. A cotton-sock factory was developed into a profitable concern, since it enjoyed a large market with no competitor within the state to raise objections. Considering in addition the excellent reform school founded at Ogden in 1889, the Mormons were justly credited by eastern critics with a successful demonstration of their capacity for statehood.

The Dakotas, enjoying a freer hand in the development of their territorial institutions, were ready for statehood when the Republican victory cleared the way to that goal in 1889. South Dakota's delegate, already in attendance at the prison congress, could boast of a complete array of state institutions in full operation, and the state hastened to create a board of charities and to endow it with powers of control. The 128 fair-sized cells at Sioux Falls were more than adequate for the small demands of this orderly community, and the prisoners found employment at a stone quarry and on the eighty-acre farm attached to the prison. A parole law was adopted in 1890 but repealed two years later, and the reformers could not secure its readoption or the introduction of grades at the prison until the early years of the next century. But the reform school at Plankington was successfully maintained, and, when at the close of the era the population at the prison finally approached the capacity, plans were projected for expansion.

North Dakota in like fashion enjoyed a slow but well-considered development. The 160-cell prison at Bismarck proved adequate throughout the period, and this circumstance may have helped to discourage the use of the parole law adopted in 1891. A harness factory, operated with the aid of a contractor, was closed by an anti-contract law in 1897, but labor on the new capitol building, on the 800-acre farm leased by the state, and at a state brickyard supplied employment during the summer months, and preparations were made for the introduction of a twine factory at state account, following Minnesota's successful experiment with that industry. No reform school was provided at this time, but the state lodged its occasional juvenile delinquents at Plankington in South Dakota. Successive governors gave close attention to penal and charitable problems, enabling the state to handle these affairs quite successfully during its first decade of self-government without the aid of a board of charities.

MAKESHIFT PENOLOGY IN THE TERRITORIES

The remainder of the West retained its great open spaces throughout the century. The era of the frontier was officially closed by 1890,
and the national Republicans hastily carved four additional states
out of the northern territories to buttress their power at Washington, but it was some time before respectable northeastern traditions
were able to dominate the institutional life of these sparsely settled
communities. The example and patterns of Missouri, Kansas, and
Nebraska on one side and those of California and Texas in other directions conflicted with those of Colorado and the Northeast, while
local exigencies played the part of arbiter. Everywhere a makeshift
penology held sway.

The federal government had the opportunity to supply leadership
but was ill-fitted for the task. The only federal measure that exerted a controlling influence was the anti-contract law of 1887, secured by eastern labor in its own interests. This law, by restricting
the employment of federal prisoners, checked the federal marshals
in charge of most of the territorial prisons from developing industrial activities. Anti-contract restrictions found their way into most
of the constitutions hopefully put forward by the territories when
seeking statehood, and few of the prisons in these later mountain
settlements provided any regular employment until after the turn
of the century. Over against the questionable value of this influence
stood the federal government's liberal land donations which considerably aided most of these states in erecting public institutions.

Washington and Montana experienced many trials with their
convicts before they took their places on the omnibus bill of 1889.
Washington Territory leased its prisoners in 1877 to a mill owner in
Seatco who made the best of their labor during the day and herded
them through a trapdoor into a log pit to spend the nights in mutual
corruption and suffocation. This structure was possibly the worst
prison in America since the closing of Connecticut's old copper mine
nearly a century before. The federal authorities built a prison on
McNeil Island and offered to take the territorial convicts as lodgers,
but the lessee was sufficiently influential to retain his profitable labor
force until the territory erected a new prison at Walla Walla in 1886.
The cell-block arrangement of the new prison represented the first
triumph of northeastern traditions, but anti-contract laws discouraged the development of industries, and the inexperienced officers

were unable to apply any but the crudest of disciplinary regulations to their idle prisoners. The attainment of statehood brought little change, although a reform school was provided for the juveniles in 1891. The prison officers made one attempt to introduce the jute industry, but, as in Oregon, the legislature failed to appropriate sufficient funds, and the experiment had to be discontinued. It was not until the turn of the century that the adoption of a parole law, the creation of a board of control, and the development of industrial activity promised better conditions for the convicts.

Montana shifted along with a small prison erected by federal authorities in 1874 at Deer Lodge. The federal marshal in charge was soon forced to crowd three men into each cell, and, although additional cells were provided, the crowded condition remained when the state inherited the prison in 1889. The new authorities quickly leased their unwonted responsibility, agreeing to pay forty cents a day for the keep of each prisoner. The constitution prohibited contract labor, making it illegal for the lessee to develop any industries, and the resulting idleness rendered it impossible to enforce the rules of silence in the overcrowded institution. Liberal land grants enabled the state to establish a reform school in 1895, and plans were projected for a new state prison at Billings in the eastern part of the state. The lessee, however, was able to persuade the state to build its new prison at Deer Lodge, and 288 fine cells were erected there, thus providing some occupation for the convicts at the old prison. A board of charities, organized in 1899, found the prison still in the hands of the lessee, seriously overcrowded, and devoid of any regular system of labor or discipline; and thus it remained for another decade.

Wyoming made even more diverse makeshifts before achieving a stable penal system. In the early seventies the federal authorities erected a wooden prison at Laramie but excessively high charges roused criticism. The territorial legislature was advised of better terms at the Nebraska state prison, and there the convicts were sent. A still better bargain was soon made with Joliet, and during the mid-eighties the large majority of Wyoming's criminals were delivered to this greatly overcrowded penitentiary where they earned their keep by hard labor. The sheriffs, meanwhile, were growing fat on the fees allowed for transporting these prisoners, and the territory finally determined to build its own prison at Rawlings. In 1891 Wyoming attained statehood and inherited the prison at Laramie, but, like Montana, she leased the entire institution to a private party, reserving only the right to appoint the warden. This compromise was of little advantage since it proved impossible to find an able man willing to stick to the job; indeed, for some time there was an average of more than one warden a year. Plans for the new prison had meanwhile prospered, and by 1897 an Auburn structure with 234 cells was completed at Rawlins. A dispute with the lessee delayed occupation until, in 1901, the state reluctantly permitted the lessee to take charge at Rawlins for the balance of his unexpired term. An adequate prison was about all that Wyoming could boast, but that was not so bad for the first decade of the smallest state of the Union.

The territory of Idaho was forced to content itself with the small federal prison. The legislature complained against the charge of seventy-five cents a day for each prisoner, and no wonder, since it required one-third of the taxes to support the convicts. As no alternative presented itself, idle convicts soon crowded the forty-two stone cells, and the construction of an equal number of steel cells in 1890 brought only temporary relief. When Idaho inherited the prison, full control was given to the warden, but unfortunately ten men succeeded one another in this office in as many years, and discipline remained chaotic. A Chautauqua reading circle, organized in 1887, provided some diversion for favored prisoners, but the majority, except for a three-hour drill in the prison yard under armed guard, remained idle in their locked cells day and night. Affairs took a turn for the better in 1900 when the population again threatened to crowd more than two into each cell; funds were provided and the convicts were set at the task of building a new cell house. At the same time a parole law was adopted and a grading system introduced —happy omens for a new era.

Three southern territories remained under federal tutelage throughout this period, but that government took no effective steps to build their prisons. New Mexico contented herself for a time with the old Spanish jails, but in 1884 the legislature voted to erect both a capitol and prison, anticipating a statehood that did not materialize for nearly two decades. No pretense was made at the Santa Fe prison, or at the Yuma prison in Arizona, of providing a cell for each man; in fact, the cells at Yuma were built to accommodate four inmates, and six were usually crowded into them. No industries were introduced into either of these prisons, and the convicts whittled away their time making trinkets to sell to visitors. Arizona created a board of control in 1896, empowered to supervise the labor of convicts outside the walls, and a partial lease system resulted, helping to relieve the prison congestion but introducing methods that were already being discarded in most of the southeastern states. Religion was the only reformatory influence in either of these prisons, and there was not much of that. The wardenship was one of the few lucrative posts open to local politicians, and it was greatly sought after by men hoping to be in the lineup when statehood was attained. Wretched penal conditions likewise remained on the waiting list.

Oklahoma, on the other hand, shirked its penal responsibilities entirely. Its criminals, who multiplied even more rapidly than its citizen body, were packed off, young and old alike, to the penitentiary in Kansas, where they were jammed into overcrowded cells and left to learn the folly of their ways while digging coal in the mine pits. Oklahoma, scene of the last land rush, had not yet sobered down, and another decade was to pass before she fully accepted the obligations of a civilized community.[2]

Thus, in a limited sense, penological technique had moved west. A few of the states, notably Colorado, Utah, and the Dakotas, had fairly caught up with their older neighbors to the east in legal and institutional equipment. Parole and indeterminate-sentence laws, after more than a decade of experimentation in the Northeast, were being enacted in the Great West, although they were nowhere genuinely applied; boards of charities were being set up, juvenile institutions were being established, and most of the states had secure prisons, nominally on the Auburn pattern; unfortunately, in most cases their cell accommodations were desperately overcrowded. But the general failure to provide any industrial activity or other form of

[2] Governor's Message, *Oklahoma Legislative Documents* (1899). Kansas charged twenty-five cents a day for each prisoner in 1891, raised it to thirty-five cents in 1898, and to forty cents a few years later.

employment was neutralizing the best efforts toward reform. Probably only Utah and the Dakotas had sufficiently considered this problem to achieve moderately satisfactory systems. The exploitation of penal labor, so prevalent in the Northeast and so unrestrained throughout the South, had been largely avoided in the Great West, except in California and Nebraska, but at a great price—the practical surrender of the objectives of the penitentiary as distinguished from the single purpose of secure confinement. Only a few of the institutions, notably those of the Dakotas and Utah, had succeeded in developing labor and disciplinary activities that justified a comparison with the newer reformatory penology of the Northeast; elsewhere the unrestrained intercourse of idle convicts was the dominant feature of the daily life in the majority of the prisons. Yet compared with the first years of the older states the record was not discreditable, for secure prisons had been established in most of the settlements, and, with the more successful development of a labor program in the first decade of the next century, many of these western states were able to achieve fairly satisfactory penal systems.

BIBLIOGRAPHICAL NOTE

The messages of the territorial governors to their legislatures or to the Secretary of the Interior are practically the only firsthand sources available before the settlements became states; then regular prison reports are included in the state documents, while the governors' messages continue to be of value. The reports of the three special investigations in California in the early eighties, the regular reports of the board of managers in that state, and the reports of the boards of charities in Colorado, South Dakota, and Utah are of great value. G. W. France, *Struggle for Life and Home in the North West* (New York, 1890), and Frank Roney, *Autobiography* (Berkeley, 1931), shed light on the development in Washington and California. *The Oregon Penitentiary* (Salem, 1917) and T. S. Ford, *History of the California State Prison* (San Francisco, 1910), are convenient historical surveys. H. H. Bancroft's volumes on the several western states, compiled in the late eighties contain many useful details on their prisons; and S. J. Barrows, *Prison Systems of the United States* (Washington, 1900), describes most of these western prisons.

CHAPTER X

THE FRUITION AND DISILLUSIONMENT OF REFORMATORY PENOLOGY

The turn of the century witnessed the opening of the third phase of the evolution of pedagogical penology. For a decade or two America was to enjoy a moderate although uneven prosperity, and many formerly retarded states were able to establish more respectable penal systems. The national reform movement, strengthened by the fresh vigor of the younger men who were shouldering its rich heritage, undertook to till the whole of America, and Europe again became distinctly visible on the horizon. The controlling influences of earlier days, such as the problems of labor and population and the organization and talents of the leaders, unfolded in unexpected ways. In the course of the first decade or so the old Auburn system was totally discarded except for its hollow architectural shell; new methods of labor and discipline were developed, and the reformatory technique, as a result of its wider application, acquired a radically different character. Improved statistical methods provided a sounder basis for the appraisal of achievements and encouraged a skepticism that turned almost into cynicism among a younger generation advancing to control during the World War period. Meanwhile the contributions of related sciences to the study of the individual and of crime causation opened the way for the development of the modern analytical science of penology.

THE MATURITY OF THE PROFESSION

The era of experimenting wardens had virtually passed with the old century, and the young men who pushed forward to fill vacancies, as well as the older men who advanced to better jobs, were primarily concerned with the more extensive application of a system already fully developed. They were forced to make numerous adaptations and in fact transformed the system more radically than had their predecessors, but this was the result of unfolding circumstances. The movement had acquired stability, integration of tradition, and organization; when radically new methods and theories appeared at the close of the era, they simply provided new viewpoints for the mature profession.

By 1900 the congresses had ceased to be round-table discussions and had become lecture tours for the education of new recruits both in prison management and in control. There was a wealth of leaders and a striking accord among them. Frederick Howard Wines, Samuel June Barrows, Hastings H. Hart, Carlton T. Lewis, Frederick J. Pettigrove, and Amos Butler differed little from the leading wardens —Joseph Scott, Albert Garvin, Henry Wolfer, and the venerable Major McClaughry—in their interpretation of the programs and the objectives of the movement. Foreign papers full of commendation were received chiefly from German admirers. The number of the delegates rose above the five hundred mark; thirty-five states were represented at Albany in 1906, thirty-nine at Chicago the next year, and thirty-four as far west as Seattle two years later. As the Association thus traveled up and down and across the continent, it revised its name to the American Prison Association in 1908, and sheer size lent weight to its theories, while the wider experience served to enrich its program. The evils of the southern lease system were discovered to be quite distinct from the possibilities for healthy outside employment, and the new plantation system received hearty approval. Colorado's honor camps on the roads attracted loud praise and helped to prepare the way for a new kind of education for citizenship. A growing appreciation of European developments stimulated more careful attention to both the causes of crime and the fate of the discharged. Thus the movement opened channels for development in the future, although its major interests continued to center around the campaign for the adoption of reformatory penology.

The reviving interest in foreign developments raised the question as to the relative merits of foreign and American achievements. The delegates of the various nations, meeting every five years in the international prison congresses started by Enoch Wines, could report few penal developments worthy of comparison with the American reformatory, but, when their more satisfactory jails and their more generous assistance to the discharged were taken into account, and especially when their less disturbing criminal trends were considered, the comparison was not so favorable to the Americans. The discussion became acrimonious when the newer criminologists of Italy, France, and Germany entered the fray, prompted by their theories of criminal types and crime causation, to belittle the service of the reformatory and to attribute the American claims of success to the optimism of the frontier. Charles R. Henderson was loudly applauded at the American Prison Congress of 1908 when he outlined and then refuted the criticisms of the European scientists. It was clear to his hearers that these men, by their emphasis on the born criminal, were seeking to justify the passive technique of the prisons of their lands. Samuel June Barrows, the other leading American student of European developments, was likewise unable to assimilate the scientific contribution and remained content to detect notes of accord between the two continents. The full impact of these ideas was not felt in America for another decade.

The Germans were the first to appreciate the full value of both contributions. It was proving difficult for some of the smaller states of the empire to build adequate prisons on the approved Pennsylvania model, and the authorities of several of the institutions were developing positive disciplinary devices to control the prisoners they were unable to keep in solitude. It was also in these years that the Borstal system was developing in England for the care of offenders under twenty-one years of age, applying devices suggestive of Elmira. As these various beginnings were discussed at the international congresses in 1895 and 1900, the Europeans began to awake to the significance of the American activities. Dr. Wolfgang Mittermaier of Heidelberg was especially discerning. He saw that, while the German interest in penology grew out of general scientific progress and therefore was primarily concerned with the philosophy of punishment, the Americans had been attracted to the problem out of a spirit of "compassionateness," and their activity was directed by their "passion for education"; he explained further that it was easy for a young people to think of criminals as individuals rather than as a distinct class, that it was natural that they should turn prisons into "institutions" and treat criminals as "inmates." He thought that, as the scientific development of his own country continued and as the contributions of anthropology and psychiatry were fully appreciated, German authorities would not hesitate to give the principle of the indeterminate sentence and the methods of the reformatory a genuine application to at least a part of their prisoners.

Some of the European states did adopt a few of the forms of reformatory penology. Indeterminate sentences of a sort, and particularly probation, found an increasing application. But the probation laws were usually suspended-sentence laws and, along with those providing indeterminate sentences, were chiefly designed to detect and penalize the recidivist. When the international gathering at Washington in 1910 voted approval of the indeterminate sentence, the resolution specifically applied only to the young and the moral degenerates. The Americans, glorying in the vindication of their principle, did not fully appreciate that their visitors had admitted the value of reformatory treatment only for the young and at the same time were indicating a desire to hold indefinitely those who were criminal by nature. The Europeans did not share the optimism of the founders of the American reformatory movement, but by this date there was not so much optimism left in America.

The national congresses frequently took cognizance of the lessons to be learned abroad, such as jail reform, the care of the discharged, and the improvement of the statistical records, but the Association was not equipped to handle these problems, especially not the jail situation. The congresses did, nevertheless, provide publicity and encouragement to a growing array of charitable societies interested in the discharged. The Central Howard Association, formed at Chicago in 1900, undertook to aid men in all states where there was no agency at work, and its activities soon came a close second to those of the New York association which was now spending around $11,000 each year in aid of the discharged. A society was organized in Kansas in the same year, and agents sent out by this body quickly organized affiliated societies in seven neighboring states. Mrs. Maud Ballington Booth continued to expand the work of her Volunteer Prisoners League units, and Commander Evangeline Booth, who had taken charge of the Salvation Army in the United States in 1904, organized Brighter Day Leagues in many prisons. One important aspect of this activity was the general disappearance of prisoners' "homes"; aid was now more frequently administered under the supervision of visitors, following the trend of general charity work.

Homeless convicts might find shelter in the increasing number of religious institutional dormitories, but these were not in any sense the criminal headquarters the old homes had frequently become. One survey listed thirty-nine aid societies active in 1911, but they hardly scratched the surface of the problem, and their services did not begin to compare with the more efficient work in this field in several European countries.

The problem of criminal records and penal statistics was a double one, and no single authority seemed to have jurisdiction over either branch. The attempts of the National Association to secure a standard pattern for prison reports was of little avail, and the intermittent surveys of the United States census investigators failed to stick to a satisfactory standard, rendering a comparative use of their successive tables most difficult. The problem of criminal identification received more attention, but the Bertillon system was proving to be very cumbersome. A new impetus was given to this activity in 1902 when New York authorities imported the fingerprint system from Scotland Yard.[1] Mark Twain's *Pudd'nhead Wilson* had popularized the system, and many prisons and police departments quickly adopted it. Again the problem of securing a central bureau appeared, and in 1907 the federal government established a clearing-house on a voluntary arrangement, accumulating 925,000 fingerprint records by 1925. It was not until this later period that America began to develop records and statistics comparable to the more efficient systems of Europe.

The reform movement continued to rest primarily on the state organizations for supervision and control. Considerable improvement in these organizations was made throughout the country during this period, but Europeans still regarded administration as one of the weakest points of the American system, chiefly because of the irresponsibility of the counties. The federal government was at last assuming responsibility for the care of some of its convicts but had no

---

[1] The Chinese had used fingerprints for centuries in connection with passports, and the English police department in India had adopted the system about 1860; Francis Galton proved it to be a reliable factor for identification in 1888; but E. R. Henry, who came from the police department in India to the new Scotland Yard, was the first to solve the many difficulties of classification, perfecting his system in 1897.

adequate agency for the direction of its program and thus failed to supply leadership to the movement.

Most of the northern states had already developed some agency for the central supervision of their prisons. The state board of charities remained the customary organization in this section, and in spite of limited powers several of them provided effective leadership, notably the relatively new board in Indiana. New Jersey still failed to create a satisfactory permanent organization, but a special commission of dependency and crime made a valuable study of the field in 1908. The reorganized Massachusetts board of prison commissioners of 1901 was the most efficient and powerful board of control in the country. New York, on the other hand, profited as much from the revival of its prison association under the secretaryship of Samuel June Barrows as from its imperfectly co-ordinated central prison authorities.

The Middle West advanced but did not complete its swing toward state boards of control. The boards of Iowa and Minnesota, created at the turn of the century, assumed full responsibility, as had that of Wisconsin a decade earlier, while the board of charities in South Dakota continued to perform control functions. Nebraska and North Dakota created such authorities toward the end of the era. Illinois, Missouri, and Kansas failed to develop central control over their prisons; fortunately Charles A. Ellwood in Missouri and Frank W. Blackmar in Kansas provided valuable if unofficial leadership to their states. The liberal uprising that upset the old political machines in several of these states had a good effect on prison developments, notably in Iowa and Nebraska where there was much to be done, but Governor J. W. Folk and his successors in Missouri proved unable to carry out the Herculean reforms they recognized as necessary in Missouri. Kansas and Illinois inaugurated new central administrations during the second decade.

Many of the southern states had established central state penal authorities in the nineties, but none of them was independent of political control. West Virginia created a board of control on the northern model in 1909, and Virginia and Tennessee created a board of charities and a board of trustees respectively. Together with the revived board of charities in North Carolina, these agencies provided inspection and some leadership, but the diversion of large numbers of the convicts from state to county authorities, where they were large-ly beyond the ken of inspectors, destroyed any gains the section might claim in the matter of administration reform.

In the Great West, agencies for control established before or at the turn of the century gained efficiency with age, especially in the mountain states where the settlements were gradually acquiring stability. Washington on the coast made a thorough reorganization in 1901 when an efficient board of control was placed in charge of state institutions; Oregon followed this example a decade later. The model board of prison managers in California had long failed to sup-ply leadership, but the formation of a conference of charities and correction in 1901 and the creation of a board of this type two years later brought fresh vigor to the cause of reform. When Oklahoma was admitted as a state, Kate Barnard became the first commission-er of charities and started a vigorous campaign for reorganization, and the state, awaking to its responsibilities, created a board of con-trol to direct the construction of a state prison and an adult reforma-tory.

Thus throughout the nation the penal systems were being institu-tionalized. The central authorities were by no means free from politi-cal influence, but in many states its disturbing power was removed a space or two from control over the major prison officials, and the ap-plication of civil service standards and tenure to the minor positions brought greater stability there as well. These changes favored the formal adoption of the program of the movement but militated against the development of new methods, and the inspiration neces-sary for the application of reformatory technique was not engendered by the process of standardization. The members of the profession were becoming practitioners, and any radically new theories or tech-niques evolved in the future would have to come from beyond their ranks.

THE TRIUMPH OF REFORMATORY TECHNIQUE

Almost all the indications were propitious for reformatory penol-ogy in 1900. The well-established profession was pledged to its ten-ets, and many of the liberal popular journals were lending their sup-port. At least a dozen institutions had already been dedicated to its application, and while these grew in size and stability others were added and secured a fine start in the same undertaking. Not only were indeterminate-sentence and parole laws spreading throughout the North and West, but court decisions were dispelling all doubts as to their constitutionality, and the laws were winning a larger application to criminals generally. Probation laws affecting adults were gaining approval in many states, riding on the crest of the wave of radical reform in the treatment of juveniles. About the only discouraging tendency of the era was the standardization and devital- ization of these measures, particularly in the case of the administration of parole. But it was not until near the end of the era that new facilities for statistical analysis made possible a revaluation of these devices and introduced a spirit of skepticism.

The adult reformatory was now a stable feature of institutional penology. Concord, Huntingdon, St. Cloud, and Pontiac were all fairly established on the Elmira pattern; each had its indeterminate-sentence law and parole officer, each its graded system with marks rewarding proficiency in academic and industrial schools as well as excellence in deportment. Such accessory features as military units, calisthenics, organized sports, institutional band and weekly paper, and special societies among the men of the top grade were fairly prevalent, and farming activities on a partial honor basis were becoming a standard feature. The newer institutions at Lansing (Kan.), Mansfield (Ohio), Green Bay (Wis.), and Buena Vista (Colo.) were rapidly developing along these same lines. Indiana was making extensive and fairly successful efforts to convert its old prison at Jeffersonville into a genuine reformatory, and the authorities at the Vermont house of correction were like-minded although seriously handicapped by an overabundance of short-term misdemeanants. Even the three earlier women's institutions were taking up some of these methods, and Ionia alone held unswervingly to its old program of reformation by hard labor, unhindered by "pedagogical fads." Only the women's reformatory at Bedford, New York, was making radical innovations in this program.

Meanwhile several new institutions of this sort were being successfully established. New Jersey opened an imposing structure at Rahway in 1901, and able officers rapidly introduced all the best features of the older reformatories, thus supplying the long-backward state with a first-rate institution. Persistent agitation in Iowa finally produced results in the middle of the decade when the agrarian politicians captured control and among other reforms transformed the prison at Anamosa into a reformatory. Washington in the Far West, awakening to the larger responsibilities of statehood, provided for a reformatory at Monroe, and this admirable institution was almost ready for occupation when the state entertained the National Association in 1909. Oklahoma and Connecticut started their reformatories in 1911 at Granite and Cheshire respectively, and Nebraska and Wyoming did the same a year or so later at Lincoln and Worland; Cheshire in particular soon became an excellent institution. After long years of agitation Kentucky finally in 1913 provided for the conversion of its old Frankfort prison into a reformatory. Each of these several institutions was provided with an indeterminate-sentence law, and the officers undertook to introduce the standard reformatory technique; most of them were fairly established before the war terminated the reformatory era.

Two specialized types of institutions experimented in new directions during the latter years of the period. Dr. Katherine B. Davis took charge of New York's reformatory for women at Bedford Hills in 1900 shortly after it was opened to major offenders and proceeded to make it the most active penal experiment station in America. A cottage system was developed to supplement the first building equipment and provide a more homelike environment; a trade department was designed to train the women for occupations open to them after discharge; special attention was given to the medical treatment of sex offenders; and in 1911 a laboratory was provided for the study of the individual prisoner. Here was a new pattern for reformatories, soon to be followed by New York's other institution for women at Albion and by New Jersey's women's reformatory open in 1913. Mrs. Jessie D. Hodder, assuming charge at Sherborn in 1911, likewise took advantage of some of the experiments of Dr. Davis. Meanwhile Massachusetts continued its experiments with the care of drunkards on the state farm, and Boston enlarged its house of correction at Deer Island. New York City created a reformatory for misdemeanants in 1905, but no very constructive program was developed until a decade later when Lewis E. Lawes took charge and moved the institution out of the city to New Hampton Farms. Before this date several other large cities were undertaking to give their minor offenders a more enlightened treatment, somewhat after the

character of the reformatory farm, and some of these applied indeterminate sentences. Several of the older city penitentiaries were extensively renovated—that of Buffalo was moved out onto a fine
farm; but the new correctional farms at Kansas City and Washington, D.C., became the model institutions of this type. Thus the reformatory theory at last broke the barriers that had kept the treatment of women and misdemeanants from its fructifying influences,
and the next era was to see a greater extension of this activity.

The reformatories in these days were frequently called upon to
give an account of their achievements. Special investigations, sometimes prompted by reports of mismanagement, sometimes arising
from complaints against country club treatment for criminals, made
old-style surveys of the character of the institutions as viewed by a
committee of observers. But the Europeans were asking for statistical reports of the performance of the reformatories, and Joseph
Scott, now at Elmira, made two such investigations of the post-insti-
tutional histories of one thousand discharged Elmira boys. Many
faults were later noted in the methods of these investigations and of
the others of a similar character, but the reformers were encouraged
at the time by the conclusion that about nine-tenths of the boys were
reformed. Meanwhile, as the original burst of enthusiasm passed,
many of the reformatories fell under the control of men less able than
the founders, and most of the new officers failed to reveal the ingenuity in overcoming obstacles that had been the chief genius of
their predecessors. There were, at the same time, increasing obstacles in the form of less tractable inmates, for the probation laws were
beginning to free many of the others from confinement even in a
reformatory. Later studies of the achievement of these institutions
were to reveal a much lower percentage of success than that claimed
at this time.

The main forms of reformatory penology continued to win their
way into the state prisons. Massachusetts, Colorado, Indiana, and
Illinois had already made their indeterminate-sentence laws mandatory for all but life sentences, although the judges, by allowing
only narrow margins between their maximum and minimum commitments, were in large part defeating the laws. Of the other states
only Minnesota gave its law any considerable application to convicts

sent to the state prison. The reformers found the task of educating the judges to an appreciation of the full spirit of the laws to be very difficult. They secured better results from the legislatures as Wisconsin, Minnesota, Michigan, and Connecticut adopted new laws extending the application of this principle to most convicts. But none of the states succeeded in hurdling the obstacle of unsympathetic judges who clung to the opinion that they were the proper authorities to measure out punishment.

The general failure to solve the problem of the supervision of parolees undoubtedly helped to cause as well as to justify judicial conservatism. Rarely did the methods of selecting men for parole from prison inspire confidence. The reformatories, with a more satisfactory technique of choosing parolees, still had generally but one parole officer to supervise their graduates scattered throughout the entire state. The arrangements for supervising parolees from state prisons were still less satisfactory. The parole authorities in Massachusetts co-operated with local probation officers to some extent; in Indiana the scheme of requiring the employer to send part of the earnings of his parolee to the prison officers for safekeeping until final discharge created a strong economic tie between the authorities and their charges; but Minnesota developed possibly the best supervision in connection with the local units of the state conference of charities. The authorities elsewhere relied largely on the monthly reports of the parolees sent in by mail, usually with the signature of a "best friend" attached.

Notwithstanding the failure to secure its genuine application, the principle of the indeterminate sentence made its way into the statute law of all the other northern states by 1915. New Hampshire took it up in 1901 and applied paroles with care for some years; Maine and Rhode Island rounded out New England's indorsement toward the end of the period. The liberal movement in politics brought the remaining states of the Middle West into line; Iowa in 1907 and Nebraska, Kansas, and the Dakotas at the end of the decade each adopted first or new laws applying this principle. Congress in 1910 finally passed a parole law applicable to federal prisoners, thus taking its place among the last straggling northern authorities to pledge themselves to the reformatory sentence.

The penological conquest of the Great West advanced apace during the first decade of the twentieth century. Colorado was the only state already equipped with a working parole system at the turn of the century, although several others had made a late beginning, but all the states here provided themselves with some sort of a parole system before 1915. Indeed, outside of California, the percentage of convicts reached by these laws compared well with that of the Northeast. Washington, Oregon, Wyoming, and Utah as well as Colorado made as extensive use of paroles during the latter years of the period as any state in the country.

These theoretical aspects of northern penology did not have much influence on the practice or legislation of the South. Kentucky's reluctance to grant paroles under the old law of 1888 was not changed by the revised law of 1900, and only the reorganization of Frankfort prison as a reformatory brought the principle into effect here. Virginia and West Virginia adopted parole laws, and the former put its law of 1904 to good use in relieving congestion at Richmond. Several of the states of the Lower South applied the principle to their juvenile offenders, but Louisiana, late in 1914, was the first among them to grant paroles to adults. Retributive justice still characterized the South and when the authorities in Georgia in 1907 reported that only 666 out of her 2,464 convicts had sentences of five years or less and 1,677 of them had terms of ten years or more, there was no popular protest.

But even in the North and the West, where the reformatory sentence had become a standard feature of the penal law, the situation was anything but satisfactory. The 1910 census reported that about fifteen thousand indeterminate sentences had been granted in the year surveyed, or about 14 per cent of the total number of felons sentenced—not a very large figure considering the prevalence of the laws. Indeed, the failure of the courts to apply the available laws was to some degree a result of the growing popular disfavor which the unsatisfactory methods of administration were earning for the reform. No effective attack was made on this problem until after the war.

Probation, an even more radical modification of the penal standards of justice, was nevertheless gaining popularity. The pioneer activities of Massachusetts in this field, extending over a score of years, had attracted world-wide attention. A few other states had made cautious experiments with the system, and the popular campaign for a more enlightened treatment of juvenile delinquency helped to carry this reform ahead with surprising rapidity. At the same time the reform promised economy, and many states welcomed the relief it promised to overcrowded institutions. The public appeared more ready to grant a convict a second chance at the time of his trial than an early parole from prison; the press was·generous with praise; and the federated women's clubs took an active interest in furthering the measure. As a result every northern state except New Hampshire adopted probation laws for both juveniles and adults by 1910, and almost every western state did likewise by 1915.

Probation was one reform that did not suffer from the growing disillusionment that was beginning to hang like a shroud over the penal system. Its timely development made probation appear to be a substitute for imprisonment, which indeed it is. Another asset was the more generous provision for the supervision of probationers, made possible by the immediate economy secured through outside care. The fact that probation developed in connection with the courts rather than out of the penal system seemed to be a point in its favor, and at all events the judges were not lined up against the system by any threat to their prerogatives. But this circumstance of its development presented the states with a new problem of centralization, and again Massachusetts and New York led the attack as they attempted to co-ordinate and direct the activities of local court probation officers. A national probation association was organized in 1907, and the establishment of probation systems throughout the country—juvenile probation, but not adult, spread into the South—added a valuable branch to the penological profession. At the same time the development contributed indirectly to the difficulties of prison and reformatory administrators. Not only were many of the more likely candidates for reform kept from the institutions, but those committed no longer regarded the reformatory as the best "break" they might have received, and their disgruntled attitudes had to be overcome before the work of reformation could go forward as in the earlier days. The fact that so many could be successfully handled on the outside re-enforced the argument that the apparent achievements of the reformatories were little better than the costly education of young men who were not really criminal. The answer that such men would quickly have become criminals if sent to the prisons did not save reformatory penology from the jar which the success of the probation movement brought to its already un-settled equilibrium.

Nevertheless, the ideology of the reformatory had finally gained an established place in American penology. The old theory, that a man could be made penitent by giving him a just measure of punish-ment to balance against the good he had received from his crime or the injury society had suffered, had been radically qualified. Un-fortunately neither the judges, the prison officers, nor the criminals had in many cases grasped the full meaning of the new principles, and the general public remained largely ignorant of the subtle revolu-tion that had taken place in the theory of punishment. Under these circumstances the portentous reformatory experiment was not re-ceiving a fair trial and suffered from the growing impatience of the public toward sentimentalists and their talk of reform. A shadow was cast over the reformatory technique so carefully elaborated dur-ing fifty years of patient experimentation, but it takes more than a vague feeling of disillusionment to scrap a well-established institu-tional equipment. The reformatory and its technique, handicapped by a loss of optimism, continued into the era of scientific penology as its most valuable heritage.

THE PASSING OF THE AUBURN SYSTEM

The half-century that witnessed the growth of the reformatory saw also the gradual disintegration of the Auburn system. The prin-ciples and technique of the reformatories helped to reshape the older prison program, but only because the population and labor prob-lems had in the course of several decades destroyed the even balance of that rigid system. By the opening of the twentieth century the authorities were everywhere turning from the old silent discipline, and many of them were attempting to introduce reformatory tech-nique in its stead. Unfortunately the task of applying these devices in the major prisons was too much for inferior staffs, and except in a few cases the final result was a lax discipline that tolerated almost everything but violence. In place of the elaborate technique of the reformatory, many officers fell back upon the fiction of a square deal as a means of controlling, if not of reforming, their prisoners. Amid the wide diversity of prisons and programs all that could safely be concluded was that the Auburn traditions had passed.

At the beginning of the century only the prisons of New York, Pennsylvania, and Massachusetts had as yet felt the full impact of the industrial upheaval. Other northern states had dodged the issue for the time, and the South was turning from its lease system in response to entirely different forces; the states and territories of the Great West had found anti-contract laws a major impediment to the development of stable prisons, but the limited number of their convicts had enabled them to shift along. Legislation against the sale of the products of penal labor became more effective during this era, but the delay had permitted the elaboration of several substitute labor systems. New York laws had outlined a model state-use system which the authorities had developed in part; Minnesota and California had developed successful state-account industries; experiments with minimum-security farm and road camps were shortly to increase in number; finally, Maryland was rehabilitating the old contract system. The prisons were dominated by the struggles of their officers to develop one or another of these systems, usually with indifferent success.

The attack on the sale of prison products was now receiving the hearty support of state and national labor commissioners. The United States Industrial Commission of 1900, accepting the views of the critics of prison contractors, even went so far as to frown at the piece-price system, still respectable in that day, and hailed the New York state-use system as the most satisfactory. The report of the United States Commissioner of Labor on prison industry in 1905 elaborately re-enforced this stand. His careful statistical analysis disclosed the tendency of prison contractors to specialize in industries that were suffering a declining market. The situation was especially grievous for the manufacturers of brooms and brushes, stove hollow ware, overalls and farm shirts, harness and wagons, cooperage, and certain grades of shoes. The investigators further discovered that prison products, manufactured at low labor cost, served to fix unreasonably low price levels in these industries. The American Federation of Labor continued to pass resolutions, and special unions, notably the Boot and Shoe Workers' Union, made aggressive attacks against the large companies operating in the prisons of several states. They protested against the system that permitted the employment of 4,253 convicts in shoe factories in twelve prisons at an average labor cost of forty-eight cents a day, dumping twenty-five thousand cheap shoes on the market every day; they protested against the depression of industrial standards and the exploitation of the convicts.

The anti-contract agitation finally began to have its way. Illinois, Indiana, and Iowa considerably limited the number that might be contracted and required industrial diversification. Ohio, Kansas, Michigan, and New Jersey in the North, as well as Oregon and Wyoming in the West, and Georgia and Texas in the South joined the leaders of the earlier period in abolishing all forms of contract labor. More than a dozen states passed laws of one kind and another to check the importation of prison-made goods from other states, but such laws had little effect until the Hawes-Cooper Bill came into effect two decades later. Only the smaller New England states, Alabama and Florida in the South, and the belt of states stretching from Maryland and Virginia to Missouri and Oklahoma stood by the old contract system with scarcely any restraint.

Industrial readjustment was a distinct problem in each prison, but various trends were dominant in different sections. Production for state use was the most usual scheme adopted in the large industrial communities, following New York's lead. The state-account system was most popular in the Middle West and along the Pacific coast as the prison authorities attempted to duplicate the success in Minnesota and California in developing industries that were enjoying a growing local market. While several of these western prisons organized thriving state-account industries, most of those of the Northeast encountered difficulties in persuading the public authorities to purchase the products they were equipping themselves to produce. New laws were passed directing the state departments to order their supplies from the prison industries, but these laws were never adequate, and prison officers had to devise other activities unless they were willing to permit the labor supply to rot in the cells as Pennsylvania was doing. More and more this became the sorry state of affairs, but many efforts were made to avoid it.

Prison farms offered the most convenient relief from the situation. The adult reformatories had for years been cultivating institutional farms, and certain western prisons had early developed such opportunities. The reclamation project started by Massachusetts on nine hundred acres at Rutland in 1900 proved the feasibility of employing certain classes of misdemeanants at such labor. City and county correctional farms were taking advantage of this form of employment, and the southern shift to plantations was dramatizing the opportunities of the system. Ohio purchased fifteen hundred acres in Madison County as a site for a new penitentiary, and, although considerations of economy defeated the plans for permanent buildings, the farm provided the base for a camp to which men were removed from the overcrowded prison and given healthy labor. In a similar way Illinois acquired a large farm as a site for a new prison in 1907, and, while the construction of Statesville was deferred, the farm provided a valuable branch for Joliet in the intervening years. Kansas and other western states put many of their convicts to work on the lands that had long been lying fallow about their prison walls, but it was Michigan that inaugurated the most extensive farming activities among northern prisons when in 1914 the 1,600-acre farm near Jackson prison was made the center of an active trucking and canning enterprise for the supply of state institutions.

The Lower South had in the meantime turned almost completely to the plantation system, although Alabama, a rising industrial state, still kept the majority of her convicts working in the mines. Texas made the most extensive investment in farms and by 1917 had a total of seventy-eight thousand acres; Oklahoma provided large farms at both her prison and reformatory; but when Georgia turned finally from the lease system, although at first putting many on farms, she soon turned the great majority into still another form of outside labor—the road gang.

The successful application of prison labor to road-building was an achievement of the West. Warden Thomas J. Tynan of Canyon City possibly deserves the credit for solving difficulties that had long obstructed this development. Colorado, as well as other states in the West and hundreds of counties in the South, had made earlier attemps to use the convicts on the roads, and the South was persisting in this activity, but the conditions had always been most unsatisfactory. Escapes were numerous, and cruel devices had been applied to check them. Living conditions were not only crude but unsanitary; only in the South did public indifference tolerate such a system. But the West was beginning to feel a greater demand for roads, and the increasing number of idle convicts prompted renewed efforts to solve the two problems together. Colorado was the first to work out a solution.

The new system of road labor was in several important respects an outgrowth of reformatory penology. Colorado's early adoption of northeastern reforms had been frustrated by overcrowding and idleness, but, when Warden Cleghorn in 1906 determined to make another experiment with road labor, he was able to take advantage of the earlier measures. Twenty-five of the men of the top grade were selected on the basis of their approaching eligibility for parole, and with promises of parole within a few months these men were stationed at a road camp some miles from the prison with but one unarmed guard as manager over them. The experiment was successful, and additional camps were sent out the next year, aided by a new highway law passed by the legislature to provide funds for this activity. Twenty escapes in 1907 discouraged Cleghorn, but Thomas J. Tynan who succeeded him as warden injected new enthusiasm, and the honor camps rapidly became so popular that the counties ready to pay the small expenses assigned to them under the law were forced to compete for the privilege. The prisoners were equally eager to earn the special parole and monetary allowances accorded them under the 1907 law, and the state soon had an average of two hundred men employed in these honor camps the year around. The West had at last found a constructive labor policy. Arizona, New Mexico, Nevada, Wyoming, and Utah quickly developed convict road camps on this pattern, but Montana made a larger use of honor road camps than any other state after 1912. Most of these mountain and other far-western states developed similar honor camps on farms some distance from the main prisons.

The good-roads movement was active throughout the nation in these first years of the automobile. Occasional counties in the Northeast employed their prisoners on the roads, and 1913 saw convicts in Illinois, Iowa, Wisconsin, North Dakota, and even New York laboring in this fashion. But it was in the South that convict road labor became most popular, threatening to displace all other penal systems. In the Carolinas the counties retained increasing numbers of the able-bodied convicts for their local chain gangs, while other states, notably Georgia, leased their prisoners to the counties for road construction. Louisiana was driven out of farming in the early part of the second decade by the ravages of the boll weevil and two disastrous floods, and the authorities leased the convicts for levee construction in order to earn funds to pay off the heavy losses in agricultural funds. The direction of these southern trends was, indeed, back to the old lease system in so far as the treatment of the convicts was concerned, for the standards of the honor camps of the West were nowhere realized. The entire development was a fearsome demonstration of the fact that, however far the South may have traveled since the dark days of reconstruction, Negro convicts had no secure safeguards against exploitation. The good-roads movement offered a desirable outlet for penal labor only in those states where the social controls over the penal system were strong enough to make the road camp a minor feature of the reformatory program of the prison; such was the achievement for a time in most of the western states and in many of the instances where this employment was developed in the North.

Meanwhile the old border states between the North and the South largely escaped these shifting experiments. Most of them stuck to the old contract system, to the great profit of their treasuries and the lucky contractors. Warden J. F. Weyler was even able to win a new respectability for the system by combining a discipline of rewards with small wages for active labor in the model surroundings of his new Baltimore prison, prompting many visitors to acclaim it the best reformatory prison in the country, but a more careful investigation in 1913 disclosed many disturbing defects. No fortuitous array of merits, however, could down the odious notoriety of the old contract system, not so long as a half-dozen wretched examples of that system still flourished from Virginia west to Missouri. Aside from their profits and the confinement they provided for criminals, the only advantages these prisons could boast were those of hard labor over "sterile tasks" and "aimless idleness"—the characteristics of many of the reform prisons of the day, as leaders in these border states were wont to remark.

Advantages of industry and economy were, nevertheless, real

merits. The retrograding tendencies of the Pennsylvania prisons and the county penitentiaries in New York when their industrial systems broke down, and the new vitality which came to western prisons with the development of road and farm activities amply demonstrated this truth. Indeed, the industrial factor was the most determining influence in penology throughout the nation in these years. The rapid elimination of the contractors forced the officers to reorganize the industries and disciplines of their prisons, but they had to do this in the face of hostile economic interests and in the midst of party rivalries for patronage that had by no means been eliminated by the elaborate development of administrative bodies. Few wardens were able to measure up satisfactorily to these new responsibilities. The result was that, instead of carrying out the reformatory theories of pedagogical penology so widely indorsed by the laws, the prisons were driven before the wind to such an extremity that their officers adopted a live-and-let-live policy and strove to keep the convicts contented within the walls.

Prison discipline seemed to be within reach of its goal in 1900. Major prisons in all parts of the North were turning to the methods of the reformatory; even in the South and the West the omens were propitious. The system seemed on the verge of attaining the destiny so hopefully mapped out by the inspired leaders of 1870. In the course of the decade the prisons of the North, with few exceptions, did achieve most of the forms of that program, and those of the Great West came into their inheritance; even the South followed its rising star for a time. But the striking changes in the industrial and population problems upset the calculations, and numerous statistical surveys began to suggest to the leaders that their goal had eluded them. New disciplinary trends brought fresh enthusiasm, but the profession was not a little inclined to skepticism as it passed on to the next generation a penal system finally freed of all the old Auburn traditions except the architectural shell.

Grading and marking devices gained for a time almost universal acceptance in penitentiary discipline. A dozen prisons had already applied this reformatory device before the old century closed. Now most of the other prisons of the North, the federal penitentiaries, and several prisons in the West likewise introduced grades. But it had taxed the ingenuity of the best reformatory officers to administer the system where the sentences were of a uniform indeterminate character; prison wardens, often inexperienced and with uncertain tenure, naturally met many difficulties in applying grades to a population variously under indeterminate sentences, definite sentences with and without eligibility for parole, and life sentences. Again and again these grading systems had to be amended, suspended, and abolished; where they persisted, institutionalization sapped their vitality. As in Indiana, the great majority of prisoners were soon enjoying the privileges of the first grade.

The greatest improvements of the period were made in the western prisons. Several of these carried out fine construction programs in the first decade—programs that were nominally, but only nominally, in line with the Auburn traditions. Prison buildings or no prison buildings, the real penological developments of this area waited upon the introduction of a labor system. When the road camp and the farm finally came into use toward the end of the decade, not only had the heyday of rigid reformatory discipline passed, but the outside labor favored a much freer technique than that of either Auburn or Elmira. These states turned rapidly to the newer recreational discipline that was so much more in keeping with their traditionally lax regulations. Their example provided an influential stimulant to the spread of the newer methods of discipline throughout the nation.

The South failed to realize in penology the full promise of its new beginnings in the nineties. Its penal history continued to be identified with the history of convict labor systems, and these took an unfortunate turn during the first decade. There were a few improvements in the border states—notably the new cell house erected at Richmond prison, the conversion of Frankfort prison into a reformatory, the great expansion of the farming activity in Texas, and the building of a prison and an adult reformatory in Oklahoma—but these were exceptions to the general trend. From the Carolinas south and west the convicts were largely put out in chain gangs on the roads. As these were usually under the inefficient control of the counties, most of the important gains of the nineties for central control were lost. The section was very much like the convict who was aptly described, when returning from a thorough lashing, as full of correction up to the neck.

If the penal authorities of the South were hard pressed for a justification of their system, many of those of the North were suffering from a strange illusion. The new officers who took charge of the New Hampshire prison in 1910 were not alone in their view that their predecessors had left "little in the way of improvements for us to do." Little to do—with the prisons jammed with criminals, most of them recidivists! Penal practitioners had traveled far from the spirit of the experimenting wardens of twenty years before. The widespread protests that were arising from the discharged prisoners did not indorse this opinion.

The prisoners were, in fact, gaining a voice in their control. They wrote as never before, describing the corruption and the horrors that still remained, but especially the stupid "slouching about their sterile tasks" that had become the prime factor of the prison environment. The whole weight of a flood of prison memoirs beat against the disciplinary traditions of the previous century and helped to push them out of the prison system. The silent opinion of the mass of the convicts was even more influential, forcing the authorities to admit practically all prisoners to the top grade and its privileges, inducing the parole boards to release men automatically at the end of their minimum sentences, and encouraging the officers to develop a more lenient discipline. But this mass opinion was not always silent, and for the first time in the age of penitentiaries a wave of prison riots broke the monotonous routine. More than ever before the wardens had to bid for the confidence and co-operation of their prisoners. The experiments with self-government that were to gain so much notoriety at the end of the period were not the sports of prison development they were sometimes considered to be, but the result of a union between idealistic officers and the upsurging desire of the mass of the criminals for more tolerable conditions. The prison populations had acquired a new character, whether as a result of changing social conditions outside or because of the disappearance of the Auburn restraints, and this new character played its part in the development of the modern prison customs under which almost everything but violence is tolerated.

Prison conditions were undergoing a slow improvement during this period. The federal government completed Leavenworth and Atlanta prisons and reopened a third at McNeil Island, housing

1,514, 1,184, and 239 in these institutions in 1915; Warden Henry Wolfer built the new model prison at Stillwater, the best penal structure in the country for many years; New York, Nebraska, and Oklahoma built new prisons, and Virginia and California constructed badly needed additions. But cell construction occupied a minor place beside the efforts to make the old prisons more tenantable. New sanitary arrangements, dining-halls, shower bathing, and out-door exercise, as well as expanded library facilities, prison journals, and more liberal mailing privileges were the order of the day. The old lock step, shaved head, and striped uniform practically disappeared for good. A more extensive provision for separate treatment of the insane and the tubercular was made in these years; even the South finally began to give attention to the problem of tuberculosis so rife among its Negro convicts. It was vain to claim any ideal solution of these problems, but virtually throughout the country the efforts of the past century to make the prisons comfortable—in a very narrow sense of the word, to be sure—went steadily forward. Only in the matter of the provision of individual cells was little done, and even here large plans were projected, only to be held up by the war and other changing forces.

The county jails continued to maintain their damnable features. Vigorous indictments of their conditions appeared from time to time, but little improvement resulted. Only those few northern states where persistent inspection by state boards had kept the facts before the public presented fair conditions, and most of these states were crowding their jails with drunkards to the questionable advancement of the public morals. The jail thus continued to be the weakest link in the penal system, and the fee system its most insidious feature; the Europeans were convinced that the American criminal problem demonstrated what happens to a chain with a weak link. The only genuine improvement was in the case of those half-dozen cities that created farm colonies for their misdemeanants. Hastings H. Hart among others saw clearly that a possible solution lay in the development of jail substitutes, such as these farms, or, in many cases, fines and probation. The "passing of the county jail" was, however, a very futuristic dream as yet.

The remarkable transformation of prisons in the second decade was the natural conclusion of the forces that had long been playing on their development. Reformatory methods had broken down the old traditions, but the prisons were failing to give the new methods the sturdy application they required. Idleness and the liberties of the top grade gave the convicts greater opportunity to make their wishes felt in prison affairs. It became difficult to intimidate them as individuals, much more so in the mass; prisoners had to be cajoled into orderliness. Fortunately the men taking charge of the prisons had the wit to see that by taking the initiative in creating a positive recreational system they retained leadership over their men.

The new recreational activities had long roots in prison customs. Since the days of Gideon Haynes, fifty years before, holiday privileges had increasingly become a feature of prison life. The "freedom of the yard" thus occasionally granted was an indefinite term, and its application had varied greatly with the nature of the prison structure and the officers in charge. Occasional lectures, musicals, and theatricals had supplied entertainment in prisons, and the reformatories had developed such features to a considerable extent during the winter months as a substitute for their outdoor military drills and organized sports. The farm and road camps were nurturing a new type of associate life, particularly in the western prisons. All these departures from the strict rule of silence culminated during the early years of the second decade in a recreational movement that swept the last vestige of the old Auburn technique out of the prisons.

The final transformation was a sudden and rapid process. The occasional half-holiday of the former era gradually became a regular Saturday or Sunday feature during the first decade in scattered prisons. Frequently the newly organized institutional bands, introduced into the prisons now that their value had been demonstrated in neighboring reformatories, provided a concert as the main feature of these half-holiday occasions. The abler wardens gave close attention to this development, but the prisoners, by their evident appreciation of the afternoon in the yard and by their spontaneous organization of games, helped to guide the final development. Beginning about 1910 regular organized sports became an accepted part of the prison curriculum in the Middle West, and by 1915 this feature had spread into practically all the prisons of the Northeast as well as those of the Great West.

Prison athletics not only proclaimed the end of the Auburn system and the triumph of one feature of reformatory technique, but presaged a new era in prison discipline. Organized sport was in direct line with the attempt to make prison life more tolerable, and its welcome was doubly enthusiastic because the lax industrial activity was failing to occupy the full time and energy of the prisoners. The wardens, through cautious experiments with their first graders, had discovered their ability to control men in masses, and, as athletics opened a new horizon in correctional therapy, many officers felt inspired to attempt to "re-create the man in prison," a popular slogan at the congresses of the day.

But this hurried shift to entertainment activities marked the abandonment of many of the pedagogical principles and undertakings of the reformatory. Grandstands were erected, indicating that the recreational possibilities of athletics were to be sacrificed to the entertainment feature of league games; the wide introduction of the movie a few years later, and of the radio still later, further emphasized the transition from the recreational program of the reformatory, with its educational motivation, to the amusement program of later prisons, seeking to keep their inmates contented. The somewhat startling experiments of Thomas Mott Osborne with self-government in Auburn, Sing Sing and elsewhere at the end of this period were cases at point. The Mutual Welfare Leagues had many roots in the reformatory tradition, and several suggestive antecedents in the form of convict societies and clubs have been noted, but "Tom Brown" Osborne's impulsive romanticism and optimistic reliance on the co-operation of all convicts, at least when held in line by the gang spirit, contrasts sharply with the forthright pedagogical technique of Brockway and his closely integrated theories about individual self-discipline and reformation. The fact is that, at the time of the outbreak of the World War, prison discipline was again in flux as it had not been since the days of Louis Dwight. Fortunately a new leadership was at hand.

Reformatory penology completed its cycle about 1910. For half a century it had run its course, an integral phase of American life. Developing within the old Auburn system the reformatory technique had slowly displaced the older traditions so that by the end of the era only the architectural shell of Louis Dwight's system remained. Reformatory theory held society responsible for the re-

generation of its criminals, and a large-souled optimism had enlivened and added power to its educational devices—both of which
features the Europeans were quick to recognize as characteristically
American. The old theory that years of imprisonment were to be
meted out to fit the crime had been almost entirely erased from the
statute books; in its place had been written the right of the convict
to his freedom, within certain limitations, as soon as he could be reformed. The organization of the system had been so elaborately
carried forward that scattered wardens were leaning back in their
chairs and blandly reporting that all reforms had been adopted, but
already several radically new considerations were appearing, indicating different trends for the future.

The creation and application of reformatory penology had been
the work of three generations spanning the years from 1865 to 1910.
A group of eclectic idealists of the late sixties had contributed the
fundamental principles, but the actual formulation of the technique
had been accomplished by the succeeding generation of experimenting wardens. The reformatory program had gained its opportunity
when Louis Dwight's older system was thrown out of gear by critical
population and labor problems. The development of new agencies
for public supervision and control had supplied a more effective
leadership for reform. But so great were the growing pains of the
nation that pedagogical penology scarcely received a fair trial in any
state. Now the third generation, after winning a formal triumph by
pledging practically the whole nation to the program, was forced to
hand on its responsibilities amid a growing feeling of disillusionment.

The almost nation-wide acceptance of the reformatory program
had been disastrous to its record. The majority of prison officers
were miserably failing to apply Brockway's carefully balanced program; growing populations were taxing the already overexpanded
institutions beyond their capacities; labor laws were restricting
the opportunities for industrial activity; and improved statistics
were revealing a startling number of repeaters whose prison and reformatory terms seemed only to have briefly interrupted their criminal careers. Reformatory penology had sought to individualize the
criminal at least to the extent of fitting his term of imprisonment to
his peculiar reformatory needs, but the effect of the general adop-

tion of the technique had been quite the reverse. The striped figures of the earlier days had been called forth from the partial seclusion of separate cells only to be submerged in the stagnant pools of humanity that characterized the idle, overcrowded, and undisciplined prisons of the day.

But a new school of criminologists, spawn of Europe in large part, was providing suggestive hints for a renewed attack on the problem. Students were at last coming to grips with the real problem—the criminal individual. He was found to have characteristics and peculiarities that seemed to have a more direct relation to the problem of his correction than either the specific nature of his crime or the ease with which he could conform to prison routine. Theories of classification and segregation emerged that were out of line with the older optimistic assumption that all convicts are corrigible. At the same time that prison authorities were considering the necessity of studying the character of each criminal, a fresh attack was being made on the environmental aspects of crime causation, stressing the need for a more intelligent and effective supervision of released convicts and relaxing somewhat the indictment against the reformatory for its failure to guide all its young men onto the right track. Many of the younger officials trained in psychiatry or sociology were inclined to disparage the work of their predecessors as unscientific, but they soon discovered that, although they might be advocates of new sciences, they were at the same time joining an old profession and assuming responsibilities in a still older institutional system. Penologists were exchanging the empirical approach of the reformers for that of an analytical science, but they were destined to encounter many bewildering problems and to suffer repeated disillusionment. The ablest administrators of the post-war period soon acquired a wholesome respect for the pedagogical technique of the better reformatories.

BIBLIOGRAPHICAL NOTE

The regular reports of the prison officers, the boards of charities, or boards of control are available for almost every state during this period. These are supplemented in some states by special investigations, such as: F. W. Blackmar, *Report on the Penitentiary* (Topeka, Kan., 1914); C. A. Ellwood, *Bulletin on the Condition of County Jails in Missouri* (Columbia, 1904); Maryland Penitentiary Commission, *Report* (1913); Pennsylvania Penal Commission, *Employment and*

Compensation of Prisoners in Pennsylvania (1917); Texas Investigation Commission, *Report on the Penitentiary* (1917); The annual *Proceedings* of the National (after 1908 the American) Prison Association, and the successive issues of the *Journal of Criminal Law and Criminology* (1910———) and *Mental Hygiene* (1917———) show the trends in both theory and practice. The United States Census, *Prisoners and Juvenile Delinquents in the United States* (1910) and United States Commissioner of Labor, *Report on Convict Labor* (1905), provide valuable statistical surveys.

Among the many volumes dealing with some phase of the developments during this period may be mentioned: R. C. Arnold, *The Kansas Inferno* (Wichita, 1906); I. C. Barrows, *The Sunny Life* (New York, 1913); Corinne Bacon (ed.), *Prison Reform* (New York, 1917); H. M. Boies, *The Science of Penology* (New York, 1901); M. A. Elliott, *Conflicting Penal Theories in Statutory Criminal Law* (Chicago, 1931); J. F. Fishman, *Crucibles of Crime* (New York, 1923); B. O. Flower, *Progressive Men and Women of the Past Twenty-five Years* (Boston, 1914); E. Grubb, *Methods of Penal Administration in the United States* (London, 1904); H. H. Hart, *The Social Problems of Alabama* (Montgomery, 1918); Julian Hawthorne, *The Subterranean Brotherhood* (New York, 1914); C. R. Henderson, *Tendencies towards Centralization in Foreign Countries* (Washington, 1903); Paul Herr, *Das moderne amerikanische Besserungssystem* (Berlin, 1907); M. M. Hurd (ed.), *Institutional Care of the Insane* (Baltimore, 1916); F. R. Johnson, *Probation for Juveniles and Adults* (New York, 1928); Collis Lovely, "The Abuses of Prison Labor," *Shoe Workers Journal* (1905); *The Oregon Penitentiary* (Salem, 1917); T. M. Osborne, *Society and Prisons* (New Haven, 1916); Prison Reform League, *Crime and Criminals* (Los Angeles, 1910); S. A. Queen, *The Passing of the County Jail* (Menasha, Wis., 1920); R. F. Quinton, *The Modern Prison Curriculum* (London, 1912); Sir Evelyn Ruggles-Brise, *Prison Reform* (London, 1924); J. J. Sanders, *Prison Reform* (Ariz., 1913); Salvation Army, *Broken Souls* (New York, 1929); F. C. Sharp, "Study of the Popular Attitude towards Retributive Punishment," *International Journal of Ethics*, 1910, pp. 341–57; J. F. Steiner, *The North Carolina Chain Gang* (Chapel Hill, 1927); F. Tannenbaum, *Wall Shadows* (New York, 1922); E. S. Whitin, *The Caged Man* (Philadelphia, 1913). The several historical surveys of specific phases of the development by H. E. Barnes, J. S. Briggs, H. H. Jackson, Philip Klein, E. C. Lekkerkerker, and E. Wisner have been noted above in the notes at the end of chaps. vii and viii. To these should be added the *History of Charitable and Reformatory Institutions of the District of Columbia* (Washington, 1927). Further bibliographical references may be found in A. F. Kuhlman's extensive *Guide to Materials on Crime and Criminal Justice* (New York, 1929).

INDEX

Administrative problems: struggle for central state control, 45, 53–57, 68, 74–75, 126–29; control seldom free from politics, 188, 192, 199, 210–12. *See* Boards of charities; Political control; *see also* under each state

Alabama: Wetumpka prison, 33, 176; lease system in, 176, 182, 222; road labor in, 188

Altgeld, John P., reform governor, 133, 138, 150

American Federation of Labor, agitation of, 105, 220. *See* Contract labor; Industries

American Prison Association. *See* National Prison Association

Arizona: Yuma prison, 204; road labor in, 223

Arkansas: "Walls" of, 33; lease system in, 175

Auburn system: origin of, 8–9, 10, 13; nature of, 8, 10–13, 38, 41; serves as model, 9, 11, 14, 17, 19, 29–35, 158; domination of, 18–19, 30, 41, 46; decline of rigor of, 87, 159, 163; abandonment of, 95, 151, 155, 162, 169, 206, 219–32; slight effect of, in Great West, 190–91, 204. *See* Dwight, Louis

Augustus, John, pioneer agent for the discharged, 44, 62, 135

Baltimore prison, as model, 29, 31, 33, 46. *See* Auburn system; Maryland

Barrows, S. J., United States Commissioner, 123–24, 169, 170, 207, 208; secretary of New York Association, 211

Batt, William J., chaplain, 116, 120

Beal, Abraham, Hopper's successor, 50, 89

Beaumont, G. A. de, French visitor, 16, 59

Beccaria, Cesare, father of penology, 1, 2, 16, 23

Bentham, Jeremy, theory of, 1, 2, 4; Panopticon of, 12

Berkman, Alexander, observant convict, quoted, 147 n.

Bertillon system of identification, 122, 194, 210

Boards of charities: first in Massachusetts, 52–53; early organization of, 53, 55–56, 74–75, 211–12; work of, 84, 126–29, 211–12; state conferences of, 129; in Great West, 199, 200, 204. *See* Administrative problems; Political control; *see also* under each state

Booth, Mrs. Maud B., work of, in prison, 160–61, 209

Boston Prison Discipline Society: quoted, 2; organized, 9–11; work of, 12–16, 18–19, 27. *See* Dwight, L.; Societies

Bradford, William, law code of, 5

Bridewell, of London, founded, 3. *See* Houses of correction

Brinkerhoff, Roeliff, at the national congresses, 119, 121, 131, 169

Brockway, Zebulon: early work of, 37, 40, 49, 51–52; at Detroit, 52, 63, 65, 77, 85; at national congresses, 70–71, 119, 120; at Elmira, 89, 108–15; achievements of, 93, 115, 137, 143–44, 169, 230; labor system of, 95, 98, 99, 112–13

Brush, A. A., Sing Sing warden, 119, 120, 122, 148

Byers, Albert G., Ohio reformer, 55, 57, 89

Cable, George W., southern critic, 180, 183

California: convict labor in, 103, 192, 193, 220; San Quentin prison, 191–92, 194, 228; Folsom prison, 192, 194; parole in, 217

Capital punishment. *See* Criminal law

Carpenter, Mary, English visitor, 28, 83, 90

Cassidy, Michael, Cherry Hill warden, 95, 119, 120, 121

Cells, size of: Walnut Street, 6; Auburn, 8; Cherry Hill, 11; Joliet and Elmira, 58 n., 154; Baltimore, 152. *See* Living conditions; *see also* under each state

Chain gangs: as used by the lessees, 172, 181–83, 188; as developed by southern counties, 185, 222, 224, 226. *See* Road labor

Cherry Hill system: developed, 8, 11, 16, 17, 19, 35; influence of, on Europe, 16, 36; abandonment of, 48, 81, 118. *See* Pennsylvania

Chickering, Hannah B., reform zeal of, 79

Civil War, effect of, on prison reform, 32–33, 48–50, 172, 173

PATTERSON SMITH REPRINT SERIES IN
CRIMINOLOGY, LAW ENFORCEMENT, AND SOCIAL PROBLEMS

1. *Lewis: *The Development of American Prisons and Prison Customs, 1776–1845*
2. Carpenter: *Reformatory Prison Discipline*
3. Brace: *The Dangerous Classes of New York*
4. *Dix: *Remarks on Prisons and Prison Discipline in the United States*
5. Bruce *et al.*: *The Workings of the Indeterminate-Sentence Law and the Parole System in Illinois*
6. *Wickersham Commission: *Complete Reports, Including the Mooney-Billings Report.* 14 vols.
7. Livingston: *Complete Works on Criminal Jurisprudence.* 2 vols.
8. Cleveland Foundation: *Criminal Justice in Cleveland*
9. Illinois Association for Criminal Justice: *The Illinois Crime Survey*
10. Missouri Association for Criminal Justice: *The Missouri Crime Survey*
11. Aschaffenburg: *Crime and Its Repression*
12. Garofalo: *Criminology*
13. Gross: *Criminal Psychology*
14. Lombroso: *Crime, Its Causes and Remedies*
15. Saleilles: *The Individualization of Punishment*
16. Tarde: *Penal Philosophy*
17. McKelvey: *American Prisons*
18. Sanders: *Negro Child Welfare in North Carolina*
19. Pike: *A History of Crime in England.* 2 vols.
20. Herring: *Welfare Work in Mill Villages*
21. Barnes: *The Evolution of Penology in Pennsylvania*
22. Puckett: *Folk Beliefs of the Southern Negro*
23. Fernald *et al.*: *A Study of Women Delinquents in New York State*
24. Wines: *The State of Prisons and of Child-Saving Institutions*
25. *Raper: *The Tragedy of Lynching*
26. Thomas: *The Unadjusted Girl*
27. Jorns: *The Quakers as Pioneers in Social Work*
28. Owings: *Women Police*
29. Woolston: *Prostitution in the United States*
30. Flexner: *Prostitution in Europe*
31. Kelso: *The History of Public Poor Relief in Massachusetts, 1820–1920*
32. Spivak: *Georgia Nigger*
33. Earle: *Curious Punishments of Bygone Days*
34. Bonger: *Race and Crime*
35. Fishman: *Crucibles of Crime*
36. Brearley: *Homicide in the United States*
37. *Graper: *American Police Administration*
38. Hichborn: *"The System"*
39. Steiner & Brown: *The North Carolina Chain Gang*
40. Cherrington: *The Evolution of Prohibition in the United States of America*
41. Colquhoun: *A Treatise on the Commerce and Police of the River Thames*
42. Colquhoun: *A Treatise on the Police of the Metropolis*
43. Abrahamsen: *Crime and the Human Mind*
44. Schneider: *The History of Public Welfare in New York State, 1609–1866*
45. Schneider & Deutsch: *The History of Public Welfare in New York State, 1867–1940*
46. Crapsey: *The Nether Side of New York*
47. Young: *Social Treatment in Probation and Delinquency*
48. Quinn: *Gambling and Gambling Devices*
49. McCord & McCord: *Origins of Crime*
50. Worthington & Topping: *Specialized Courts Dealing with Sex Delinquency*
51. Asbury: *Sucker's Progress*
52. Kneeland: *Commercialized Prostitution in New York City*

* new material added

* new material added   † new edition, revised or enlarged

For continuation of list, write for catalog.